# RELIGION
## IN THE
## NEWS

# RELIGION
# IN THE
# NEWS

Faith
and
Journalism
in
American
Public
Discourse

## Stewart M. Hoover

SAGE Publications
*International Educational and Professional Publisher*
Thousand Oaks   London   New Delhi

*For information:*

SAGE Publications, Inc.
2455 Teller Road
Thousand Oaks, California 91320
E-mail: order@sagepub.com

SAGE Publications Ltd.
6 Bonhill Street
London EC2A 4PU
United Kingdom

SAGE Publications India Pvt. Ltd.
M-32 Market
Greater Kailash I
New Delhi 110 048 India

Printed in the United States of America

*Library of Congress Cataloging-in-Publication Data*

Hoover, Stewart M.
    Religion in the news: Faith and journalism in American public
discourse / by Stewart M. Hoover.
        p.    cm.
    Includes bibliographical references (p.    ) and index.
    ISBN 0-7619-1677-6 (acid-free paper)
    ISBN 0-7619-1678-4 (pbk.: acid-free paper)
    1. Mass media—Religious aspects. 2. Journalism, Religious. I. Title.
P94 .H657 1998
302.23′0973—ddc21                                            98-9072

This book is printed on acid-free paper.

98  99  00  01  02  03  04  7  6  5  4  3  2  1

| Acquisition Editor: | Margaret H. Seawell |
| Editorial Assistant: | Renée Piernot |
| Copy Editor: | Joyce Kuhn |
| Production Editor: | Astrid Virding |
| Editorial Assistant: | Denise Santoyo |
| Typesetter/Designer: | Christina M. Hill |

# CONTENTS

# PREFACE

This book comes at a time when it is far more common to raise questions about religion in the media than was the case when I first began looking into them. In an era when television programs with religious themes are among the highest rated on the air, when public broadcasting stations use religious and quasi-religious headliners to help raise money during their pledge weeks, and when major newspapers and news magazines run religion cover stories at times *other* than Easter and Christmas, it seems almost too obvious a step to write a book about religion journalism.

When this project began, however, things were very different. Religion was much less present in journalistic and entertainment content. It is probably the case, moreover, that things have not really changed all that much. It is entirely possible that the trends we see around us now are more ephemeral than permanent. Certainly, the sorts of things I have found during my investigations (and that now appear in this book) would lead me to suspect that whatever high-water mark of religion-in-the-media we might have achieved at the late midpoint of the decade of the 1990s, there are very good reasons why we may backslide at some point.

What will not be undone, however, is the increasingly sophisticated *discourse* that has begun to develop about these issues. This discourse has both scholarly and popular voices. Important new books and research articles are appearing all the time, conferences are being planned and carried out, and an ever-growing network of people inside and outside the academic community are beginning to take the intersection between religion and the media more seriously.

As this discourse has developed, it is important to see that it has had some distinct concerns within it. There are the questions of religion's *use* of media. Studies of televangelism fit into this category. Then there are questions of the use of religion *by* the media. This book is an example of this latter focus. Other studies have looked at the construction of religious symbolism in entertainment or leisure media, and this is, of course, an important task, too. Each of these foci has proved to be exceedingly rich and interesting, particularly as new theoretical and methodological perspectives have been brought to bear.

However, there is a whole package of issues that moves beyond these questions. As a logical extension of the tentative speculations in this book about the nature of contemporary religious practice and its potential to center on popular arts, popular culture, and the media, there is an emerging focus on the religious practice of the media age per se. That is to say that in addition to understanding what happens in the construction of media texts we must also understand what audiences *do* with those texts. An emerging scholarship of religion in the media age is coming to stand beside the other areas of emphasis.

In short, there is a great deal more to be done. The intent of this book is to center itself in one of the many fields of inquiry now beginning to address the nexus of media, religion, and culture.

# ACKNOWLEDGMENTS

$S$ ome of the research that supports this book's arguments began nearly 10 years ago. It thus stretches back across a number of institutional locations and has benefited from a long and complex network of collegial and informative relationships. Each of these institutions and each of these colleagues deserves credit for having played a role in this product. Any value in it is to their credit. Any defects are mine.

Most recently, the project has benefited from a concerted time of study and reflection made possible by my university and the resources and excellent scholarly atmospheres at the Swedish Collegium for Advanced Study in the Social Sciences (SCASSS) and the faculty of Sociology of Religion at the University of Uppsala, both in Uppsala, Sweden. I particularly want to recognize the directors of the SCASSS, Björn Wittrock, Barbro Klein, Göran Therborn, and Bo Gustafsson, and, of course, the staff. At the University of Uppsala, thanks are due Dean Carl-Reinhold Bråkenhielm of the Faculty of Theology, Professor Thorleif Pettersson, and Dr. Alf Linderman.

At the University of Colorado, I particularly want to recognize Dean Willard Rowland and Garda Meyer of the Dean's Office for their assistance. Members of the university staff whose help also was invaluable include Pat Meyers, Susan Schneider, Diane Willian, Dave Martinez, and Judy Jensen.

Much of the research was supported by two major grants from the Lilly Endowment, Inc., of Indianapolis. The staff there, including Robert Wood Lynn, Craig Dykstra, and James Wind, was very supportive and provided intellectual as well as material input on the project.

Initial phases of the work took place while I was at Temple University in Philadelphia, and I received very helpful support from faculty and staff colleagues there.

I have also been privileged by the quality of student collaboration and assistance I have had along the way: Paula Britto, Barbara Mastrolia (Hanley), and Martin Radelfinger at Temple University and Shalini Venturelli, Douglas Wagner, Joseph Champ, and Lynn Schofield Clark at the University of Colorado.

Professional and scholarly networks have also been invaluable. I want to thank the Religion Newswriters' Association and particularly John Dart and Ed Briggs for their help. Judy Weidman has been of great assistance both during her time at Religion News Service and more recently at United Methodist Communications. Thanks also are due Joan Connell of RNS, David Briggs of the Associated Press, Danny Miller of WHYY-FM, Diane Winston of Princeton University, Jimmy Allen, Sue O'Brien, Everette Dennis, Kenneth Briggs, Bill Moyers, Jim Castelli, Lois Anderson, Terry Mattingly, and Roy Larson.

Valuable academic and scholarly advice came from Robert Wuthnow, Wade Clark Roof, Martin Marty, Fred Denny, Don Shriver, Jim Carey, Judy Buddenbaum, Bill Wyatt, Ted Glasser, Mark Silk, Conrad Cherry, and John Ferré. Harry Cotugno at the Gallup Organization and David Roozen of Hartford Seminary provided important support to the survey research phases. My colleagues in the Uppsala Group (a scholarly collegium dedicated to the development of research and theory on media, religion, and culture), Knut Lundby, Alf Linderman, and Jolyon Mitchell are a valued reference group, as is Robert White.

The studies and this book would clearly have been impossible without the cooperation of over 200 individuals who agreed to be interviewed. Those from professional ranks are identified herein, the laity remain anonymous. It is to them, in particular, that I want to convey a note of gratitude. Those of us who are professionally involved in the knowledge industries take the task of opining in stride. These private individuals gave much in terms of their time and attention to my questions.

At Sage Publications, I'd like to recognize my editor, Margaret Seawell, and her assistant, Renée Piernot. Three anonymous reviewers provided priceless advice and feedback to the manuscript.

A major project such as this always has implications for home and family. I want, finally, to thank my wife, Karen, for her advice and support, and my father-in-law, Carl Woody, and my mother, Miriam Hoover, for their proof-reading help during what otherwise were holidays in Sweden.

# RELIGION IN THE NEWS

This book begins with a deceptively simple question: Why is it that in the United States, the most religious of the western industrial countries, the coverage of religion by the secular press continues to be so controversial? To answer this question requires a breadth of effort because the worlds of religion and the media are so complex and so nuanced, and because to answer this question we also have to address some fundamental realities—seldom examined in these considerations—about the state of American polity and American cultural discourse at this point in history.

The fact that few seem to be happy with the way religion is covered by the press masks a deeper, more profound reality: significant segments of the various religious communities, the public, and the press, have no expectation that religion will be covered at all. It has simply been such a minor component of the news historically that many people have no basis on which to make a judgment about either its quantity or its quality.

1

But this serves to underscore, rather than undermine, the notion that religion news is a problem and that serious and troubling examples of press treatment can be found. New kinds of religion stories have presented themselves that have strained journalistic conventions. A number of these have emerged on both the national and international level as the end of the millenium approaches. In spring 1997, international attention was drawn to the mass suicide of the "Heaven's Gate" group in Southern California. Members of *Aum Shinrikyo* in Japan set off poison gas on a Tokyo subway in spring 1995. And in April 1995, the Federal Building in Oklahoma City was demolished by a bomb, allegedly to mark the second anniversary of a deadly confrontation with the Branch Davidian sect led by David Koresh in Waco, Texas in 1993.

The seige of Waco had been one of the most dramatic news stories of 1993 and has implications that stretch far beyond the outcome of the legal battles surrounding it. One of these is that the incident, and its aftermath, continued to call into question the place of religion in the policy and practice of the public media. The *Kansas City Star* engaged this issue directly by publishing a carefully researched account[1] of how the situation might well have been resolved peacefully had its fundamentally *religious* nature been better understood.

The *Star*'s Bill Tammeus revealed that public officials had systematically refused to take seriously the religious authenticity of Koresh and his followers. Classifying Koresh and certain of his followers "terrorists" and others among his group "hostages," civil authorities chose a course of action that seemed to make a confrontation inevitable. According to Tammeus, the key to understanding the crisis was Koresh's particular reading of the Book of Revelation, something that some religious experts had begun to decode as a result of tentative contacts with him via his lawyer.

In a critical turn of events, Koresh revealed late in the crisis a willingness to surrender once he had completed an exegesis of the "seven seals" of Revelation. This was seen as a delaying action by the FBI, who were quoted by Tammeus as dismissing, at this critical moment, any notion that Koresh was anything other than a common criminal.

What Tammeus argued for was, in the first instance, a better, more sensitive treatment of religion by civil authorities. He was able to report that, as a result of some self-criticism, both the Bureau of Alcohol, Tobacco and Firearms and the Federal Bureau of Investigation were taking steps in this direction.

However, there is a deeper, more ominous, and more profound implication to the Koresh incident. That is, there was a set of *public perceptions* that guided both the governmental action and the media treatment of this crisis. As the public became more and more aware of the incident, one that was—not incidentally—deeply embarrassing to government agencies, a great deal of discussion naturally ensued. The outcome therefore needed to be one that "made sense" in a fundamental way. The outcome needed to *appear* to be both *just* and *appropriate.*[2]

It is at just this level of the "appropriateness" of public action that media coverage operates. Journalists write in a mode of generality that is articulated into broad public discourses about policy, sentiment, taste, and value.[3] Public perceptions of David Koresh and the Branch Davidians—and the media coverage on which those perceptions would have to be based—were therefore also implicated in the misunderstanding documented by Tammeus and other critics of the handling of this incident.

Thus questions that can be raised about the inadequacy of FBI understandings of fundamental religious issues can also be raised about "the media." An example from National Public Radio illustrates this point. On the Sunday, March 7, 1993, *Weekend Edition* program (during the "standoff" in Waco), host Liane Hanson introduced a live report from John Burnett, the correspondent on the scene:

HANSEN: So it's been very difficult to get information, very difficult to cover this story. And you're boning up on your Bible studies. Are your colleagues doing the same thing?

BURNETT: Listen to this piece of tape and you get an idea of the kinds of Sunday School lessons that we're all having to go through.

RELIGIOUS SCHOLAR: They would often refer to Revelation, and sometimes to the Books of Daniel and Ezekiel which share a lot in common with Revelation, to justify this position.

REPORTER: Where do we find this book of Revelation? I'm not very knowledgeable.

RELIGIOUS SCHOLAR: Okay, it's the last book in the Bible in the New Testament.

REPORTER: So it's in the Bible in the New Testament?

RELIGIOUS SCHOLAR: Right, uh-huh, uh-huh.

BURNETT: What's happening is after the news conferences there usually are—in this case there was a professor from Baylor University, a religion professor, who are sort of painstakingly and patiently instructing reporters on, you know, the finer points of the Book of Revelation, the last book of the Bible. And this is a particularly difficult book to understand under the best of circumstances . . . so if nothing else comes out of this, David Koresh has certainly taught a very large press corps some Bible lessons.[4]

The religious illiteracy demonstrated by this anecdote is assumed by many observers to be widespread. But this situation is also one that has received increasing attention in recent years. Perhaps spurred on by high-profile religion stories, more and more people both inside and outside the media have begun to talk about the way religion is treated in the nation's newspapers and on its airwaves. In her review of the "year in religion," Lynn Neary of National Public Radio said of 1997 that

this seemed to be the year that the media discovered religion. I mean, for a long time there've been surveys showing that Americans tend to be more religious than most other nationalities, but this year the media caught up with that fact, and you saw stories about religion and spirituality on all the covers of major magazines—*The New York Times,* even *Mother Jones.*[5]

A particularly notable example of this new attention was a November 1997 issue of *New York Times Magazine,* which was entirely devoted to emerging religious practices across a wide range of religious movements.[6] The Fall 1997 *Nieman Reports,* the journal of Harvard's Nieman Center, was likewise devoted entirely to consideration of religion journalism.[7]

Such examples of change work into a larger discourse about religion coverage *itself.* As this discourse has evolved, it has begun to look for answers in a logical place: the role and status of the religion "beat" at the nation's newspapers. Until recently, religion specialization has been exclusively a feature of the print media and has been concentrated in the major metropolitan dailies. And its place there has been a marginal one. It has labored under a set of received definitions that were surprisingly consistent nationwide.

In general, this "received view" held that religion was not a serious object of press scrutiny; that it deserved limited and compartmentalized treatment; that the journalists who would cover it were less professional because it demanded less professional treatment; that its readers were largely older, less educated, and less important; and that general readership interest was low.

These beliefs about religion news are very revealing not only for what they might tell us about its consequences for coverage but for what they can tell us about the media themselves, about American religion at this point in history, and about American religious discourse in general. The purpose of this book is to unpack each of these beliefs in some detail and in the process to look at the received understanding of religion in the news and consider a fuller picture of the relations between American religion and American media.

## ▪ The Sources of Change?

At some time in the recent past, the prospects and practices of religion news began to change. This was not the result of any specific incident at any fixed point but an evolution of events over a recent history in which the nature of American religion itself began to change by becoming more public. The following way points (indicated by italics) seem to be important ones.

The 1976 presidential campaign of *Jimmy Carter* stood in sharp contrast to precedent. Unlike in the election of 1960 where (for vastly different reasons) the winning candidate had to distance himself from his religion, Carter was quite open about his. By 1980, both major candidates would need to declare themselves "born-again Christians."

Also in the mid-1970s, a new form of *religious broadcasting* emerged on the national scene. Changes in federal regulation allowed alternative satellite-fed television networks to develop to service the growing cable television market, and the ministries that collectively came to be known as "televangelism" began drawing national attention. A number of these televangelists also began to verge into politics, generally supporting conservative social issues.

The rise of televangelism was part of (indeed, perhaps a major explanation for) a larger movement in *evangelicalism* away from a former political quietude into *political activism*. Conservative Christianity had traditionally been satisfied with the protected space of the private sphere. Through televangelism and political involvement, evangelicals became a force on the national scene.[8]

In 1978, *The Rev. Jim Jones* came to international attention as the leader of an apocalyptically inspired group living in the jungles of Guyana. A global media audience was horrified by pictures of the mass suicide that followed the assassination of a U.S. congressman by members of the group.

In 1979, *a revolution in Iran* (which involved Muslim traditionalists) installed an Imam, the Ayatollah Khomeini, as head of state. This was a shocking turn of events for a global political establishment steeped in twentieth-century ideals of secularism in politics.[9] The Islamic Revolution also introduced the misnomer "Islamic Fundamentalism" into the popular (and journalistic) lexicon.

The 1980s saw an acceleration of these sorts of religion news events. Conservative Christianity continued its movement toward political involvement during the Reagan years. A new, more media-friendly Pope began a series of high-profile travels throughout the world. In the mid-1980s, televangelism erupted into a series of spectacular scandals. In 1988, a prominent televangelist, Pat Robertson, ran for the Republican nomination for the presidency, completing a transition to political prominence that has become even more secure since.

The nature of American religion has also begun to change fundamentally as the millenium approaches. Increasingly, religious practice is something that takes place in the public marketplace rather than only in the privacy of homes, churches, mosques, and synagogues. As a result, a new range of religious symbols and practices now present themselves for press scrutiny.

But, looking back, the events in Iran in 1979 may well have been the watershed for the religion beat. An unprecedented amount of soul-searching seems to have resulted from the failure of the media and the political establishment to understand the depth of the role of Islam in what was thought to be—by all rights—a "purely" political movement. Religion scholar Ruel Tyson suggested at the time that the press's inadequate appraisal of the situation in Iran did not bode well for similar events in the future. In an introduction to a report on religion and the media,[10] Tyson noted the range of expert commentary on the topic available in the major media, among them a February 20, 1979, letter to the *New York Times* from cultural anthropologist Mary Catherine Bateson. Referring to its contents, Tyson observed,

> Professor Bateson noted the deep failure of understanding regarding the "fundamentally religious base" of movements such as that of the Imam Khomeini. She noted that this "failure is all the more frightening since we can expect it to be repeated unless we undertake a fundamental reappraisal of the role of religion in the world today."[11]

Tyson's thoughts appeared in an introduction to a set of papers produced by a number of scholars and media professionals who had been called together for a 1980 consultation on religion and the press sponsored by the Rockefeller Foundation. Several themes seemed to develop as that meeting considered the status of religion coverage. Some participants appealed to notions of journalistic *professionalism* as a potential antidote to the ills of the past. John Dart, a well-known religion writer at the *Los Angeles Times,* was a prominent voice in this direction, based on his reading of the history of religion journalism. Against a backdrop of what he called the "pious, dutiful" coverage that preceded it, Dart saw religion journalism on the upswing in 1980:

> I suppose it hasn't been all that miraculous, but the reporting and writing of religion news has improved greatly, and improved as the nation's newspapers, wire services, and newsmagazines have improved in general.[12]

Others among the Rockefeller conferees suggested that the issue could be laid at the feet of the particular society or culture of the news business and its inhabitants. Peter Steinfels, at that time the editor of the independent Catholic magazine *Commonweal* (and later to become a religion editor at the *New York Times*), steered the discussion in the direction of journalists and news decision makers and their own *perceptions* of the importance of religion. It was their outlook, he suggested, that led them to overlook the powerful role that religion played in the revolution in Iran.[13]

A third set of explanations emerged as well: Beyond the question of professionalism and its improvement and beyond questions of the interests or commitments of the people who work in the nation's newsrooms lay a more fundamental issue, the nature of American public discourse *about* religion. In his remarks, Steinfels stressed that the traditionally "privatized" nature of American religious experience meant that it crossed the boundary into public discussion only rarely and in inadequate ways.[14] Tyson suggested that as public discourse is largely the province of intellectual elites in the culture, their perceptions of these issues can be seen to be determinative:

> The manner in which religion is understood, or is not understood, among the various intellectual elites in publishing, the academy, and the professions profoundly affects the ways in which religious events and

movements are understood; and, in turn, these understandings implicate both the writing of religious news and the manner in which it is arranged for publication and viewing by the public at large.[15]


The Rockefeller conferees saw some room for optimism from the vantage point of 1980. Dart's suggestion that religion coverage was improving overall, along with the general sense that Iran and Jonestown had been lessons learned, seemed to indicate that there would be no going back to either the era of polite deference or a time of religion's relegation to the margins. And, indeed, some of the trends already apparent in the early 1980s have seemed to continue. Dart listed seven major metropolitan dailies that in 1980 had no religion writers.[16] Today, all of those on Dart's list that have survived *do* employ religion specialists, some of whom are among the best in the nation. Further, it is hard today to find *anyone* at any level of the news business who will argue that religion is trivial or that it should *not* be covered. And yet, as will be seen, the situation is still not settled.


## Looking for Answers

Clearly, all these considerations underscore the fact that the prospects and practices of religion news are embedded in a larger set of questions about the nature of American religious culture and relations between the worlds of religion and the media. It also seems clear that to in any way account for this complex story, we must address it along the lines predicted by those Rocke-feller conferees nearly two decades ago. We must understand religion cov-erage through the experiences and actions of *those who do the job:* working journalists and editors in the print and nonprint media. We must also under-stand the extent to which those journalists work within a *specific cultural surround:* the culture of the newsroom and the larger news business. Finally, we must understand the extent to which the media, as they contemplate religion, do so within a *larger context of public discourse.*

Journalistic practice can be seen as a kind of broad generalism that has as its goal the creation of narratives that speak to heterogeneous audiences. Even journalistic "specialization" is oriented toward a realm of public perceptions and public discourse that is general in nature. Journalism does not alone create these perceptions and discourses. Instead, it speaks both *to* and *for* them. Ruel Tyson has described this role as one rooted in the notion of *consensus* and by extension *reflexive* consensus; that is, it is both "consensus made" and "consensus making":

> The reason that newspapers and other media are consensus-making and consensus-made institutions is that stories fit a range of cultural preconceptions of news. The cultural preconceptions are expressed, not as such, but rather in the "fit" of the facts, the fit of a news story into available conventions for writing that story. To study the way the media cover religion is to study the constitutive rules that govern the display of stories in the media, rules that are never stated as such but that are presented through the conventions of news writing.[17]

Tyson's point has been more famously put in Robert Darnton's recounting of a waggish turn on the *New York Times*'s motto: "all the news that fits we print." Mark Silk credits Darnton with the sophisticated understanding that the conditioning of stories to fit the newspaper is both a common practice and a functional one:

> Unlike many critics of the media, Darnton does not accuse newsfolk of distorting reality to suit their own sovereign prejudices. He understands, as only a practitioner fully can, that the cultural preconceptions found in reporting are stock sentiments and figures that journalists share with their public—and from which they learn not to deviate too far.[18]

As the historical instances we have discussed and some we will look at in succeeding chapters illustrate, the media—and the public discourses into which they write and speak—regularly suffer from a lack of expertise in, and attention to, the fundamental nature of religious experience and practice and its role in contemporary life. This sentiment has been expressed in some prominent places in recent years, and by some prominent—and contrasting—voices in the public sphere. Commentator Jeff Greenfield put it this way in a broadcast of *ABC World News Tonight:* "When it comes to the day-to-day presence of religion in America's media, it's a very different story. In fact, usually it's no story at all."[19]

At a time when the amount of religion coverage seems to be on the upswing, we must ask whether it is enough to suggest that more coverage of religion *alone* will solve the problems implied by the widespread criticisms of the religion beat or that a more "professional" approach *alone* will necessarily suffice. The *nature* and *depth* of coverage are also important questions when considering the legacy of Waco and other important religion stories. This implies that some *normative* standards of religion coverage need to be applied.

These concerns can be said to reside in three separate but related domains: the *profession of journalism itself, contemporary religion,* with its many and varied practices and institutions, and *public discourse,* the broadest of the three, into which both journalism and religion fit and to which they both contribute to a greater or lesser degree.

Journalism and religion share the need to "make sense" to the broad cultural environment of contemporary life. As Ruel Tyson suggests, the relationship between the practice of journalism, the reality of religious practice, and the sphere of public discourse is a symbiotic one. As he puts it, journalism is "consensus made" and "consensus making." Each of these three domains is heavily interconnected with the others. Where they become *distinct* is at critical points of controversy or crisis, as demonstrated by, for example, the Koresh and "Heaven's Gate" incidents. In those cases, the realm of public discourse and public perception functioned to establish the extents and limits of civil action and the demand for the journalistic product, that is, the "news." The domain of religion provided the concrete incidents in the first instance but also presented competing claims as to their representativeness and legitimacy as various religious spokespeople strove to define themselves vis-à-vis these "aberrations." Finally, the domain of "the media" faced the challenge of interpreting "the religious" within the conditions of the contemporary public sphere along with its necessary expectations and definitions.

### ■ A Larger Question

The relations between "religion" and "the media" have long been contentious, and there are some fundamental reasons why this will always be the case. *Religious beliefs and practices* present a particular kind of challenge to journalism. Over and above the intrinsic problem of interpreting something that defies the evidential processes of conventional journalism (that is to say, that it is "intangible") is the fact that in contemporary (media-saturated) public life religious *people* and *institutions* have an incentive to engage in "publicity" efforts of various kinds. Leaders of movements such as "Heaven's Gate," the Branch Davidians, or the Church Universal and Triumphant seek to appeal to the "court of public opinion" but so too do their definers and critics from elsewhere along the religious spectrum. The world of religion is thus a "moving target" for journalists, and as it undergoes change, our understandings, definitions, and coverage of it will also change.

In the final analysis, journalistic practice vis-à-vis religion and religious practice vis-à-vis the media are defined by the *broader realm of public discourse* and its definitions and expectations of both "religion" and "the media." The way the media handle religion is deeply embedded in a set of historical, cultural, and political perceptions about religion's natural, proper, or desirable place in democratic public life.

## ■ Quantity or Quality?

As commentators stand outside this system and look in, their criticisms of media treatment of religion seem to follow two lines of argument. There are questions of *quantity* and questions of *quality.* Arguments about the quantity of attention given to religion can be made simply and starkly and, indeed, have been made by some rather prominent voices. Columnist Terry Mattingly, writing in *Quill,* the journal of the Society of Professional Journalists, has noted that figures as diverse as Norman Lear, Billy Graham, and Shirley MacLaine are of one voice on the matter:

> For years, Graham has asked why newspapers assign thousands to cover sports and only a handful to religion. And [Shirley] MacLaine preached a similar sermon in an April address to the American Society of Newspaper Editors.[20]

Jimmy Allen, coauthor of a report on religion and media, echos those sentiments:

> At most papers you have one-tenth or less the number of people on religion that you have on sports. Yet many more people go to church weekly than go to sporting events. You have to wonder whether that balance is right.[21]

The late George Cornell, the long-time religion editor at Associated Press, once suggested that the proportionality is not as important as the simple question of religion being ignored. As a voluble element of contemporary life, it deserves to be represented in the news.

Religion is a determining element in the human story, a powerful ingredient of the social mix. To disregard religion in chronicling that story prevents any intelligent perspective on conditions in this society or any other. Certainly no one can understand America, its history and present forces without understanding the nature and the history of its religious life. After all, that was mainly what brought settlers here in the first place. The news media have begun, slowly but surely, to record this provocative dimension of American life more completely and competently.[22]

Questions of quality of coverage are more difficult to address. Indeed, it is largely the purpose of this book to elaborate the extent of the qualitative purchase of the media on religion. We know that the religion beat has traditionally been marginalized and misunderstood. We also have reason to suspect that its prospects are changing for the better. It is now seen as more necessary and more interesting than in the past, and more space and time have been devoted to it. But, we must ask, "What *is* the coverage that is evolving?"

Media treatment of religion can be seen as a kind of indicator of the broader role and status of religion on the contemporary scene. That the media have so easily and tacitly accepted the notion of the secularization of society as a guiding principle of coverage does suggest the extent to which this idea is embedded in American social, political, and educational philosophy. However, the media also have an educational function. They do inform public discourse. Thus their role is more than just a litmus; they also contribute something to public knowledge.

But it can be further argued that, for very good reasons, the media must move beyond a mere "informational" role. The success of the American experiment depends in part on our ability to engage in a kind of public discourse that successfully takes account of the diversity of religious values and sentiments present in it. Because of their prominence in that discourse, the media—and particularly journalism—are implicated in this task to a greater degree than they might realize.

To see the way ahead, it makes sense to address issues surrounding the dimensions already discussed: the necessity of understanding two interacting sets of dimensions. First, we must look at *journalism itself,* along three related lines: the work of the *journalist,* the *institutional context* of the journalist, and the *public discourse* that surrounds those practices and is specific to them. Second, we must understand that this construct actually makes up one of a larger set of domains. We must also investigate how *journalism* about religion relates to the domains of *contemporary religion* and of *public discourse*. This book is dedicated to this task. It wishes to address the question with which I began this chapter, but it is clear that this question in turn begs a number of other ones.

## ▉ The Structure of This Book

This book pursues these questions by moving along several related lines of inquiry. The most basic data used here came from interviews with *journalists, readers,* and *listeners* and from a series of national surveys conducted over the course of several years of formal research. Empirical sources are, however, not enough. They must be understood within the contexts of the social and cultural discourses of which they are a part. Therefore, this volume "bookends" empirical findings with chapters dealing with the history, policy, and culture surrounding relations between "religion" and "the news."

I begin, in Chapter 2, by placing these considerations in contexts of history and practice. The way we talk about religion coverage, both inside and outside the media, is largely determined by our collective memory and by canons of professional practice. Whatever change may be under way must build on these received understandings. This historical review of religion coverage is followed by a look at the context of the experience of working religion journalists, as they reflect on their own senses of the expectations and defnitions that surround their work.

Chapter 3 looks at relations between the private and public faces of religion. Relations between religion and the press are rooted in history and culture, and we need to take account of how the construction of religion in the media is embedded in broader understandings of American religious discourse.

What is the evidence that the treatment of religion is changing and in what ways? A number of vocal critics of the media hold that the secularism of media institutions makes it impossible for religion to be fairly and reasonably treated. Others suggest that it is not antireligion but *irreligion* that describes the situation. Still others contend that religion treatment is, in fact, rooted in a fundamental, consensual civil religion, of which it tacitly approves. Chapter 4 considers these issues in more detail.

Chapter 5 looks at the religion beat in more detail in further discussions with working journalists. American religious culture is in a period of change and ferment, and this change is reflected in the day-to-day work of the press as it approaches the religion story.

In Chapter 6, individuals from a variety of religious backgrounds talk about their expectations, experiences, and understandings of religion coverage. Although the received wisdom in the media regarding religion news has some rather narrow understandings of reader interests and wants, the informants in this chapter widen the envelope by displaying some remarkably sophisticated understandings of the nature of news and the relations between religion and public discourse.

Chapter 7 reviews national survey data on public interest in the religion beat. There has been surprisingly little research done on this topic, and these numbers are quite revealing. They significantly broaden our understanding of the religious nature of the news audience and its expectations and interests.

Chapter 8 considers the tension between religion and the press as a function of a fundamental conflict between these institutions. The realm of publicity and mediated public culture is a context increasingly determinative of institutional action. This chapter looks at some recent issues and incidents in religion and the press for insights into these matters.

Chapter 9 introduces both a historical and a contemporary analysis of broadcast treatment of religion. Broadcasting provides an interesting case study of policy making regarding the coverage of religion and a valuable insight into the self-conscious crafting of religion content for a new context.

Chapter 10 considers evolving understandings of journalistic practice vis-à-vis religion, evaluates competing prescriptions for improvement, and suggests normative standards by which religion treatment might be judged.

Finally, in Chapter 11, I return to critical questions facing the profession of journalism. Considering the nature of contemporary media, public discourse, and religious evolution, what should the role of journalism be? What are its prospects, and what can reasonably be expected of it?

## ▇ Defining Religion

Scholars of religion have long held that there are two major ways of defining and understanding it. The first of these focuses on its *essential* or *substantive* characteristics. In this view, religion is best accounted for in terms of its substantive dimensions of meaning and practice. In this view, something is religion if it is "essentially" religion. Mircea Eliade's works on the nature of religion are important and central sources of this perspective.[23] The second way of understanding religion has been called *functionalist* in that it focuses on the purposes, meanings, and practices that surround those areas of culture we think of as religious.[24]

This distinction clearly relies on overgeneralization and has recently come under scrutiny within the field of religious studies. Those debates are beyond the scope of the task here other than in the sense that they help us understand that the "functionalist" approach is the most significant one to us. Debates over the distinction have helped illustrate the extent to which essentialist ways of understanding religion rely too heavily on formal categories that may blind us to the ebb and flow of contemporary religious evolution.

This point has been forcefully made in important recent works by Stephen Warner and others.[25] Warner points out that a wide range of religious forms, meanings, and practices now dot the cultural landscape, many of which are simply unaccounted for if we use only the measure of their formal or essential "religiousness." Instead, religion scholarship is beginning to focus more and more of its attention on practice, where symbols, values, meanings, and rituals can be observed as they form, shape, and evolve.

This is particularly helpful to the considerations here, because (as will be seen) the range of phenomena that present themselves as religious or potentially religious in the sphere of public and media discourse is wide indeed. In a sense, then, this book does not have a definition of religion of its own, if by that is meant a formal or essentialist one. The book does consider many definitions of religion, particularly those that emerge in the experience of working journalists and others within the media whose task it is to account for the religious in those contexts. But the purpose here is not to define or classify or legitimate religion or "the religious." There are two fundamental reasons for this. First, as will be seen, it is not clear that to do so would help clarify or solve any of the dilemmas that underlie the basic challenge of covering religion. Second, as religion scholars are telling us, the range of things that are now emerging, which we must consider as "religious," is wide indeed and would defy any attempts at a summative definition.

Therefore, the extent of phenomena that might fit under the umbrella of religion in the considerations here is very wide. Traditional religions are of course included but so are many emerging or "new" religious movements. It can be argued, in addition, that contemporary religious ferment also includes a panoply of practices and symbols that are not movements but exist and find presence in other ways.[26] The complexity of this landscape seems to have two major implications for media. It makes the field covered by religion journalism very broad and in some ways diffuse. It also centers the practice of journalism within the emergence of religion in a rather fundamental way. If the purpose of journalism is to be in the middle of public discourse, then with the emergence of new cultural forms, which are by their nature public (as most religious trends and movements eventually become), journalism has a role in investigating and interpreting these developments for the culture at large.


## Notes

1. Tammeus, Bill. 1994. Religious freedom under fire. *Kansas City Star,* April 17, p. K1.

2. Indeed, public opinion data suggest broad public support for government action against the Mt. Carmel group. This sentiment of course derived from the level of public knowledge available at the time. See Silk, Mark. 1995. *Unsecular media: Making news of religion in America.* Urbana: University of Illinois Press, p. 97.

3. Schudson, Michael. 1987. *Discovering the news: A social history of American newspapers.* New York: Basic Books; Tuchman, Gaye. 1978. *Making news: A study in the construction of reality.* New York: Free Press; see also Silk, *Unsecular media.*

4. *Weekend Edition/Sunday,* National Public Radio, March 7, 1993.

5. Interview, *All Things Considered,* National Public Radio, December 31, 1997.

6. God decentralized. *New York Times Magazine,* Sunday, November 30, 1997.

7. Nieman Reports. 1997. The faith of journalists: Does their religion help or hinder them professionally? *Nieman Reports* 51(3).

8. Balmer, Randall. Address to the annual convention of the Religion Newswriters' Association, Colorado Springs, July 15, 1995.

9. Brown, Warren. 1979. CIA didn't forsee "national revolution" in Iran, chief says. *Washington Post,* February 5, p. A5.

10. Tyson, Ruel. 1981. Introduction. In *The religion beat: The reporting of religion in the media.* A Rockefeller Foundation Conference Report. New York: Author, pp. 1-7.

11. Ibid., p. 3.

12. Dart, John. 1981. The religion beat. In *The religion beat,* pp. 19-26.

13. Steinfels, Peter. 1981. Public news, private religion. In *The religion beat,* p. 28.

14. Ibid., p. 31.

15. Tyson, Introduction. In *The religion beat,* p. 1.

16. Dart, The religion beat. In *The religion beat,* p. 22.

17. Tyson, Ruel. 1987. Journalism and religion. In *The encyclopedia of religion,* edited by Mircea Eliade. New York: Macmillan, pp. 121-7.

18. Silk, *Unsecular media,* pp. 49-50.

19. Greenfield, Jeff. *ABC World News Tonight,* August 13, 1993.

20. Mattingly, Terry. 1993. Religion in the news: Are we short-changing readers and ourselves with biases that filter news? *Quill,* July/August, p. 13.

21. Allen, Jimmy. Informal remarks to the winter meeting of the National Council of Churches Communication Commission, Chicago, February 10, 1994.

22. Dart, John and Jimmy Allen. 1993. *Bridging the gap: Religion and the news media.* Nashville, TN: Freedom Forum First Amendment Center, p. 54.

23. Eliade, Mircea, ed., *The encyclopedia of religion.* See also Eliade, Mircea. 1959. *The sacred and the profane: The nature of religion.* New York: Harcourt Brace Jovanovich.

24. For an important commentary on the distinction, see Berger, Peter. 1974. Some second thoughts on substantive versus functional definitions of religion. *Journal for the Scientific Study of Religion* 13:25-33.

25. Warner, R. Stephen. 1993. Work in progress toward a new paradigm for the sociological study of religion in the United States. *American Journal of Sociology* 98: 1044-93. See also, Albanese, Catherine. 1996. Religion and popular American culture: An essay. *Journal of the American Academy of Religion* 4:733-43; and McDannel, Coleen. 1995. *Material Christianity.* New Haven, CT: Yale University Press, pp. 1-16.

26. As an example, the coming of the millenium has seemed to spark an impressive array of new trends and movements. The Associated Press reported that millenium thinking has now suffused a number of traditional congregations and organizations (Millenium more than just a number to some. *Boulder Daily Camera,* January 2, 1998, p. 4B).

# 2

# APPROACHES TO
# UNDERSTANDING

I f religion is a troublesome topic for the news business, that unease is felt first and most often in the experience of the working religion journalist. There are relatively few such positions in American media, most of them confined to the major metropolitan dailies and the newsmagazines. A recent account reported the total membership of the Religion Newswriters Association at 200, with fewer than half that number working full-time.[1]

Only since 1990 has there been more than an idiosyncratic one or two working in broadcasting nationally and locally. The numbers there are still not overwhelming. ABC hired the first network-level television religion reporter in 1994. Three or four local television stations seem to have added religion staff during the 1990s. And, in spite of a raft of religion coverage in television newsmagazines and other places on the dial as the millenium approaches, the engagement of actual religion specialists continues to be limited.

On one level of analysis, this relative paucity of personnel seems to suggest a ready solution to the problem of the quantity of religion coverage: employ more reporters. However, things are not that simple. Religion has long been a part of the American news business. Had it found a more comfortable place there, the question of numbers would have resolved itself as a matter of course. Instead, religion's role in news has always been a problematic one, and this has been both ironic and curious in light of history. Religious publishing was, in fact, integral to the formation of the American media industries. Among the first printing enterprises were those devoted to the production of Bibles, tracts, and newsletters.[2] Early American journalism even included a category of commercial journalism that was more self-consciously "religious" than we would be comfortable with in the "secular press" today.[3]

A major defining moment came with the development of the "penny press" in the early 19th century. Before that time, journalism itself was extensively compartmentalized. What we would think of as general-interest newspapers today were heavily influenced by partisan interests; others were devoted to various commercial and mercantile purposes. The development of mass-circulation newspapers changed that situation. The early innovators of the form saw great potential in the development of large-circulation publications that could balance income lost from lower cover prices with income gained from advertising. Advertisers would be attracted by the efficiency of reaching large numbers of readers. This recognized a fundamental demographic reality: Larger populations of working-class immigrants were crowding American cities, and the penny press became a way of reaching them with what has been called a more "democratic" medium.[4]

The commercialization and democratization of American journalism created a new, more independent role for the publisher. Before the era of the mass press, publication was more closely tied economically to formal political and commercial interests. With the mass press emerged the "press baron." Even though the reputations of publishers and editors such as William Randolph Hearst, Joseph Pulitzer, Horace Greeley, and James Gordon Bennett approach legend, it is important to realize that these were editorial innovators who had to find ways to make their papers continually compelling to increasingly diverse audiences of mixed educational, political, and economic backgrounds.

Bennett discovered early on that religion could sell papers, not in the form of religious content per se but because religious *controversy* made "good copy." Bennett's *New York Herald* set an entirely new tone by introducing religion as news into its pages. This was at some variance with prior practice, where religious journals, like their political and commercial counterparts, had pretty much controlled their own turf.[5] Just as was its practice with business, politics, and other topics, Bennett's *Herald* covered religion from its own point of view, and the result was volatile. He was roundly criticized by religious leaders and the religious press. What journalism saw as independence, religion saw as rampant secularism and a threat to its authority.[6]

Besides simply covering religion from the outside, Bennett took the step of *editorially* addressing religion, which further alienated him from the religious institutions and leaders who were the objects of his criticism and who organized pressure on him. Although it has been demonstrated that Bennett continued to provide substantial coverage of religion, some of it neutral, even positive,[7] Bennett's approach, and the controversy it stimulated, has entered journalism's collective memory as religion coverage's "myth of origin." That myth tends to remember the controversy, and an eventual mediation toward less controversy, but not the more traditional ways the *Herald* and competing papers treated religion. Bennett, for example, began the practice, finally abandoned by the *New York Times* in the 1960s, of covering the Sunday sermons in the leading city pulpits. It is also often forgotten that his approach to religion maintained readership interest by applying the classic Bennett formula of the essential human interest angle.[8]

By the latter half of the 19th century, the world of religion had gradually become used to the idea that it might be scrutinized by the secular press. There was still criticism from religious leaders over such things as the sensationalized sex and crime that continued to dominate the mass-circulation press and the move to Sunday editions by many papers. But a kind of domestic tranquility seemed to evolve, along with a kind of domesticated coverage. Major revivals and other happenings in the world of religion received press attention, but the kind of critical editorial commentary Bennett himself had pioneered faded from view.[9] The evolution of the Sunday edition (which, in an appeal to respectability, fashioned itself as "family fare") may have had something to do with this domestication, as did the evolution of the "church page," which became a staple of Saturday editions. Thus the "myth of origin" tends to remember both the controversy of the early years and the eventual modulation of the treatment of religion.

It is a widely held view that commercial considerations played a role in these matters, particularly in the evolution of the Saturday "church page." To this day, there is a suspicious eye cast on these pages, where, particularly in small markets, there seems to be a correspondence between the size and number of paid ads and the largely honorific stories of local religion that appear.

The cultural memory of religious controversy is long and continued to provide a justification for domesticated coverage for many years. Few spokespeople have been as clear on this point as was Lawrence C. Martin of the *Denver Post,* who told an audience of journalism students in 1940,

> Religion is a fruitful source of controversy; I mean by that the creeds, sectarian differences and denominational quibbles which are among the human perversions of true religion. In times past, newspapers got into so many scrapes over these religious squabbles that most editors drew in their horns and actually barred from their columns any but the most harmless and noncontroversial items about churches or religious topics. Even today you will find most editors refusing to print letters from readers on religion, for fear of inciting a riot. Thus through the years there grew up, with good reason, a journalistic feeling that religion in the paper was dynamite.[10]

Relatively quiet and noncontroversial coverage thus served the purpose of appearing to account for religion without opening up to controversy. The convention of a church page, and its placement on Saturday (where its ads would be more useful for attracting Sunday attendence), was an ideal forum for this approach. To the extent that the Saturday page became the only location where religion could appear, this practice established a practical barrier to hard news approaches to religion. Saturday is not an important news day. Holding religion stories, which might appear earlier in the week, for the Saturday edition further delegitimated them. The result was a convention that, by the 1950s, had religion news defined into a rather narrow set of expectations, most of which were at some variance with the canons of conventional news.

Historians and observers are split on the question of the nature of religion coverage between 1900 and 1950. Although the domesticated approach appears to have held sway, there were prominent exceptions. The Scopes trial of the 1920s received widespread "hard news" and editorial treatment. The revivals led by Billy Sunday, Charles Fuller, "Fighting Bob" Shuler, and Billy Graham received widespread coverage. The fact that William Randoph Hearst directed his papers to give Graham favorable coverage is a widely recounted anecdote in journalism history.

In a recent review of the record, journalist and historian Mark Silk takes issue with the received view that religion news between Bennett and the emergence of the religious controversies of the 1970s and onward was predictable, pat, and otherwise nonexistent. Silk identifies a number of major religion stories of the first half of the 1950s, and ponts out that leading thinkers of mainstream religion received their share of coverage in the mainstream media. Why this period appeared to be one of quietude on the religion front was that the stories were "good" ones:

> Ecumenism was a good thing, Billy Graham was a good thing, Vatican II was a good thing. Religious support for the civil rights movement and religious opposition to the war in Vietnam would seem like good things, too. It was when religion no longer appeared to be always on the side of the angels that it once again became problematic for the news media to cover.[11]

Thus, according to Silk, the coverage that religion received before 1970 was so naturalized that it often did not register. But it cannot be denied that this naturalization involved a certain amount of standardization and generalization. According to Silk, historian Kenneth Nordin has argued that this, in fact, helped maintain religious consensus during the period.

In this reified and standardized formula and structure for religion coverage, the role of the religion journalist was made problematic. It appears that the practice of naming a designated religion writer emerged along with increasing specialization in beats after the so-called reform era of journalism in the 1920s. While no comprehensive scholarly history exists, scattered accounts suggest that before the founding of the Religion Newswriters' Association (RNA) in 1949 religion writers attempted to approach coverage in ways consistent with the general expectations of the journalistic profession but continued to face opposition from entrenched views of the relations between religion and the press and of the proper place of religion in the press.

In fact, George Cornell, the long-time religion editor for the Associated Press (and arguably the most widely read religion journalist of the 20th century and now deceased) contends that the founding of the RNA had the dual purpose of upgrading the professionalism of the beat and the promotion of the beat and improvement of its status among the media industries.[12]

That religion journalism required such efforts is an indicator of the broader nature of its position as a focus of the relations between the media and religion in the 20th century. It struggles against both the myth of origin of religion in the news and a set of contemporary received understandings of its role and status.

The consensual strategy toward religion that has evolved has been rooted in an understanding of religion as largely an institutional story. The kind of domesticated coverage that emerged after the turn of the century (and which achieved its firmest expression during the Eisenhower era) was, in fact, rooted in the religious culture of the 19th century, where Bennett found religion news in the actions of formal religious institutions and their leaders. Ninteenth-century American religion, it must be pointed out, was profoundly less diverse than is the case today, and so reticence based on the complexity and controversy of the religious landscape seems today almost ironic by comparison.

The approach to religion in the period before 1980 was also one that included a good bit of *deference* to religious leaders and institutions. It was a "polite" era, as described by veteran *Los Angeles Times* religion editor John Dart, when that which was not treated with deference was relegated to the margins.[13] This deferential attitude was also expressed in the convention of he Saturday church page, which symbolized the relationship between newspapers and religion as service provider and client rather than journalist and object of scrutiny.

Dart recounts his own movement into the beat as a moment of transition from the past of polite deference to a present of professionalism. In a small but significant anecdote, he recalled that his predecessor on the beat, Dan Thrapp, had always answered his phone with the words "church editor," even though the *Times* had long since given him the more general title "religion editor."[14] The distinction is a significant one along two lines. To say that one is covering religion and not the church is to recognize a point of view that can account for specific churches or organizations and their actions without necessarily assuming that they are coterminous with the world of religion. Further, to say that one is covering religion and not just the church begins a process of gradual liberation from the domestication of the Saturday page.

In the experience of the working journalist, the received understanding of religion is felt in the expectations of readers and sources who have been conditioned by traditional approaches to coverage. But the received view is more powerfully felt through the newsroom culture within which one must work. Far from being a craft that finds its models for action in reified formal standards of professionalism and professional action, journalistic practice has been shown to be strongly influenced by its professional cohorts. Journalism is a cultural practice involving the crafting of narratives within expectations that are powerfully enforced by colleagues.[15]

Dart expresses the marginalization of the beat in an anecdote:

> I like to say that if the second coming did happen, the general-assignment people would do the main story and they would ask the religion writer to do a side-bar or two. So, religion news, no matter who it is covered by, is getting more coverage, but not necessarily by religion writers.[16]

Most working religion reporters have direct experiences to share. Don Lattin of the *San Francisco Chronicle* reports that when first assigned to the beat he encountered numerous colleagues who expressed amazement at his interest in it: " 'Why would you want to do that?' they'd ask." The traditional way of seeing religion journalism was rooted both in the domesticity of it and in the sense that the beat reflected negatively on the professionalism of anyone who would be interested in taking it seriously. This is a situation that is now changing, as we shall see, but its outlines continue to provide the backdrop of the beat's status and prospects across the board.

One of the first challenges facing religion journalism is the definition of the beat itself. Exactly what *is* religion news? Conversations with working religion reporters reveal a range of answers to this question. Interestingly, few of them revert to a definition that depends on the actions of religious institutions—itself a significant turnabout from the view held since the time of Bennett. Most instead assume religion to be something independent of what denominations, churches, and their leaders are up to:

> Religion coverage is coverage of anything having to do with philosophy of life or attitudes toward life and death. The secular paper has to explain these things to the wider public.

> Religion news is where, in order to understand a story or understand a development, some explanation of the religious aspect needs to be included in it.

> News is news, whether it is about religion, politics, sociology, crime, etc. If it ain't *news,* it ain't religion *news.*

> Religion is news because it affects large numbers of people.[17]

What these definitions have in common is the assumption of a normative category one might call "newsworthiness."[18] That is, religion news must fit some conventional notions of what is or is not news. This approach directly resolves two very important challenges to religion journalists. First, it clearly integrates their work into the professional domain of the news business in general, denying received notions that the religion beat is somehow separate, protected, or marginal space. Second, it addresses the pervasive and un-resolvable problem with religion: how to deal with the fact that some of its claims are *substantive* ones that lie outside the empirical realm. Tom Brisson, religion editor of the *Bakersfield Californian,* put it this way:

> At a newspaper, it is a matter of *survival* to cover religion as a matter of *behavior.* You must try to be *objective* in the news business—it *must* be from a *news* standpoint. If it is not, then you're finished [collegially *and* professionally].[19]

Teresa Wasson, managing editor of the *Nashville Tennessean,* understands the limitations of the approach but agrees that journalists must necessarily confine themselves to the empirical realm.

> We do cover what religion "thinks it is about." It thinks it is about faith and belief, and here in the Bible Belt it is tied to belief in the resurrec-tion and things like that. We take as a matter of fact that many people have spiritual needs. We focus on how they go about fulfilling those needs.[20]

This is a widely shared view among religion journalists, that the force and effect of the beat is to address religion in terms of its observable behaviors. The existence and substance of faith and spirituality is more or less "brack-eted," and the journalist goes on from there. This approach stipulates that such things can be taken as a precondition of the behaviors and attitudes that are the subject of stories and can be assumed to be involved in the particular story in question. The story can then be written without sacrificing conven-tional news judgment by focusing on the behaviors and attitudes instead of the "substance."

One of the outcomes of the domestication of religion news has been its definition primarily in *local* and *parochial* terms. This makes sense as part of the logic that created the Saturday church page. If the primary (and uncontroversial) purchase of religion on the public imagination is in the local context, then little else by way of religion news will find its way in. Helen Parmley, former religion editor of the *Dallas Morning News,* describes this criterion as nearly absolute: "Religion is a local story, primarily. Religion usually must have a local angle to get in, at least religion as *we* cover it."[21]

This localizing tendency is, of course, not unique to religion. One of journalism's historical cycles throughout its various epochs has been toward, and then again away from, the local.[22] Presently, the competitive nature of the metropolitan news business has pushed papers toward an increasing emphasis on localism. What is merely cyclic for other beats, however, tends to be an endemic construction for religion, even at major papers that seem to take a particularly "hard news" approach to the beat.

Religion's parochialism is a related matter. An often-heard view of the business is that "the complaints we get from readers are when we don't cover their church's bake sale." But there is a less pecuniary end to this assumed parochialism. In the traditional view, readers are most concerned about their own faith and little interested in others. This also seems to be based on perceptions gained from those readers who call or write to complain.[23]

The assumption of localism and parochialism, the fear of controversy, and the traditional sense that religion is not "hard news" have combined to marginalize the religion beat, something that the working religion journalist must still face on a fairly regular basis. Appeals to professionalism become a symbolic response to this marginalization. Most religion reporters point to conventional ideas of professionalism as an antidote. Pam Schaeffer of the *St. Louis Post-Dispatch* put it this way:

> The bottom line is trust. We have to get the editors, readers, public, etc., to trust us. We have to *sell* the story to *all* of these contexts. . . . We have to be skilled as journalists and knowledgeable about our sources beyond the *obvious* stories.[24]

Teresa Wasson of the *Tennessean,* a paper that has developed a reputation for sophisticated religion news, echoes this view:

> Religion is very rich turf, in news value, and many editors don't know that. That is because *they have not seen it demonstrated.* The models of the kind of religion coverage as "hard news" that we do, are few and far between, and most editors and reporters have not seen it done like this before.[25]

Thus the common approach seems to be one of supporting increasing professionalism and the treatment of religion as a serious, newsworthy beat. This is all well and good at the *output* side of religion journalism. The outcome of serious coverage justifies itself, according to this calculus, and with some considerable success. Don Lattin reports that he was rather quickly able to turn skepticism around by the kinds of stories he covered and the way he covered them when he took on the beat. But what of the *input* side? What about the controversy that has so troubled the news business about religion? And controversy is related to the complexity of religion. There are, in short, so many religions (or so the thinking goes) and with adherents of any one of them ready to complain about the slightest offense, the challenge of good religion news hardly seems worth the effort.

However, controversy can be seen differently. Although it continues to be a concern, it is becoming less of a disincentive to coverage. As is discussed in more detail in Chapter 5, the decline in concern about controversy may be related to the erosion of the deference with which religion was once treated. This change in attitude toward religion seems to be directly related to changes in the nature of American religious culture in general. Frank Sotomayor, who has supervised the religion beat at the *Los Angeles Times,* sees the change against the backdrop of the traditional approach:

A lot of religion coverage was very soft [in the past]. Mostly features on denominations and preachers, and if you go way back, a lot of papers were covering Sunday sermons, and that would be religion coverage. I think the coverage itself has improved. There are models of people doing it right, and that has helped to change peoples' attitudes.[26]

In other words, in the "establishment era," coverage of the establishment's religious *institutions* could suffice. Now that the institutions themselves have become more diverse and now that much of what we would want to call religion takes place outside these traditional institutions, coverage has become more complex and nuanced. John Dart sees it this way:

That was back in the fifties when the Protestant mainliners were inherently more of an influence. As people became more aware of the broadening pluralistic religious scene, Protestantism wasn't seen as representative of American religion anymore. Catholic homilies were short, fundamentalists only quoted scripture, rabbis did it on the wrong day. It [the concentration on coverage of institutional statements and

sermons] was really a holdover from when the *New York Times* used to
have copy boys going out and doing it.[27]

As dominant religious institutions have declined in legitimacy so has the
tendency to treat them (and indeed, the whole of the religion story) with
*deference*. Religion has more easily become *news* when it has resembled
other beats, and that has also affected the general way it is regarded by the
news business. Gustav Niebuhr, whose career included stints at the *Atlanta
Constitution, Wall Street Journal,* and *Washington Post* prior to the *New York
Times,* sees the change in deferential attitudes as stemming from a general
willingness to be more aggressive toward religion as well as other beats.

> The whole situation has changed. Papers are now much more receptive
> to "stepping on toes" than in the early days. Most papers are now seen
> as dull, and our editors are interested in controversy, religious and not.[28]

The reflections and experiences of working religion journalists begin to
describe for us the outlines of the *received view* of religion in the news at
this point in history. With change clearly in the wind, this view is the
backdrop against which this change is taking place.

First, unnamed in the background of the received view of religion is the
idea of *secularization*. Secularization holds that as societies and cultures
become more modern, more advanced, and more rationalized, they necessarily also become more *secular*. Peter Berger has provided the definitive
description of this process:

> By secularization we mean the process by which sectors of society and
> culture are removed from the domination of religious institutions and
> symbols. . . . As there is a secularization of society and culture, so is
> there a secularization of consciousness. Put simply, this means that the
> modern west has produced an increasing number of individuals who
> look upon the world and their own lives without the benefit of religious
> interpretation.[29]

Secularization is thus seen to be the underlying structure against which
trends must be judged. Its inevitability has achieved canonical status in
American intellectual life, although it is now under considerable challenge
in the scholarly community.[30] Controversy over it notwithstanding, much of
what we have seen in the development of American religion over the past

half-century could be taken as supportive of an overall secularizing trend. Religious institutions have indeed faded in prominence. However, as Wade Clark Roof[31] and Robert Wuthnow[32] have observed, the decline of the formerly prominent institutions can also be seen as an evacuation of certain modes of religiosity in favor of others. In fact, according to many scholars, the fundamental religiosity of the American public has persisted and even shown remarkable vitality and adaptability, as people have begun to explore new avenues of faith expression, from the "megachurches" of the religious "right" to the "new religiosities" (such as the "new age" movement) of the "left."

And yet, if we look only at the prospects of traditional religious *institutions,* these trends could appear to support the overall theory of secularization. Therefore, a deterioration in press coverage of religion in the years following the Eisenhower era might well have appeared justified, as religion itself seemed to be deteriorating.

The second component of the received view of religion is that religion is fundamentally a *private* matter. Stephen Carter has provided an important recent account of this idea of religious privatism. Religion is seen as a "hobby," says Carter, something that is accorded legitimacy in private experience but is largely outside the realm of acceptable public modes of knowing and doing. It is thus not like politics or business or education. It is unique both in its modes of legitimacy and in its locus of action.[33]

The third element of the received view, and one already discussed here, is the fact that religion makes claims *outside the empirical realm* and thus outside the realm of the concrete and knowable. Journalistic practice is all about verification and sources, and religion is fundamentally unverifiable. As former CBS correspondent Bernard Kalb put it on a CNN broadcast, "the media deals [sic] in facts, religion in faith."[34] Jeff Greenfield of ABC concurs: "News and drama rely on conflict, action. The quiet, daily influence of faith is hard to cover. Then there's the nature of media people—more skeptical, more secular."[35]

Fourth, as has already been noted, religion is thought to be *complex.* Many journalists and editors express the sentiment that "there are so many of them" and that it is hard to choose among them. Implicit in this argument is the idea that the journalist's task of "objectivity" is made particularly difficult when there exists a multiplicity of perspectives from which to choose. In their study of these issues, John Dart and Jimmy Allen quote correspondent Judy Woodruff: "It is difficult in a secular news program to fit them in. We're dealing with an audience of every conceivable religious background."[36]

And again, Jeff Greenfield: "Add to this the sheer complexity of covering religion in a country with dozens of different faiths and denominations, each with its own theology."[37]

Fifth, linked to this notion of complexity is the assumption, often verified in concrete experience, that religion is inherently *controversial*. That is, regardless of which religious issue is covered, the journalist or editor or broadcaster can expect to hear criticism, garnering more response than that received in most other arenas covered. This impression is hard to prove or disprove, but it is widely held.[38]

Finally, there seems to be a sentiment in some quarters that the special status granted to religion and the press under the First Amendment somehow implies separation between all three. Thus, in addition to an obligation to disentangle religion from the state and the press from the state, it is necessary to maintain a separation between religion and the press. Although this is clearly not stated in the First Amendment, it has served to underscore the "special" status of religion in thought about journalism.

These received understandings of religion in the news are not static. What further change we can expect depends to some degree on the challenges faced by the media as they continue to address the world of religion. But the extent and limits of change are also set by the various perspectives—journalistic, political, religious, and public—that surround religion journalism. The balance of this book is devoted to a careful investigation of these perspectives.

## Notes

1. Dart, John and Jimmy Allen. 1993. *Bridging the gap: Religion and the news media.* Nashville, TN: Freedom Forum First Amendment Center.

2. Noord, David Paul. 1984. The evangelical origins of mass media in America, 1815-1835. *Journalism Monographs* 88. Columbia, SC: Association for Education in Journalism and Mass Communications.

3. Olasky, Marvin. 1988. *Prodigal press: The anti-Christian bias of the American news media.* Westchester, IL: Crossway, pp. 20-22.

4. Emery, Michael and Edwin Emery. 1996. *The press and America.* Boston: Allyn & Bacon, pp. 103-4. See also Michael Schudson, *Discovering the news.*

5. Sweet, Leonard. 1993. Communication and change in American religious history: A historiographical probe. In *Communication and change in American religious history,* edited by Leonard Sweet. Grand Rapids, MI: Eerdmans, pp. 40-47.

6. Emery and Emery, *The press and America;* Silk, Mark. 1995. Unsecular media: Making news of religion in America. Urbana: University of Illinois Press, pp. 17-18.

7. Buddenbaum, Judith. 1987. "Judge . . . what their acts will justify": The religion journalism of James Gordon Bennett. *Journalism History* 14:54-67.

8. For an excellent recent account of the Bennett era, see Silk, *Unsecular Media,* pp. 17-22.

9. Ibid., p. 25.

10. Quoted in Arthur Robb. 1940. Shop talk at thirty. *Editor and Publisher* 73 (April 27), p. 106; also quoted in Silk, *Unsecular media,* p. 26. It is interesting to note, however, that Martin's overall argument was *in favor* of *increased* attention to religion, in a turn that echoed Tocqueville and presaged arguments such as that of Stephen Carter, to which we will turn later. He was speaking on the topic "The Place of Journalism in Fostering Religion in the Community" and noted, among other things, "that religion is an essential of our democracy for the reason that it is today the one remaining champion of the sanctity and integrity of human personality." On the subject of constitutional issues, he said, "we, therefore, must put religous freedom on a plane of importance with freedom of speech and of the press. And insofar as we give the matter thought at all, I believe that as a people we do acknowledge that all our liberties rise or fall together."

11. Silk, *Unsecular media,* pp. 29-30.

12. Cornell, George. 1990. The evolution of the religion beat. In *Reporting religion: Facts and faith,* edited by Benjamin J. Hubbard. Sonoma, CA: Polebridge Press, pp. 25-6. See also Wright, Elliott. 1993. *RNS reporting: 60 years of Religious News Service.* New York: Religious News Service.

13. Dart, John. 1981. The religion beat. In *The religion beat: The reporting of religion in the media.* A Rockefeller Foundation conference report. New York: Author, pp. 19-26.

14. Dart, John. Personal interview, March 6, 1989. Throughout the book, quotations from personal interviews originated in a several-years-long study of the religion beat, supported by the Lilly Endowment. In the basic study, which ran from 1988 to 1991, interviews were conducted with leading members of the Religion Newswriters' Association along with their editorial supervisors as well as with working religion journalists at a sample of small and medium-size newspapers. Denominational communication officers were also interviewed as part of that study. Focus-group interviews were conducted with laity in four congregations and are reported in Chapter 6. Data from national surveys conducted as part of that study are reviewed in Chapter 7. In a subsequent study from 1992 to 1995, also supported by the Lilly Endowment, additional interviews and surveys were conducted, fleshing out both the data and the range of informants contacted. For detailed descriptions of the methodologies of these studies, see their technical reports: Hoover, S., B. Hanley, and M. Radelfinger. 1989. *The RNS-Lilly study of religion reporting and readership in the daily press.* Philadelphia: Temple University and New York: Religious News Service; and Hoover, S., S. Venturelli, and D. Wagner. 1994. *Religion in public discourse: The role of the media.* Boulder: University of Colorado School of Journalism and Mass Communication.

15. For detailed scholarly accounts of the profession, see Schudson, Michael. 1987. *Discovering the news: A social history of American newspapers.* New York: Basic Books; and Tuchman, Gaye. 1978. *Making news: A study in the construction of reality.* New York: Free Press.

16. Dart, John. Personal interview, March 6, 1989.

17. Quotations from personal interviews with, respectively, Jeanne Pugh, February 14, 1989; John Dart, March 8, 1989; Russell Chandler, March 7, 1989; and Beth Pratt, June 3, 1989.

18. It must be noted that such normative ideas about the essential nature of journalism have been put to the test in scholarly studies of the profession. In most of these, notions such as "newsworthiness" are seen to be more relative and less absolute than is assumed by professional practice.

19. Brisson, Tom. Personal interview, December 18, 1988.

20. Wasson, Teresa. Personal interview, February 16, 1989.

21. Parmley, Helen. Comments made at an open forum on religion news held by the American Academy of Religion, Chicago, November 7, 1988.

22. For a comprehensive history, see Emery and Emery, *The press and America.*

23. An issue that deserves fuller attention than can be provided here is the relative paucity of hard research data available to news decision makers about reader interest in religion. The 1989 study whose results appear in Chapter 7 was the first comprehensive readership survey about religion coverage conducted in decades. What research was available before 1989 suffered from a range of defects that limited its utility to the larger question of real reader interest in religion. The most common of these defects in market research were the tendency to base surveys on reader experience with actual extant coverage—where there was little coverage, reader interest was hard to gauge—and the tendency to classify as religion coverage only those stories that fit a rather narrow definition of the beat, something that both readers and religion writers have begun to contest as a constraint, as we shall see.

24. Parmley, comments at forum, November 7, 1988.

25. Hoover et al., *RNS-Lilly study,* p. 103.

26. Ibid., p. 105.

27. Ibid., p. 106.

28. Ibid.

29. Berger, Peter. 1967. *The sacred canopy.* Garden City, NY: Anchor, pp. 107-8.

30. For a recent discussion, see Warner, R. Stephen. 1993. Work in progress toward a new paradigm for the sociological study of religion in the United States. *American Journal of Sociology* 98:1044-93.

31. Roof, Wade Clark. 1993. *A generation of seekers: The spiritual journeys of the baby boom generation.* San Francisco: Harper San Francisco.

32. Wuthnow, Robert. 1988. *The restructuring of American religion.* Princeton, NJ: Princeton University Press.

33. Carter, Stephen. 1993. *The culture of disbelief.* New York: Basic Books.

34. *Reliable Sources,* CNN, December 5, 1993.

35. *ABC World News Tonight,* August 13, 1993.

36. Dart and Allen, *Bridging the gap,* p. 21.

37. *ABC World News Tonight,* August 13, 1993.

38. In a recent guidebook for religion writers, John Dart refers a number of times to the issue of controversy over religion stories, suggesting that controversy may well be a measure of a poorly reported story: "A Hot, Sensitive Topic, when presented fairly and completely, often draws little public response. But a story reported poorly, replete with technical mistakes, or one edited severely enough to destroy the story's fairness: That's the one that will draw fire—as it should." Dart, John. 1995. *Deities and deadlines: A primer on religion news coverage.* Nashville, TN: Freedom Forum First Amendment Center, p. 6.

# 3

# DISCOURSES OF
# CONTEMPORARY RELIGION

If religion is not fading from the scene under a culture of secularism, then what *is* happening to it? Were we only to refer to the prospects of the traditional religious institutions it might appear that religion has been on the decline. It is probably more accurate to suggest instead that what has been happening is what Robert Wuthnow has called a *restructuring* of American religion.[1]

This "restructuring" has been typified by at least the following trends:

■ A decline in the salience of the formal religious institutions, expressed through a decline in denominational loyalty, a decline in the cultural and political prominence of the traditional religious bodies, and a decline in the legitimacy of those institutions as measured by such things as public confidence in their leaders. This decline has also been signaled by the increasing prominence of independent churches and congregations, such as the new "megachurches" of evangelical Protestantism.

■ The rise of nontraditional religious groups and activities, including increased participation in so-called "para-church" or "special purpose" religious groups. For example, Wuthnow notes that the Gallup Organization has documented the extent to which religious volunteerism is a powerful force in contemporary life.

■ The emergence of so-called alternative or "new" religions, including "New Age spirituality," "native spirituality," and interest in Eastern religions and Eastern mysticism. A related development has been the "therapeutic" movement, including such things as the booming "12-step" programs, which are seen by many observers as at least "quasi-religious."[2]

■ The development of what Philip Hammond calls "personal autonomy" in matters of faith. Hammond argues that underlying all of these other developments is the tendency for adherents to see contemporary faith experience to be entirely in their own hands and no longer something on which the traditional institutions and histories have particular claims.[3] Thus contemporary faith and spirituality can be seen to be a kind of "cafeteria" where the individual crafts a personal theology and cosmology out of a range of (often quite disparate) beliefs and values.

Some have called this latter mode of religiosity "Sheilaism," after a subject of the landmark study of contemporary meaning, *Habits of the Heart*. In that book, a woman called Sheila Larson, when asked to describe herself religiously, said,

> I believe in God. I'm not a religious fanatic. I can't remember the last time I went to church. My faith has carried me a long way. It's Sheilaism. Just my own little voice.[4]

The authors, Robert Bellah and his associates, do not see this as self-worship or narcissism. Instead, Sheila expresses a mode of religiosity that is directed toward the transcendent sphere. It is just that she herself is the final authority over the nature and relevance of her faith. Traditional institutional claims and loyalties hold less power for her than they might have in the past.

It is important to see that this new religiosity is not *privatized* in the classic sense of that term.[5] Instead, it takes place in a rather public way, in the sense that the various forms and influences that come to bear on it exist and find legitimacy in the public sphere. In his study of religion in the "baby boom" generation, Roof details how religious and spiritual quests among that group rely on a wide range of cultural and social symbols and ideas, many of which are accessed through such *public media* as books, cassette tapes, self-help groups, and other publications.[6]

## A New Perspective

This argues for a new way of understanding religion. The received view of religiosity by the news media holds that religion is a private matter, that it is receding in influence, and that its adherents are largely concerned with their own particular faith and that they construct that faith within rather rigid historical and institutional boundaries. We need a way of seeing religion instead as something that can be described in more general, less parochial terms. It seems to persist as an authentic and vital component of the contemporary scene and can be found expressing itself in social, cultural, and political spheres. Thus, although religion is, on some level, personal and individual, it also finds expression outside the private sphere. It is no longer defined by the traditional institutional boundaries. It is now more diffuse perhaps but no less important.[7]

The Waco tragedy, seen in this light, is portentous. We are entering an era where, more and more, such groups can be expected to appear on the scene and where our definitions of "the religious" increasingly will be stretched thin. It will be an era where the *fundamental claims* of particular faith perspectives come to the fore, replacing historically received categories. Individuals and groups will need to be religiously defined more by what they *believe* than by where they *belong*. Further, this trend transcends the so-called new religions and is becoming a phenomenon in all religious categories.[8] This means that, just at the moment when journalism seems to be taking religion more seriously, the character and nature of religion itself is rapidly changing. The definitional issue is thus becoming more significant all the time.

A seasoned radio interviewer proposed an approach to definitions that fits well with the reality described here. In response to a question of how her radio program comes to delve into religious issues so frequently, she responded,

> One of our big beats tends to be identity. So, in that sense issues like race and religion and gender and sexual orientation are just coming up all the time in first-person interviews with people. If I'm interviewing somebody on a first-person kind of way, about their life as opposed to their area of expertise, . . . if the spiritual life has been an important part of their life, it will likely come up in the interview.[9]

This "definition" of religion is one that speaks of an era where belief, faith, and spirituality revolve around the *self* more than the *group*. This tacitly recognizes the restructured mode of religiosity identified by Wuthnow, Roof, and Bellah. This is obviously not, at the same time, a general or *normative* definition that necessarily would be applicable in other media forms or genres.

But such general definitions must be developed if news treatment of religion is to continue to mature. In their study, John Dart and Jimmy Allen warned of the danger that this newly restructured religion may itself become a disincentive to coverage:

> If religion is increasingly a subjective experience, ineffable, private, and nontranslatable, then how is it to be captured by the busy reporter? If religion no longer provides the paradigms for understanding the meaning of life, then how important can it be?[10]

Ironically, none of this is news to professional religion journalists, many of whom have been following these developments for years and have described them in very competent published accounts. There are religion writers who are as knowledgeable about contemporary "lived and practiced" religion as are the recognized scholars. What must happen is that these new understandings, in turn, come to define the general practice of religion journalism itself. This is not a problem for the majority of expert religion writers. It is a problem for those media just now beginning to take religion more seriously as they contemplate their own evolving policies and practices. There is a danger that each of them will begin by "re-inventing the wheel" and for that wheel to be one embedded in some of the old assumptions about the nature of contemporary religion and demands of coverage.

## ■ American Discourse About Religion

The context we have called *the realm of public discourse* defines the general sentiments and definitions within which journalists in the public media must work. We have seen how journalistic treatment of religion can be attributed to a set of perceptions and practices within newsrooms themselves. However, the news business is naturally articulated into the preconceptions, perceptions, tastes, and interests of "the general public." As was suggested in Chapter 1, these dimensions of public sentiment define the third major domain of religion coverage: *public discourse.*

These dimensions are not static but fluid. They occur in a kind of continuing, self-regulating public "conversation" that cultural scholars call "discourse." Discourses are more than mere conversations. The term has come to imply a range of social and cultural attributes that are almost structural.[11] This rather expansive use of the term *discourse* implies therefore at least four components: a language, a set of boundaries with principles of inclusion and exclusion, a master narrative or narratives, and a "public" or set of "publics."

Thus the realm of public discourse is a structured one in the sociological sense, having attributes that are as important as class, education, race, or gender in explaining such things as public perspectives on the role and place of religion in public life. The narratives and definitions that are specific to the realm of American public discourse (and its particular construction of the "religion story") have a history that is deeply rooted. These narratives and definitions also have implications beyond the media, particularly in education, where their impact is self-evident (pervading both the modes and media of instruction), and in political processes and the courts, where they come to establish such things as "community standards" for everything from speech to commercial activities.

American public discourse is rooted, at its base, in the principles of Western rationalism inherited from the Enlightenment. The German sociologist Max Weber has been most influential in his articulation of the relations between Enlightenment thought, modernism, and the industrial revolution. Weber's basic premise has to do with the gradual effacement of the public dominance of religion by the rationalism that came to define modernity.

This line of argument holds that in the primordial past one's religious, social, and economic life were coextensive. People lived, worked, and worshipped in very localized and integrated contexts. Intergenerational relationships were strong, and the institutions of religion and the family were ultimately determinative. Weber observed that with modernity—and industrialization—this began to change. The scientific rationality that typified modernity had little room for religion. Secular "ontologies" competed with those presented by religions, and the "secular/rationalist" approach began to win out.

The impact on religion has been rather profound. The rationalist order leaves only two options for religious belief systems. First, they may be quite extensive and well integrated in *private,* so long as they do not intrude too far into the *public* sphere. Once in public, religious ontologies must compete with secular ones in a rationalist discourse that applies its own criteria for ascendancy. Weber[12] suggested that the dominant criteria are *consistency, lucidity,* and *coherence.* These are quite rational categories and, at the same time, quite different from the substantive categories of meaning that define religion.

The second option for religion is to become rationalized *itself,* to integrate into the secular realm by structures and processes of organization that allow it to compete with the meaning systems of rationalism. One of Weber's best-known contributions is his observation that Christianity—and Protestantism in particular—seems uniquely suited to this task.[13] There is much evidence that this *dualistic* notion of religion is the one that defines our discourse today. On the one hand, there is substantial scope for religion to take place in the private sphere. Its role and purpose there is extensive and profound, and it is granted much leeway. On the other hand, when religion does become "public," it does so within the confines of a set of rational and bureaucratic definitions. It is most comfortably understood as one among many public institutions that competes with others for definition and presence in public discourse. Its construction—particularly by "the media"—is most comfortable when religion appears to be "like" other things.

Removing religion from the public sphere, or domesticating it when it does appear there, makes some historical sense. Richard John Neuhaus, a prominent conservative commentator on the public status of religion, has suggested that the secularist doctrines of the 18th century (of which the Constitution of the United States can be said to be an example) were crafted with fresh memory of European wars of religion in the century just preceding.[14]

In an important historical study of the postrevolutionary period, historian Nathan Hatch[15] describes how the privatization of religion in that period arose amid a fluid process of religious evolution and change. The "establishment" religions of the colonial period came under spirited assault at the hands of the "new religious movements" of Methodism, "Christian-ism," and the original Campbellites:

> A diverse array of evangelical firebrands went about the task of movement-building in the generation after the Revolution. Intent on bringing evangelical conversion to the mass of ordinary Americans, they could rarely divorce that message from contagious new democratic vocabularies and impulses that swept through American popular culture. Class structure was viewed as society's fundamental problem. There was widespread disdain for the supposed lessons of history and tradition, and a call for reform using the rhetoric of the Revolution. The press swiftly became a sword of democracy, fueling ardent faith in the future of the American republic.[16]

This process, which Hatch calls the "democratization of American Christianity," was fueled by a vibrant activism that included, interestingly, powerful and effective use of media, both "private" and "public." These movements did not at the same time move to achieve the social, cultural, political, and class *ascendancy* enjoyed by the "establishment" religions of the time. They eschewed such status, choosing instead to work their way on the gray boundary between the private and the public realms; denying the legitimacy of the powerful institutional and clerical orders that had long controlled religion in the public sphere and maintaining a vibrant claim to authenticity outside that realm altogether. Over the years, these "democratized" religions (which have become the largest Protestant denominations) have continued to leave the public sphere vacant of any *natural* claim they might make to presence there (based, for example, on their size). They could, therefore, be said to have acquiesced to a definition of their role that has made little pretension to a place beyond their base in the private sphere. These faiths are not, of course, the whole of American religion today. But as the inheritors of the legacy of the democratization process Hatch describes, their prospects can be said to have had an important role in defining American religious culture.

In his book *The Culture of Disbelief*, Stephen Carter makes the point quite explicitly that the particular American version of religion's "proper place" results from a conscious, rationalist balancing of competing claims:

> We are trying, here in America, to strike an awkward but necessary balance, one that seems more and more difficult with each passing year.

On the one hand, a magnificent respect for freedom of conscience, including the freedom of religious belief, runs deep in our political ideology. On the other hand, our understandable fear of religious domination of politics presses us, in our public personas, to be wary of those who take their religion too seriously.[17]

Carter goes on to note, as others have, that this role and position is ironic in a nation that is the most religiously active in the Western industrialized world. As a nation we are balanced on the cusp of dilemma over competing demands: deeply religious, on the one hand, and deeply committed to the protection of public institutions *from* religion, on the other. The result, according to Carter,

is that we often ask our citizens to split their public and private selves, telling them in effect that it is fine to be religious in private, but there is something askew when those private beliefs become the basis for public action.[18]

Carter surveys the many consequences of this duplicity that express themselves in personal, social, political, and legal spheres. The most profound of these is the most basic. Religion is treated as a *hobby,* says Carter, an affectation that is expected to fairly easily yield to a secular-rational calculus (as Weber would have predicted) at appropriate moments:

The consistent message of modern American society is that whenever the demands of one's religion conflict with what one has to do to get ahead, one is expected to ignore the religious demands and act . . . well . . . *rationally.*[19]

On one level, this merely confirms our observation that religion is problematic in public discourse in the same way that it is problematic in newsrooms, with the latter context assumed to naturally reflect more general public sentiments. But the effect of the situation we have described is somewhat different from a case of mere *reflection.* If, as a number of studies have shown, people in the news are less religious on average than the general public, the resulting contrast is even more stark. As Carter notes, the media are *particularly* prominent in their disregard for religious faith and practice.

Carter's view stands in sharp contrast to that of Mark Silk, who addressed this issue as the central concern of his book on religion and the press, *Unsecular Media.* He concludes there,

> I have tried to show that the news media, far from promoting a secularist agenda of their own, approach religion with values and presuppositions that the American public widely shares.[20]

Unlike observers from within the world of religion (in particular), Silk argues that the dominant mode of religion coverage in the press is of a general, inoffensive, and consensual kind. In attempting to understand why this view is not more widely shared, he observes that

> people fail to register what gives no offense. From reports on good works to exposés of "cults," a lot of religion news does not strike most consumers of news as reflecting any point of view, precisely because it is a point of view they share.[21]

Acknowledging the seeming inconsistency between this view and the general sense that more and more religion is appearing in the news and in the form of controversial, not consensual coverage, Silk turns the discussion around to point out that the primary source of the discourse is the media:

> At the same time, the most important news from the religion front over the past two decades has been turbulent and contentious. . . . The main story line for the end of the twentieth century is that people of faith are leading a counterrevolution against a morally impaired, if not bankrupt, secular society—of which the mass media are the most familiar expression. What has escaped notice is that the media have told this story largely from the standpoint of the religious themselves.[22]

There are several implications in Silk's argument. First, he clearly suggests that the debate about religion coverage needs to be open to an approach that is broad and consensual (and thus inoffensive). This makes some intuitive sense, particularly when we consider the fact that the media do function in a commercial marketplace that enforces a kind of conformity and generalism of all media content. Second, he points out that the media can become a particular target of scrutiny in contemporary cultural struggles over the modern order. The location of the media within modernity make them particularly obvious targets regardless of how much the canons of journalism might assume a kind of transparency. Finally, he observes that the source of most of what we know about these issues and developments we know via the media themselves. They are in the curious position of participating in the developments they cover.

These themes are discussed in more detail elsewhere in this book. We will see that various media practices vis-à-vis religion have spoken to each of these implications. Broadcast media have tended to rather self-consciously choose an approach to religion that stresses this consensual "broad truths" understanding. Critics on the Right from both professional and lay ranks clearly demonstrate a discomfort with modernity and secularity as they are most obviously represented by media texts. Critics on the Right and the Left regularly foreground the role of the media themselves in the formation and shaping of cultural discourse.

To resolve a disagreement such as that between Carter and Silk, it is necessary to investigate the questions in more detail, as we are presently doing. This analysis must recognize two primary bases for analysis. First, religion is far from a settled issue for American culture in general. Second, there is little natural tendency among media practitioners to "push the issue" of religion in their coverage of the contemporary American scene.

## ■ A Normative Claim

But why should they? What arguments can be marshalled to suggest that their "irreligion" (admittedly an oversimplification) should be transcended in favor of some more extensive approach to religion? As has been seen, an argument can be made that due to the sheer level of religious interest in America, the media space and time devoted to it seems out of balance.

Would a "re-balancing" alone serve the purpose? It would not satisfy Carter's critique, for one. He clearly holds that the constraints placed on religion in the public square are more profound than would be remedied by increased media attention alone. Indeed, he presses a normative argument for an appropriation of religious discourse into public discourse in a new and invigorated way.

Carter bases his normative call (as have others) on the ideas of the early chronicler of American democracy, Alexis de Tocqueville. Tocqueville has loomed large in considerations of the development of American democracy (and American public discourse) because he was such an astute observer at an early stage of its development. More important though, he is revered for his early observation about the essential underlying conflict that continues to define American polity to this day—the conflict between individualism and democratic consensus.

Tocqueville admired America as a place where public virtue and public-mindedness were commonplace but feared for the consequences of individualism. He wrote that he knew of no country "where the love of money has taken stronger hold on the affections of men and where a profounder contempt is expressed for the theory of the permanent equality of property."[23] Yet at the same time he recognized (and respected) the civic virtues evident in the populace of the new republic.

## Religion and Public Discourse

Tocqueville saw an important role for religion in these matters, a role that had a number of facets. First, he saw religion as having clear and necessary *political* implications. The spheres of religion and politics were not separate; instead, religion had specific value and moral claims that could and should suffuse the political environment. Second, he saw that various religious perspectives had *unique claims* they could make and that the religious sphere could provide alternative ontologies that would enliven and enrich democratic discourse. Third, he saw that religion could serve as an *"intermediate institution"* between the people and the state. Tocqueville observed that religion shared with other voluntary associations the capacity to be a focus of individual action in the pursuance of common ends, something that totalitarian states arrogate to themselves.

Carter describes two important roles for religion derived from Tocqueville's thought:

> First, they can serve as the sources of moral understanding without which any majoritarian system can deteriorate into simple tyranny, and, second, they can mediate between the citizen and the apparatus of government, providing an independent moral voice.[24]

This voice speaks not from outside the democratic process but from within, directly engaging in discourse about solutions and the future. "Religion . . . must be regarded as the first of political institutions" said Tocqueville,[25] for it alone is capable of bonding political freedom to an ethical foundation.

Thus, we might argue, the question of how religion is covered by the media is also the deeper question of how religion enters into the public discourse that is the unique turf of mediated communication. The connection between the media and public discourse is a fundamental one. In an address to the Religion Newswriters' Association, Bill Moyers stressed both the necessity of such discourse for the maintenance of democracy and the essential role of media in framing it:

> In a democracy, we have a responsibility to discuss and debate our value systems in the "marketplace of ideas" because here our collective identity and our governing consensus and indeed our social peace are secured or lost. Once the marketplace of ideas was the marketplace. In late 20th-century America, our television sets have become . . . a primary source of ideas and information about the world.[26]

And yet, as practiced, journalism has tended not to see those ideas that are *religious* as important elements of its purview:

> A reporter seeking comment today on an issue such as assisted suicide or American intervention in Bosnia will ask an economist, politician, psychologist, sociologist, lawyer, almost everyone but a member of the clergy, or a philosopher, or an ethicist, or a theologian—even though life and death, right and wrong, war and peace are the very heart of religious concerns. Sometimes it appears that the "wall of separation" that is meant to keep the government from giving any specific religion a privileged position in American life is interpreted as a rampart dividing all of religion from the rest of American life.[27]

Moyers cited Lawrence Sullivan's arguments regarding the meaning of the Branch Davidian tragedy. According to Sullivan, what was missing from the public calculus there was any sense of the important, constitutive role of religion in society. And, we might add, what is as important as this *realization* about the necessity of introducing religion into the public sphere is the necessity of establishing *means* whereby this can take place. Those means have to be rooted in a *discourse,* according to Robert Wuthnow:

> I consider the problem of public discourse among the most important.
> . . . How can we communicate with one another about basic values, the collective symbols on which our society rests, the goals and ambitions

to which we aspire as a people? Our way of life, our future as a society—the future of any democratic society—depends on arriving at effective answers to this question. Our freedom depends on being able to contribute to the public debate over collective values.[28]

Tocqueville identified a role for the media in the development and maintenance of American democracy, and among the most important demands was for mediated discourse to account for religion, to allow for religious values to enrich democratic debate. This is a particularly important and formidable challenge today, at a time of tremendous religious struggle and religious diversity. And it can be argued, as James Davison Hunter has, that religion is at the root of the most significant contemporary struggles, those Hunter calls the "culture wars."[29]

Bill Moyers sees the challenge here as one of consensus building. "One has to wonder if it will be possible to develop a new cultural myth that combines this robust religious pluralism within the traditional American consensus that everyone belongs."[30] A former managing editor of a metropolitan newspaper agrees:

It's all about the politics of meaning. It's out there. We want meaning in our lives and we're willing to talk about it. And it's partly the result of the realization that the world is changing and what do you have that is stable and meaningful? Well, you've got values and religious rights. But it's all about the same thing, I think, people looking for meaning in their lives, and to the extent that that gets discussed in the public domain.[31]

Both of these voices contend that this discourse about meaning, infused as it is with religious sensibilities, will continue to be a particular challenge for journalism. "The struggle over this consensus is one journalists will be covering well into the next century," says Moyers.

And how will that coverage be done? This is an important normative category for the practice of journalism and deserves some careful thought and consideration. Joan Connell, the religion and ethics correspondent for Newhouse News Service in Washington (and more recently managing editor of Religion News Service), observed at a roundtable discussion of these issues that the central problem is, indeed, a discursive one, a problem of "language." This problem is rooted in deeper questions of diversity and religious legitimacy, however:

I think it is a question of language and that we lack a particular language. Every religion has its own primary language. Its scripture, its moral universe, its values and ethics. Religion writers or journalists of religion are supposed to be familiar with each one of those languages.[32]

This familiarity with these "primary languages" is an important part of the journalist's role. Claims of special expertise are based on the ability to decode and interpret these languages. However, the process does not end there, says Connell:

We also need a second language to write about religion and to talk about religion. We need a neutral, cool, informed language, which is the language of journalistic objectivity. But, because we are basically ignorant of most religions other than our own and the ones closest to it, we get confused. Correspondents get confused between the primary language and the secondary language, and that is not really competent or professional journalism. If we are going to make progress as newspaper writers or television producers, we have to be fluent in both those languages.[33]

This is a telling point. The Tocquevillian call for a meeting place where democratic discourse can take account of the moral claims of the religions of the private sphere (spoken in their own "primary languages") depends on the development of a general "secondary language" as well. This secondary language is the one that needs to be articulated into the realm of public discourse and is the one that should be, as Connell points out, the natural *lingua franca* of the journalistic project.

Connell's view was challenged by Diane Winston, a historian of religion and communication and a former religion writer herself:

I agree that religion has its own language and I think we need to develop an empathetic ear. . . . But don't all "specialty beats" have a "language near" and a "language far"—the language of the people inside and the language that you have to write about in the newspaper?[34]

Connell's response evoked Tocqueville's notion of the special status of religion in public discourse:

The difference is that there is a moral dimension to religious discourse, and while there is also a moral dimension to such things as the environment, religion resonates on a deeper, more primary level. Religion has historically reserved the right to prescribe and proscribe human action. And, it is something qualitatively different. It is all mixed up with magic and transformation and mystery. That is part of religion and that is what is so difficult to grasp. It is not empirical.[35]

And yet it must be accounted for. Tocqueville—and Carter—contend that the status of religion as a potential contributor to public discourse derives from the simple fact that it exists. It is a fundamental dimension of human life and human consciousness, and it makes natural and powerful claims on human action. The core challenge posed by religion is that of allowing it to enter into democratic life in such a way that its claims can be recognized and realized and in such a way that democracy can benefit.

The tension between the languages and sentiments of the private and the public binds together a number of the critical issues in religion coverage. The *complexity* and *controversy* of religion are rooted in the nature and power of its fundamental claims. The problem of accounting for those claims gets at the heart of the role of media practice in legitimating contemporary institutions and symbols (including religious ones). The religion journalist must ultimately develop an expertise both in decoding and in understanding the often arcane languages of the various meaning systems that present themselves as religious. The journalist must further articulate those languages and claims into a realm of public discourse that requires a more general language. Finally, there is some expectation that the media will take a determinative role in that discourse.

Lynn Neary of National Public Radio provides a contemporary case study of this issue, reflecting on the experience of covering the "culture wars" by looking into the lives and experiences of two families—one progressive (liberal), one fundamentalist (conservative)—in Colorado Springs. The "culture wars" controversies are textbook examples of the kind of issues Tocqueville had in mind. Private sentiments, heavily infused with religious values and sensibilities, have been bubbling to the surface of public and political action. How are these to be accounted for and understood?

Both families were quite compelling. There was a basic authenticity to their faiths and to the moral consequences of that faith in their own lives:

They were both very sincere and very committed to their beliefs. The difference between them was profound, and on one important level. The conservative family saw morality in terms of prescriptions and proscriptions. With the other family, the sense was that the parents were trying to demonstrate morality to their children through their own actions.[36]

Both "sides" of this divide did see it as a point of struggle. "There is a sense on both sides that they are a minority and are dispossessed," said Neary. For the conservatives, it was a feeling that humanism dominates public life; for the liberals, it was a feeling that conservatives want to dominate the sphere of private choice.

Both "sides" were further prone to activism, as Neary's story, as broadcast, made clear. The conservative pastor referred to (what he termed) a prior "political pacifism" on the part of conservative Christians, a situation that he felt had changed. For him, this activism included such things as direct actions against family-planning clinics. The liberal mother saw her actions in defending these clinics as the front line of a battle. Thus, on the personal level of moral action, there appeared to be an almost irreconcilable demarcation. "What you have is both sides saying what they want is for their kids to stick by their beliefs," observed Neary, "and both of them felt their actions were serving as important lessons to their children."

This story and her role in covering it define for Neary the core challenge of the relationship between religion and the sphere of public discourse:

> What was missing was a sense that we have to sort these things out in a public way. This all does have to be played out publicly, we can't just leave it to individual sentiment and choice.[37]

And that is the key issue. Is it enough for coverage of such issues to describe the "sides" well, to account for the authenticity of beliefs and claims, or does not journalism have a responsibility to do its accounting in a way that contributes to public understanding?

The question of journalistic responsibility is itself controversial. In response to the comments of Connell and Winston presented earlier, Jimmy Allen rejected the notion of an obligation of journalism to do anything other than be "good journalists":

> I'm a little troubled by the idea that journalism has an obligation, a social obligation to cover religion. It seems to me that journalism has an obligation to be good journalism. Religion is so taprooted into the lives of people that you really don't cover the story unless you come to it with the religious questions as well as the personal questions. If you

come from the perspective of being socially obligated, you'll run out of obligation real soon. If you come into it to say we really want to tell the truth and be truthseekers, religion is part of that truth.[38]

Diane Winston responded to this idea by affirming the notion attributed to Ruel Tyson earlier in this book, that journalistic practice actually exists within a system of conventions that articulate it into broader social structures and discourses:

> To say that it is all about "professionalism" is to ignore what is behind those conventions, which are the questions of "what is news" and "what is journalism." Journalism is about a reinforcement of the status quo. Journalists are upholding certain social, political, and economic beliefs that all of us take for granted.[39]

There may not, in fact, be a contradiction between the Tocquevillian model and the kind of "professionalism" implied by John Dart and Jimmy Allen. The key question is whether the religious, as a category, is enabled through journalistic practice to enter into the consensual sphere of discourse. This is not an easy task. Years of separation into a "private" sphere of authentic action and a "public" sphere of truncated civic symbolism have not equipped public discourse with the tools and sensibilities to easily account for religious claims.

Yet democratic processes demand that this happen. As Lynn Neary notes, at some point along the line private claims must make their way in public discourse and public dialogue, and it is this public dialogue that is the particular province of journalism. The seeming contradiction between views that confirm and deny journalistic responsibility may be resolvable through the almost constructivist tone of Connell's notion of a "public language." That "neutral, cool, informed" language is *necessarily* a *public* language, a language of public discourse. The question becomes, then, how well journalism is doing in identifying and interpreting the "private" languages of religion in the public sphere.

This is a bit more subtle and nuanced than the kinds of criticism normally leveled at religion coverage by voices outside "the media." It is also somewhat removed from the conventional senses of the challenges of the religion beat from within these industries. The next chapter considers the former. Succeeding chapters attempt to unpack the latter.

# Notes

1. Wuthnow, Robert. 1988. *The restructuring of American religion.* Princeton, NJ: Princeton University Press.

2. Roof, Wade Clark. 1993. *A generation of seekers.* New York: HarperCollins; Mainline religion in transition. In *Religion and America,* edited by Mary Douglas and Steven Tipton. Boston: Beacon, 1983.

3. Hammond, Philip. 1992. *Religion and personal autonomy: The third disestablishment in America.* Columbia: University of South Carolina Press.

4. Bellah, Robert, Richard Madsen, William Sullivan, Ann Swidler, and Steven Tipton. 1985. *Habits of the heart: Individualism and commitment in American life.* Berkeley: University of California Press, p. 221.

5. Luckman, Thomas. 1967. *The invisible religion.* New York: Macmillan.

6. Roof, *A generation of seekers.*

7. Warner, R. Stephen. 1993. Work in progress toward a new paradigm for the sociological study of religion in the United States. *American Journal of Sociology* 98:1044-93.

8. Marty, Martin E. 1993. Where the energies go. *Annals of the American Academy of Social and Political Science* 527:11-26. See also Stewart M. Hoover. 1997. Media and the construction of the religious public sphere. In *Rethinking media, religion, and culture,* edited by Stewart M. Hoover and Knut Lundby. Thousand Oaks, CA: Sage, pp. 283-97.

9. Gross, Terry. Personal interview, March 24, 1993.

10. Dart, John and Jimmy Allen. 1993. *Bridging the gap: Religion and the news media.* Nashville, TN: Freedom Forum First Amendment Center, p. 34.

11. Wuthnow, Robert. 1989. *Communities of discourse.* New York: Oxford University Press.

12. Weber, Max. 1948. "Politics as a vocation" and "Science as a vocation." In *From Max Weber: Essays in sociology,* translated and edited by H. H. Gerth and C. W. Mills. New York: Oxford University Press, pp. 77-158.

13. Weber, Max. 1930. *The Protestant ethic and the spirit of capitalism,* edited by T. Parsons. London: Allen & Unwin. (Original work published 1904-5)

14. Neuhaus, Richard John. 1984. *The naked public square: Religion and democracy in America.* Grand Rapids, MI: Eerdmans.

15. Hatch, Nathan. 1989. *The democratization of American Christianity.* New Haven, CT: Yale University Press.

16. Ibid., p. 7.

17. Carter, Stephen. 1993. *The culture of disbelief.* New York: Basic Books, p. 8.

18. Ibid.

19. Ibid., p. 13, emphasis in original.

20. Mark Silk. 1995. *Unsecular media: Making news of religion in America.* Urbana: University of Illinois Press, p. 141.

21. Ibid.

22. Ibid.

23. Tocqueville, Alexis de. 1945. *Democracy in America,* edited by P. Bradley (2 vols.), vol. 1. New York: Alfred A. Knopf, p. 53. (Original work published 1834 and 1840)

24. Carter, *Culture of disbelief,* p. 36.

25. Tocqueville, *Democracy in America,* p. 248.

26. Moyers, Bill. Address to the convention of the Religion Newswriters' Association, New York, April 29, 1994.

27. Ibid.

28. Wuthnow, Robert. 1992. Introduction. In *Vocabularies of public life,* edited by R. Wuthnow. New York: Routledge.

29. Hunter, James Davison. 1991. *Culture wars: The struggle to define America.* New York: Basic Books.

30. Moyers, address to RNA convention, April 29, 1994.

31. Taylor, Belinda. Personal interview, August 10, 1993.

32. Connell, Joan. Comments to a roundtable on religion and the news, held at the Freedom Forum Media Studies Center, New York, October 4, 1993.

33. Ibid.

34. Winston, Diane. Comments to a roundtable on religion and the news, held at the Freedom Forum Media Studies Center, New York, October 4, 1993.

35. Connell, comments to roundtable, October 4, 1993.

36. Neary, Lynn. Personal interview, April 21, 1994.

37. Ibid.

38. Allen, Jimmy. Comments to a roundtable on religion and the news, held at the Freedom Forum Media Studies Center, New York, October 4, 1993.

39. Winston, comments to roundtable, October 4, 1993.

# THE SOURCE
# OF THE PROBLEM?

*C*ritics of media treatment of religion could not have imagined a better example of press calumny than a February 1993 *Washington Post* article in which staff writer Michael Weiskopf detailed the activities of religious conservatives in the public debate over military policy toward homosexuals. In attempting to explain the strength of this movement, Weiskopf asserted,

> The strength of fundamentalist leaders lies in their flocks. Corporations pay public relations firms millions of dollars to contrive the kind of grass-roots response that Falwell or Pat Robertson can galvanize in a televised sermon. Their followers are largely poor, uneducated and easy to command.[1]

By the next day, the *Post* had received so much angry response that it issued a correction:

An article yesterday characterized followers of television evangelists Jerry Falwell and Pat Robertson as "largely poor, uneducated and easy to command." There is no factual basis for that statement.[2]

This incident was not entirely unique. In December 1995, National Public Radio apologized on-air for a commentary by poet Andre Codrescu in which he discussed the millenarian belief in the "rapture":

The rapture, and I quote, "is the immediate departure from this Earth of over four million people in less than a fifth of a second," unquote. . . . The evaporation of four million who believe this crap would leave the world an instantly better place.[3]

There is no doubt that in the flow of journalistic and media comment there will always be those stories and statements that will offend someone. The larger question, and the one that concerns us here, is whether those statements and stories belie a systematic attitude on the part of "the media" and whether that attitude is one that is consistently or irresolutely antireligious. These questions are focused in the first instance on the practice of journalism as it considers religion (as in the case in the Weiskopf article). As such, they fall into a rather narrower area of discourse, that of the news business.

Scholars who study the practice of journalism have come to question the notion that it is clearly and unequivocally a search for truth. Instead, most observers concede that a set of conventions influences or determines the selection and interpretation of fact in the press. Conventional narrative structures (story styles and formats) and the institutional constraints within which fact is processed into those structures are the cultural determinants of the news product. These forces are necessary but not sufficient explanations, however. In all beats, these internal forces interact with certain external forces (events, outside pressures, *and* the broader context of public discourse) to determine what will appear in the daily newspaper.[4]

In all of this, the field of religion journalism has continued to be problematic. In a thorough review of this field, Judith Buddenbaum[5] has suggested that recent apparent improvements in religion coverage have come about as a result of the weight and momentum of religion news itself: there are many stories that now simply *must* be covered. However, she also presented four areas of continuing criticism of religion coverage: that there still isn't enough of it, that there isn't enough variety in what is covered, that the coverage tends to be too shallow, and that coverage sometimes appears biased either against religion in general or against particular religious expressions.

These criticisms have traditionally been based on some serious consideration and empirical research. A range of studies[6] suggested that coverage has been too meager until recently. Other voices, such as those who are advocates for particular sectarian or political worldviews, hold that the major deficit in religion news is that it fails to promote or defend particular religious groups and expressions and is therefore biased against them. Charges of bias are hard to confirm or deny empirically, although a great deal of effort has been made to do so.

More recent research, taking account of the renewed public profile religion has gained in the past decade, has begun to see change. *Los Angeles Times* reporter David Shaw documented the growing interest in religion at newspapers by interviewing religion writers and outside observers in the early 1980s. He found a growing consciousness and commitment to religion on the part of newspapers but continuing problems with uneven levels of coverage, a tendency for coverage to underplay the implications of religion for broader cultural and social issues, and a continuing overall sentiment on the part of the newspaper industry that failed to grasp exactly how significant religion *is* to much of its readership. Shaw quoted Ben Bradlee, executive editor of the *Washington Post,* as feeling that religion coverage is only justified by the presence of church ads. The paper simply needs to fill the space on those pages.[7]

Shaw concluded that religion had been pushed to the front burner for the daily press by a series of important events, beginning with the Second Vatican Council in the early 1960s, followed by the activism of churches and clergy in the American civil rights movement. This impetus developed momentum throughout the social revolution of the 1960s, the Carter presidency, the rise of the Evangelical New Right, Fundamentalist Islam, and the Reagan years. As a result, Shaw concluded, daily newspapers of all sizes have taken more and more interest in religion. This had resulted in a number of them expanding the traditional "Saturday church page" from a thinly veiled cover for church ads to a "religion section" of some moment and significance. Other papers had moved religion out of an identified section altogether. Shaw noted, "The best papers also carry religion news in the regular news pages when the stories warrant the play."

Syndicated religion journalist Terry Mattingly has frequently commented on the perceptions of the religion beat within the newsroom itself. "The role religion plays in America and the world has been a well-kept secret in most of the nation's newsrooms," he observed in *Quill,* the journal of the Society of Professional Journalists.[8] Although he saw momentum, progress was slow in the early 1980s. Mattingly identified one major explanation for continuing resistance: that the majority of media decision makers do not find religion very important *personally* and therefore have a blind spot as they consider how to cover it. This together with the perception that religion is a "soft" beat means that religion is unique in constantly having to defend itself against the suspicions, ignorance, and indifference of editors and colleagues.

Mattingly identified several other aspects that help explain uneven coverage. Religion is a *complex* beat that combines tangible and intangible elements. Religion seems to fit best when it satisfies standard news categories, such as when the story happens to be a scandal. Religion is thought by many journalists to be a uniquely *personal, private,* and *local* matter. In the final analysis, Mattingly saw hopeful signs on the horizon—for example, that more and more religion writers were coming to the beat with the professional training and education that qualified them as "experts" and that more and more papers were seeing religion as an expert beat.

Both Shaw and Mattingly thus saw signs of change in the early 1980s, based on anecdotal evidence from interviews with working journalists. More recent studies have tended to confirm that the quantity and quality of religion coverage improved during that decade. In 1986, E. C. Hynds surveyed religion editors at papers with circulations above 100,000 and found that all of them had expanded religion coverage over the previous 10 years. Interestingly, the greatest emphasis was placed on *local* coverage, with more than half of the papers reporting that they had expanded in that area as opposed to smaller percentages that had expanded coverage of national or international religion news.[9]

Most of the respondents to Hynds's survey were convinced that the religion beat generally is expanding and improving, "moving out of the ghetto as the stepchild of the newsroom," as he put it. There was general consensus that the major reason for this improvement was that religion had become more *credible* due to the surge in stories where religion is seen to impact other areas such as politics, government, and international relations. The major indicators of improvement identified by Hynds's study were the increase in the number of full-time religion writers at the nation's newspapers, the increase in the number of papers moving to a "religion section" and away from a ghettoized "church page", movement of religion out of an identified section to occasionally appear in the front section—even the front page—of the paper, and a general sense that editors and colleagues are coming more and more to respect the beat and the people who cover it.

Although no comprehensive history of religion coverage exists, Judith Buddenbaum's analysis used both historical and survey sources to come to similar conclusions. To the dimensions identified by Hynds she added the indicator that the people who cover religion are now better qualified, noting that "even at smaller papers, they are generally better educated in both religion and journalism and more experienced than their counterparts at the largest newspapers a decade ago."[10]

The most comprehensive and detailed study of the religious perceptions of people in the news business was conducted by Robert Wyatt, who surveyed clergy, working religion writers, and members of the Associated Press Managing Editors Association.[11] Like earlier studies, Wyatt's found a high degree of religious involvement and interest on the part of the religion writers themselves and surprisingly high levels of religious interest among their supervisors, the managing editors, 72 percent of whom said that religion was either important or somewhat important to them.[12]

But these studies have done little to quell continuing criticism of the way the press treats religion. Delving through them, the conditions presented as reasons for continued resistance to religion by the press fall into the following general categories. First, some suggest that it is merely a question of *ignorance.* That is, for any number of reasons and regardless of their own religiosity, decision makers in the media are simply unaware of the role of religion in contemporary life, are not particularly interested in religion, and do not know whether or not there is potential readership interest. Others put it down to *indifference.* Decision makers often *are* aware of religion but may simply be indifferent to it as a topic. Finally, some suggest that the situation is actually the result of active *hostility* toward religion on the part of media people.

But how has this situation been allowed to continue and develop in a context like the United States? There are a number of perspectives here, too.

*The pluralism explanation.* There are those who argue that religion is problematic because of American religious *pluralism* or *diversity.* In a pluralistic society many religions are valid, so how are secular authorities to choose among them? How do they avoid playing favorites? It is functionally impossible to treat all religions equally, so reluctance to treat religion at all results.

*Media cohort explanation.* Some critiques have at their base the idea that the institutional cultures of the mass media, the formal journalistic training programs, and the social and professional cohorts of journalists all contribute to a consciousness that is at least indifferent to the importance of religion. Most notably, the Rothman-Lichter "media elite" studies have proposed that journalists are *both* more irreligious and more politically liberal than their readers and the public at large. Although there is some controversy over those specific studies (discussed later in this chapter), the cohort argument is a powerful one, given what is known about how news organizations function and about the functioning of cohort networks in corporate and other "institutional cultures." Some observers also have suggested that some journalists may have had conflicts in their own lives over the issue of religion and may as a result actively *resist* religion coverage.[13]

*The "historic secularism" explanation.* It has been suggested by some[14] that establishment perspectives (including media establishment perspectives) on the role of religion are largely shaped by the historic secularism of American education. Since the Supreme Court's school-prayer decision, schools and universities have maintained a greater and greater measure of distance from religion. The First Amendment protects religion from government and vice versa. It affords the same distance between government and the media. The powerful idea that these two institutions are to be distinct from government seems to lead naturally to the notion that they should also be distinct from one another. For most of us, the model of such a delicate distance is in the educational system and the clear boundaries drawn there over the past 25 years.

But there are those who argue to the contrary—that America has never been a secular state but, instead, was founded on clear religious (while nondenominational) principles. Robert Bellah has been particularly eloquent on this point.[15] A critique of the press from this direction might say that media reluctance to deal with religion, while understandable, is in fact inconsistent with the historic roots of American polity. And the facts *can* be said to not support the notion of broad-scale secularity or secularization. Church membership declines in some denominations have been made up in others. Stable majorities of the population continue to respond to national polls that they are, in fact, interested in religion and that they hold basic religious beliefs.[16]

More prominently, religion has seemed to be on the "upswing" in the *public environment* in recent years. The Christian Right, the Islamic revolution in Iran, and many, many other incidents and phenomena have demonstrated that religion has not faded away and has no prospects of doing so any time soon.

Some things about religion *have* changed, however. There is much evidence that religious faith has become increasingly *privatized* and, by extension, *noninstitutional*.[17] This contrasts with the era of the religious "establishment" described by Will Herberg as a time when it could be said that "to be a Protestant, a Catholic, or a Jew are today the alternative ways of being an American."[18] America was defined by religion, in a sense. And religion was defined by its institutions.

Today, *diversity* of belief and practice is the order of things. Along with increasing diversity has come a decline not of *religion* but of certain religious *institutions* and the idea that those institutions define religious faith and practice for most people most of the time. The "establishment era" has given way to a time of noninstitutional and increasingly diverse expressions of faith and practice.

The implication is that this decline of institutions could easily be mistaken for the larger decline of religion itself. As shall be seen, there is evidence that such confusion lies beneath some press perspectives on the importance of religion coverage.

Regardless of which explanation for the state of religion coverage seems most convincing, much of what we have seen in journalistic attitudes about religion resides in the context of a set of ideas and practices—a "received history"—of the religion beat. Although there appears to be much evidence that these ideas are changing with the times in positive ways, the received wisdom is nonetheless in the background. It becomes the standard against which change is judged. There are a number of elements to this received perception of religion news, but two of them seem to cut across all of these analyses.

From the evidence seen thus far, the received perception of religion coverage holds that religion is a *local* beat. That is, it is of primary interest to people locally, is a local story, and needs concentrate on local churches and local interests. Much previous research into news practices around religion has revealed this to be a basic orientation and assumption.

It further seems that members of the press perceive that religion readers are *parochial* in their news interests. They want to hear or read about their own church or faith group or the churches and faith groups most like their own. This particularism would reinforce the idea of localism, suggesting that newspapers would do well to cover their local communities as broadly and thinly as possible.

As interest in, and commentary about, religion and the press has increased, the public controversy around the question of whether media professionals are biased *against* religion has persisted. The evidence most often cited comes from a 1980 study by S. Robert Lichter, Stanley Rothman, and Linda Lichter where half of the respondents in the media industries were found to hold no religious affiliation at all and 86 percent said they "seldom" or "never" attended religious services.[19]

These findings have had remarkable staying power in part because they can be used so effectively to describe a gulf between the American people and the media who cover them. Here is a recent example from CNN's *Crossfire* program. The speaker is Ralph Reed, at the time head of the Christian Coalition:

> On the one hand, you have mainstream, middle America, which is devout, church-going, prays daily. . . . They're more devoutly religious, more devoutly of faith, but on the other hand you have the media elites, which according to sociologists Stanley Rothman and Bob Lichter, 86 percent said that they go to church either infrequently or not at all, and what happens is you have that syndrome . . . which perpetrates stereotypes of people of faith—in the same way that blacks were once stereotyped and women were once stereotyped.[20]

The Lichters and Rothman drove home the point in their book: "Thus, members of the media elite emerge as strong supporters of sexual freedom, and as natural opponents of groups like the Moral Majority."[21] This idea, that the natural inclination of media decision makers is to be either antireligious or at least irreligious, is widely shared. The implication is that those who determine the construction of "the religion story" in the nation's newsrooms have a natural disinclination to do it well or to do it fairly. Morton Kondracke, a prominent conservative commentator speaking on *ABC World News Tonight,* suggested that this results from a certain perception of religion:

> I think what religion has represented to them is something that's confining and oppressive and old-fashioned and bourgeois. And what they're interested in is the social frontiers, and so they're not interested.[22]

In *Bridging the Gap,* an influential report on religion journalism prepared by John Dart (of the *Los Angeles Times*) and Jimmy Allen (former president of the Southern Baptist Convention) for the Freedom Forum First Amend-ment Center in Nashville,[23] the authors are particularly critical of the Rothman-Lichter study and the way it has been indiscriminately applied to American journalism. They point out, correctly, that the Lichters and Rothman confined their 1980 survey to representatives of what they called "the media elite," or those newspapers and broadcasting outlets assumed to be the most prominent "flagships" of contemporary journalistic practice. In fact, their study included only the *very most* prominent of such outlets: the *New York Times, Washington Post, Wall Street Journal, Time, Newsweek, U.S. News & World Report,* and the news operations at the three commercial networks and PBS.

Dart and Allen note the seeming fallacy of using data such as Rothman's and the Lichters' as an adequate sample of *all* media and all journalists. They counter with data from a larger number of news outlets, representative of a wider range of markets nationwide. First, they cite studies by journalism researchers David Weaver and Cleveland Wilhoit that found a much less pervasive liberalism than appeared in *The Media Elite* sample and called into question the pervasiveness of the impact of those northeastern media on the rest of the country.[24] Against Rothman's and the Lichters' figure on *religious attendance* of 86 percent attending infrequently or never, Weaver and Wilhoit found that religion was "not important" to only 28.2 percent of their sample.

Dart and Allen also presented data from Robert Wyatt's sample of 266 managing editors nationwide, among whom he found a much *higher* level of interest in religion than among the Rothman-Lichter interviewees (as was noted earlier): 72 percent responded to Wyatt that religion was at least "important" in their lives.[25]

Stanley Rothman and Robert Lichter replied to Dart and Allen in an October 1993 letter to the *New York Times.* Their overall assessment was that the Dart-Allen data are not directly comparable to their own for two reasons. First, as Dart and Allen also point out, the Rothman-Lichter *sample* included a variety of staff categories at only the "most prominent" national news outlets, whereas Wyatt surveyed only religion writers and managing editors at newspapers in small to midsize cities. Rothman and Lichter also ques-tioned the potential of *response bias* in Wyatt's study, where only half of the surveys were returned.

Second, Rothman and Lichter noted that the questions asked are not directly comparable. The most often cited statistic from their research—the 86 percent figure—was for religious service *attendance,* a question not included in Wyatt's survey. Thus, as Rothman and Lichter put it, "Without this information, we cannot know how their professed attitudes relate to their behavior."

What can we learn from the seeming contradictions in the data? A great deal, with some careful parsing. First, there is little doubt that there is some distance between the religiosity of the media and that of the public. Against a general-public figure of 58 percent who consider religion "very important" in their lives, Wyatt found a much smaller figure among the managing editors in his survey. Rothman and the Lichters, asking a sample of editors and reporters from the most prominent national media about *religious service attendance,* found only 14 percent professing to be regular attenders.

Second, even if we accept the notion of a gap between the media and the public, comparison of these figures still does not tell us very much about the religiosity of the people who *actually cover religion.* Here the numbers are quite a bit different. Wyatt's survey of *religion writers* found that an even higher percentage than among the general public (75 percent as opposed to 58 percent) consider religion "very important" in their own lives.

Finally, the Rothman-Lichter hypothesis (or, to be fair, the critique of media coverage that consciously refers to Rothman and Lichter for its empirical basis) rests on several premises that deserve careful consideration. The first is that not all media are created equal. To put it simply, attitudes of professionals at a very few prominent media outlets are inordinately influential. Thus, a pervasive atmosphere or set of professional attitudes regarding religion is established by the institutional cultures of the most dominant media and "filters down" to the rest.

The second premise of the Rothman-Lichter critique is that the measured attitudes and religious behaviors of these "media elites" actually determine the way religion is *covered* at both the dominant outlets and elsewhere. The implication is that no level of journalistic professionalism can overcome the fundamental misunderstanding with which journalists must eye religion.

The third premise, stated clearly in several of the quotations presented here, is that "media elite" attitudes and practices regarding religion go beyond mere ignorance or indifference to outright suspicion and hostility. Rothman and the Lichters themselves tend not to see this as antireligious but as socially progressive or liberal/reformist. "Like other privileged Americans, the media elite . . . hold the cosmopolitan, anti-establishment social views fashionable since the 1960s," they wrote in *Washington Journalism Review* in 1982.[26] Others are not so charitable. Conservative columnist Cal Thomas put it this way during a discussion on CNN's *Reliable Sources:*

The press more than ever now sees the church, religion, particularly of the conservative variety, as being the final blockade to the enhancement or to the implementation of the liberal, philosophical and political worldview, particularly when you have a Pope who . . . [is] widely ignored by the mainstream press, which preferred the public opinion polls, rather than what the Pope said. I think they see the church as the final barrier to the implementation of that agenda and therefore a threat to that agenda.[27]

What most of the critics seek to deny, therefore, is the role that journalistic or professional *values* might play in ensuring that, in spite of personal preferences and attitudes, professionalism would dictate an approach that might still afford religion fair treatment.

Herbert Gans of Columbia University wrote a spirited refutation of *The Media Elite* in *Columbia Journalism Review* in 1985, in which he addressed this point:

Journalists, like everyone else, have values, the two that matter the most in the newsroom are getting the story and getting it better and faster than their prime competitors.[28]

Unlike Rothman, the Lichters, and Cal Thomas, Gans considers reformism and progressivism to be positive values that have been expressed in American journalism since the earliest days of the republic.

None of these observers contends, therefore, that journalism is entirely an objective enterprise. It has values and commitments. The question seems to be one of characterizing those values and commitments as normatively positive or negative vis-à-vis religion. And all of these observers in the end call for a kind of religion coverage that transcends traditional categories, that moves beyond domesticated coverage of institutions (or the political conflicts thereof), and that more seriously and carefully accounts for the substantive nature of religion in the lives of people and nations.

The work of Marvin Olasky, one of the most vocal critics of journalism's treatment of religion, is helpful in clarifying what these perspectives share in common. Olasky, himself a professor of journalism, contends that the problem is a more fundamental one than that implicitly addressed by the Rothman-Lichter versus Dart-Allen debate. He takes the historical view, holding that before the rise of the mass press in the 1830s a kind of religion journalism existed that naturalized "the religious" rather than objectifying it. He argues that the change in coverage represented by James Gordon Bennett and the *New York Herald* introduced a secularized, irreligious type of coverage that has evolved into an antireligious humanism today.[29] In contrast to the Rothman-Lichter critiques, Olasky contends that no amount of "professionalism" or "balance" can be expected to right the wrongs of religion news. What is needed instead is a separate, *religion-centered* coverage.[30]

Mark Silk, in *Unsecular Media,* considers Olasky's argument and finds it perhaps too narrowly drawn. Echoing the larger debates over responsibility in coverage, he notes,

> It is well to recognize that there comes a point when no common journalistic discourse will be able to satisfy believers and nonbelievers alike or, perhaps more important, all groups of believers. Yet even editors as spiritually committed as Olasky may find virtue in reporting the news according to commonly accepted journalistic norms.[31]

Where does this leave us? Olasky's more radical critique aside, we can set up Dart-Allen and Rothman-Lichter as—admittedly—straw arguments and can see answers *and questions* emerging from each. In reporting that "media elites" hold certain attitudes of indifference or even disdain toward religion, Rothman and the Lichters are merely confirming something that is widely accepted anecdotally. Dart and Allen, and much of what is considered here, provide ample evidence of the extent to which religion is misunderstood and undervalued in America's newsrooms. What these "media elite" critics—including Olasky—fail to recognize, at the same time, is the extent to which very competent religion coverage takes place every day at most of the same outlets surveyed by Rothman and the Lichters.

Dart and Allen provide valuable information on the nature and extent of religion interest in newsrooms at newspapers across the country. They present a persuasive defense of the profession of religion journalism. However, their approach fails to fully appreciate the extent to which religion continues to face challenges within the news business. Their recommendations are good and sound and would, if implemented, do much to close the gap between the media and the world of religion. However, the professionalism they call for is only part of the answer. We must recognize the extent to which there is still a powerful uneasiness about religion in America's newsrooms. As long as this atmosphere holds sway, even the most energetic and dynamic religion reporter will face significant obstacles.

Terry Mattingly described some of those obstacles in a 1993 article in *Quill.* The state of religion news can be attributed to four "biases": *space, time, and resources,* where religion writers rarely have the institutional support in these areas afforded other beats; *knowledge,* where religion journalism often suffers from a lack of expertise; *worldview,* meaning that the culture of the newsroom is one where religion is not held to be important by newspeople themselves; and *prejudice,* or those cases where religion is actually targeted for unfair or negative coverage. Mattingly sums it up this way:

> Many on the right like to blame all poor, negative, or shallow religion coverage on this fourth bias. They note surveys indicating that about nine of ten journalists back abortion rights and a large majority supports gay rights. . . . I believe the first three biases play the primary roles in shaping religion coverage. With the "bias of world view" being the most important.[32]

Mattingly's view, then, is that the problem is not one of *antireligion* so much as it is one of *irreligion.* "It is hard to write a good story if you don't know that it exists," he says.

Against these arguments over the antireligion or irreligion of the news media, Mark Silk contends that what religion coverage represents is a kind of consensual consonance between American civil religion and civic values and a benign—even supportive—news media. Rather than representing irreligion or antireligion, the media represent a kind of *consensual religious* approach. To Silk, this flows understandably from the nature of the news business:

> The news media, far from promoting a secularist agenda of their own, approach religion with values and presuppositions that the American public widely shares. . . . Newspapers, in particular, preoccupied with their declining market share, are at great pains to give readers a product that meets their needs and sensibilities. Hostility to religion is hardly the order of the day.[33]

It does seem important to consider that the status of religion at the nation's news outlets does not derive from the perspectives of individual journalists or editorial decision makers alone but is more deeply rooted in the status of religion in American public discourse. Professionalism alone, for instance, will do little to change the perceived status of religion as exclusively a *private* matter. And until we come to understand religion in a way that can introduce it successfully into the *public sphere,* we will still only be hearing part of the story.

## Notes

1. Weiskopf, Michael. 1993. Energized by passion, the public is its calling; Gospel grapevine displays its strength in controversy of military gay ban. *Washington Post,* February 1, p. A1.

2. *Washington Post,* February 2, 1993, p. A3. Writing in the *Washington Times,* conservative media watchdog Reed Irvine contended that this terse apology had, in fact, been more fulsome in early editions of the *Post,* including demographic evidence of the social and educational status of evangelicals to undermine Weiskopf's original assertion. See Irvine, Reed. 1996. Call-in democracy from the third house. *Washington Times,* February 7, p. B3.

3. *All Things Considered,* National Public Radio, December 19, 1995.

4. For the most comprehensive and scholarly recent description of these processes, see Michael Schudson. 1987. *Discovering the news: A social history of American newspapers.* New York: Basic Books.

5. Buddenbaum, Judith. 1990. Religion news coverage in commercial network newscasts. In *Religious television: Controversies and conclusions,* edited by Robert Abelman and Stewart Hoover. Norwood, NJ: Ablex.

6. For example, see Liroff, D. B. 1971. *A comparative content analysis of network television evening news programs and other national news media in the United States.* Ph.D. diss., Northwestern University; Buddenbaum, Judith. 1988. The religion beat at daily newspapers. *Newspaper Research Journal* 9:57-69; Buddenbaum, Judith and Stewart Hoover. 1996. The role of religion in public attitudes toward religion news. In *Religion and mass media: Audiences and adaptations,* edited by Daniel Stout and Judith Buddenbaum. Thousand Oaks, CA: Sage, pp. 135-47; Buddenbaum, Judith. 1996. The role of religion in newspaper trust, subscribing, and use for political information. In Stout and Buddenbaum, eds., *Religion and mass media,* pp. 123-34; Ferré, John. 1980. Denominational biases in the American press. *Review of Religious Research* 21:271-83; Rockefeller Foundation. 1981. *The religion beat: The reporting of religion in the media.* New York: Author.

7. Shaw, David. 1983. Coverage increases: Media view religion in a news light. *Los Angeles Times,* December 28, p. A12.

8. Mattingly, Terry. 1983. The religion beat: Out of the ghetto, into the mainstream. *Quill,* January, pp. 13-19.

9. Hynds, E. C. 1987. Large daily newspapers have improved coverage of religion. *Journalism Quarterly* 64:444-8.

10. Buddenbaum, "The religion beat at daily newspapers."

11. For a detailed report of Wyatt's findings, see Dart, John and Jimmy Allen. 1993. *Bridging the gap: Religion and the news media.* Nashville, TN: Freedom Forum First Amendment Center.

12. Ibid., p. 39.

13. Mattingly, "The religion beat."

14. See, for example, Neuhaus, Richard John. 1984. *The naked public square: Religion and democracy in America.* Grand Rapids, MI: Eerdmans.

15. Bellah, Robert. 1997. Is there a common American culture? Plenary address to the annual meeting of the American Academy of Religion, San Francisco, November 22; Bellah, Robert,

Richard Madsen, William Sullivan, Ann Swidler, and Stephen M. Tipton. 1985. *Habits of the heart: Individualism and commitment in American life.* Berkeley: University of California Press.

16. In December 1997, a widely circulated report by Pew Research Center found that by certain measures American religiosity is actually on the increase. For example, 71 percent of respondents to the Pew survey said they never doubt the existence of God, up from 69 percent in 1987; 61 percent said they believe that miracles come from God, up 14 percentage points from a decade earlier; and 53 percent said prayer was important in daily life, compared to 41 percent in 1987 (*Los Angeles Times,* December 22, 1997, p. A20). For a comprehensive discussion of American religiosity patterns, see also Caplow, T., H. Bahr, and B. Chadwick. 1982. *All faithful people: Change and continuity in Middletown's religion.* Minneapolis: University of Minnesota Press.

17. Luckman, Thomas. 1967. *The invisible religion.* New York: Macmillan. For a more detailed description, see Hoover, Stewart M. 1997. Media and the construction of the religious public sphere. In *Rethinking media, religion, and culture,* edited by Stewart M. Hoover and Knut Lundby. Thousand Oaks, CA: Sage, pp. 283-97.

18. Herberg, Will. 1956. *Protestant, Catholic, Jew.* New York: Doubleday, p. 256.

19. Lichter, Robert, Stanley Rothman, and Linda Lichter. 1980. *The media elite.* New York: Adler & Adler.

20. *Crossfire,* CNN, December 29, 1993.

21. Lichter et al., *The media elite.*

22. *ABC World News Tonight,* August 13, 1993.

23. Dart and Allen, *Bridging the gap.*

24. Ibid., p. 43.

25. Dart and Allen note, in passing, that the expressed religiosity of Wyatt's interviewees from the media was still at some variance with the religiosity of the general public, as determined by regular Gallup polls. Data reported in a later chapter here, for instance, found that the percentage of respondents choosing the most extreme category of "importance of religion"— "very important"—was 58 percent, whereas the percentage among Wyatt's sample of editors choosing that response was quite a bit smaller: 35 percent.

26. Lichter, Linda, Robert Lichter, and Stanley Rothman. 1982. The once and future journalists. *Washington Journalism Review,* December, pp. 26-7.

27. *Reliable Sources,* CNN, December 5, 1993.

28. Gans, Herbert. 1985. Are U.S. journalists dangerously liberal? *Columbia Journalism Review,* November/December, pp. 28-33.

29. Olasky, Marvin. 1988. *Prodigal press: The anti-Christian bias of the American news media.* Westchester, IL: Crossway, pp. 20-26.

30. Ibid., p. 152.

31. Silk, Mark. 1995. *Unsecular media: Making news of religion in America.* Urbana: University of Illinois Press, p. 144.

32. Mattingly, Terry. 1993. Religion in the news: Are we short-changing readers and ourselves with biases that filter news? *Quill,* July/August, p. 13.

33. Silk, *Unsecular media,* p. 141.

# LOOKING AT RELIGION

If there is an enduring sense anywhere that religion is somehow fading from the national or global scene, recent events should have laid it to rest by now. Whatever its ultimate prospects or ultimate shape as we enter the new millenium, religion today continues to play an important role in social, cultural, and political trends domestically and internationally. Global fundamentalisms persist, and seemingly become stronger and more influential.[1] The Evangelical New Right continues as an important element of American politics at both the local and national levels.[2] Patterns of immigration have resulted in a vibrant religious diversity continuing to grow in many urban areas of the country, adding to the array of faiths already present in the American pastiche.

What we see is a fundamental tendency for interest in things religious to persist among the very classes and groups that supposedly would be most likely to abandon spiritual explanations in favor of more rationalist ones. Wade Clark Roof's comprehensive studies of baby boom religiosity provide persuasive evidence of the continuation of religious sensibilities, although in new guises.[3] In place of religious practices lodged in traditional settings such as churches, with their historical and doctrinal claims, the baby boomers (and presumably the postboom "Generation X"ers) are turning to modes of spirituality and consciousness, which are no less fundamentally—and none-theless powerfully—religious.[4]

The "New Age," interest in Eastern and Native American spirituality, the therapeutic 12-step movement, encounter groups, and crystal healing are but a few of many such modes of spirituality available to the baby boom generation. These combined with a still-vibrant conventional religiosity among boomers on the Christian "right" (involved in evangelicalism and the charismatic movement) and "left" (those returning to more liberal churches) and the so-called mega-churches that lie somewhere inbetween reflect the persistence of religion in the face of long-predicted secularization.[5]

The summer 1992 issue of the *Newsletter of the Religion Newswriters' Association* initiated an interesting colloquy regarding the contemporary state of the religion beat as it contemplates this ferment and change. David Crumm, the religion writer for the *Detroit Free Press,* wrote a reflection that made the point that religion writing had achieved an unprecedented status and profile. Pointing out that some prominent newspapers and journalism think-tanks had begun to take religion more seriously, he argued against the then-common assumption among the RNA membership that, after a period of growth, religion coverage was on the decline at the nation's papers.

Crumm was challenged in the next issue by Julia Duin, a former religion writer for the *Houston Chronicle.* Although there were some positive signs, she granted, the overall trend was not up but down:

> My reply . . . is David, have you tried job hunting recently? If not, give it a whirl . . . you may find out there are lot less enlightened attitudes out there than exist at the Free Press. . . . I've been job hunting since January and [not] run into the kind of open . . . attitude about religion and spirituality that you say exists among your editors.
>
> . . . Let's read the signals that editors at other newspapers are giving. Since 1990 nine major newspapers . . . have had openings on their religion beats. These are good papers. They all have filled them (some with part time) from within. . . . What [this] says is that religion is not a beat worth hiring a specialty writer for. It's a beat "anyone" can do.[6]

There is, in fact, evidence on both sides of this issue. *New York Times* Religion Editor Peter Steinfels noted a number of positive signs in a story written to coincide with the 1994 meeting of the RNA.[7] Many of the larger newspapers have maintained an emphasis on religion in the face of tight economic times in the news business. A few have even expanded their religion staffs. A prominent case of decline cited by Duin was the *Los Angeles Times;* however, in 1993, a former senior environment correspondent was assigned full-time to the religion desk there. The 1994 meeting of the RNA witnessed a remarkable panel of editors from the *Dallas Morning News, New York Newsday,* and Newhouse News Service, who claimed that the religion beat was definitely on the upswing.[8]

As David Crumm had noted in his RNA *Newsletter* column, the Poynter Center, a major journalism think-tank, has for a number of years conducted training events in the area of religion coverage. They were joined in 1993 by the Knight Center for Specialized Journalism at the University of Maryland, which held its first week-long symposium on religion that year. At about the same time, George Cornell, long-time religion editor at the Associated Press and the dean of American religion writers (now deceased), conducted an inquiry into the status of religion in journalism education and found some hopeful signs of change amid a background of general disregard of the beat. Sources at Gonzaga University in Washington, Temple University, Columbia, Northwestern, and Marquette all reported to Cornell that plans were under way to offer formal courses or majors in religion journalism.[9] Indeed, both Temple University and Northwestern's Medill School of Journalism have now established formal master's courses in religion journalism held in cooperation with religion departments or seminaries.

The Freedom Forum (formerly the Gannett Foundation) made major contributions to the beat during 1992-1993. The Freedom Forum Media Studies Center in New York appointed Donald W. Shriver, former president of Union Seminary, as a senior fellow, allowing him to develop a joint Union-Columbia course in religion and the media that he team-taught with James Carey, the distinguished former Dean of the College of Communication at the University of Illinois. In October 1993, the Media Studies Center sponsored (in cooperation with a research project supported by Lilly Endowment, Inc.) a national conference on "Religion and the News." The Freedom Forum's center in Nashville also undertook a study of the religion beat, directed by Dr. Jimmy Allen, former president of the Southern Baptist Convention, and John Dart, the distinguished religion editor at the *Los Angeles Times.* Their work resulted in the important report *Bridging the Gap.*[10]

There were also important developments in broadcasting. Attendees at the October 1993 Freedom Forum conference in New York heard Peter Jennings of ABC speak of his intention to hire the first full-time religion correspondent in network television news history. In February 1994, Peggy Wehmeyer, who for years had been one of only two religion correspondents at *local* television stations (she was at WFAA in Dallas), began work as a member of *The American Agenda* staff on *ABC World News Tonight.*

There were also developments in public broadcasting. Bill Moyers continued his important documentary work on public television, airing multipart series on the book of Genesis and on religious historian Huston Smith in 1996 alone. Many PBS stations carried *Mine Eyes Have Seen the Glory,* an exploration of American evangelicalism written and hosted by Randall Balmer of Barnard College, *Faith Under Fire,* produced in cooperation with the Lilly Endowment, and *Searching for God in America,* an assessment of American religion hosted by Hugh Hewitt. In 1997, a new program for public broadcasting, *Religion News Weekly,* appeared.

Most surprising to many observers was the increased attention given to religion by National Public Radio (NPR). In 1992, Pew Charitable Trusts began supporting coverage of religion within the general range of NPR news.[11] In 1993, the NPR cultural desk assigned one of its top correspondents, Lynn Neary, to cover religion and announced its intention to expand the beat to a full unit. That same year, NPR's *Talk of the Nation* devoted several programs to issues of religion, including a 10-week series on the Ten Commandments.

But the glass can always still be seen as "half empty." *Bridging the Gap,* the study by John Dart and Jimmy Allen, noted that even though there are over 200 members of the RNA, only 67 newspapers have full-time religion writers, a decrease in recent years and, as one reviewer pointed out, "a trifling number" compared to beats such as education, business, and sports.[12] Dart and Allen provide a telling anecdote as to the persistent marginalization of religion at CNN, one of the most important contemporary media outlets:

CNN falls short on religion news, admitted Ed Turner, executive vice president for news at CNN. "Along with the other major TV networks, we just don't do it well," he said in an interview. The round-the-clock news channel does not have a specialist in religion as it does in sports or business. "That would take a special kind of person," Turner said. Even then, he added, "in these tough economic times, the religious reporter would be the first to be cut."[13]

So, is the religion "beat" on the upswing or downswing? It would appear that most signs are positive. It is at least new and unprecedented to have such nationally prominent sources as ABC and National Public Radio getting on the religion bandwagon. Some observers predict that now that these "flagship" media have begun to take the beat seriously other media will be inspired to follow suit. As has already been suggested, a good deal of the explanation for religion treatment can be found in *implicit* definitions and standards of appropriate coverage. The fact that ABC has begun to (quite self-consciously) cover religion will have a symbolic effect on these definitions and standards, quite apart from the specific approaches taken.

All of this means that there is now more religion in the news than ever—that the problem of time and space raised by Terry Mattingly in Chapter 4 has in part been addressed. While it cannot be said for certain that these trends will continue, it seems appropriate to assess the character and nature of this evolving religion coverage so as to be able to judge it according to criteria beyond mere *quantity.*

In the first instance of course, an argument for quantity does make some sense. The proportion of coverage devoted to religion, as opposed to other beats, has been patently out of balance when measured against the fundamental religiosity of the American public. Jane Greenhalgh, a producer at National Public Radio who participated in re-evaluating that network's approach to religion, sees this as a fundamental justification for increased and improved coverage. When she and her staff looked into the matter, she says,

> [we] found that people thought the media don't do a very good job of covering religion, and then this great statistic that 92% of Americans have at least a nominal religious affiliation, we said this is *unique,* and it is something *significant.* Those figures are far different from Europe and most other countries. Most of them are not that devout, or active, but it does mean that it is something very important for people.[14]

This finding is echoed in sentiments attributed to Billy Graham and Shirley MacLaine by Terry Mattingly in his article for *Quill:*

> For years, Graham has asked why newspapers assign thousands to cover sports and only a handful to religion. And [Shirley] MacLaine preached a similar sermon in an April address to the American Society of Newspaper Editors.[15]

Jimmy Allen has made the proportional argument this way:

> At most papers you have one-tenth or less the number of people on religion that you have on sports. Yet many more people go to church weekly than go to sporting events. You have to wonder whether that balance is right.[16]

Dart and Allen end *Bridging the Gap* with an appeal for a "re-balancing" of attention to religion. They and others[17] have made strong arguments for improvement in coverage on a moral basis as well. A 1989 report on research into the status of the religion beat at daily newspapers took this perspective:

> Religion is a diverse, rich beat. It has become complex, as religious faith and practice have become diverse, idiosyncratic (in some cases) and privatistic. As one interviewee said, " . . . it has it all, scandal, sex, power, money, hopes, dreams, corruption, altruism. . . . " As it has become easier for newspapers to cover, many of them have taken the opportunity. Perhaps to oversimplify, religion's "special" status has begun to fade, along with the "establishment," and this has allowed journalism to feel emboldened to look into its closets.
>
>     Thus, what the journalists and readers interviewed here are calling for is a type of religion coverage which fits the present age. They want to see religion news in the mainstream of newspaper practice. By developing categories and definitions of religion that are sufficiently broad and diverse, categories such as those elucidated by our interviewees here, religion news can find such a place.[18]

To move beyond arguments for greater *quantity* of coverage toward questions of *quality* begins to raise a larger and more complex set of issues, however. Ultimately, the task is the development of what we might call *normative* standards of coverage. Such tasks have been undertaken by previous studies. One basis on which to approach normative standards is through structural and procedural approaches to religion within the newsroom itself. The same 1989 study[19] proposed that the following set of criteria be applied to the newsroom context.

*Is religion a "hard news" or a "feature" beat?* "Hard news" clearly has the highest status among both journalists and readers. For journalists, the hard news conventions are the most comfortable ones. Most journalists seem to regard exposure in the "news" section of the paper or broadcast as an important goal. Readers concur, as Chapter 6 will show. Their desire for coverage that confirms that religion is a part of daily life is expressed in their judgment that religion should therefore appear in the "news" sections of the paper or during the "hard news" segments of television programs.

*Is religion a local or a nonlocal story?* Readership surveys suggest that religion should be seen as a story that often transcends local contexts. That is not to say that a local angle is not important but that reader interest in religion extends to stories of national and international import. Yet much of the contemporary discourse about religion, however, still evidences this localism bias. For example, when Dart and Allen interviewed journalists across the country in *Bridging the Gap* they found some in favor of writing the "small" stories (Debra Nussbaum Cohen of the Jewish Telegraphic Agency), "getting out in the trenches" to determine faith's effect on people's lives (Sandy Dolbee of the *San Diego Union-Tribune*), and providing coverage more specific to a local area (Mark Hass, an editor of the *Detroit News*).

*Is there a religion "section" or "department"?* This is a mixed issue, with some working religion reporters advocating for a section and the relative freedom and autonomy it brings, and others arguing against the "ghetto-ization" that a section implies. It is clear that having a defined section does give readers and others a point of reference for religion interests, and papers have often been surprised at the level of reader loyalty they engender. However, many journalists and readers are coming to think of religion as something that can and should move outside the defined boundaries of a section.

*Is religion "run of paper" or "run of broadcast"?* That is, can it appear anywhere, in any kind of story, or is it confined to certain contexts only? This of course is related to the question of a defined religion section and to the question of the status of religion as "news" in a functional, practical sense. The readers met in Chapter 6 and most religion writers and other observers see religion as something that should transcend the narrow confines of its received definition. This confinement seems to have two dimensions. First, religion has not been treated as "newsworthy" *on its own terms,* and second, the *religious dimension of other stories* has often been left out or under-reported. The remedy is seen to be acceptance outside the narrow confines of the feature or religion pages. As the *RNS-Lilly Study of Religion Reporting* put it,

Placement in sections outside the identified religion section (if there is one) or placement in the news section of the paper, is the most sought-after by the writers we interviewed. Certainly, many of them would point out that longer-form "feature" pieces are a necessary outlet for religion coverage, but they all spoke with the greatest satisfaction of the times when their material made it to the news section or to page 1A.[20]

*Is there a religion specialist on staff?* This would seem an obvious question to ask. Most observers assume that the depth and complexity of the religion beat dictates specialist treatment. For example, this would address the second of Terry Mattingly's "biases" of coverage discussed in Chapter 4. Having a specialist, however, can also militate against the kind of general scope implied by the desire to have religion be "run of paper." Where is the specialist to be lodged? To whom does this person report? Is the specialist considered as the only source of religion stories? Is everyone else therefore "off the hook"?

*Is the level of religion coverage based on the interest and commitment of the religion specialist?* Several observers have suggested that, at least in the past, many papers' approach to religion was dictated by the religion writer, who sometimes had been on staff for many years and thus commanded a good deal of respect for that reason alone. There are also some cases where the departure of a prominent religion writer occasioned the downgrading of the religion beat.

*Is the religion specialist the only one who does religion? What is this person's relationship to other beats and desks?* These are complicated questions. On one level, it would appear a confirmation of the importance and weight of religion that more than just the religion writer is assigned to cover religion stories. Yet, on another level, it can be a measure of lack of respect for the beat when other reporters "step in" if the stories are particularly "important." John Dart of the *Los Angeles Times* put it this way: "If the Second Coming were to occur, . . . a general-assignment reporter would cover it, and the religion writer would do a sidebar."[21]

The 1993 visit of Pope John Paul II to Denver resulted in a variation on this theme. Most newspapers assigned their religion reporters to lead the coverage, yet the "size" of the story resulted in many general-assignment and other reporters also being put on it. This revealed a second sort of problem in this area: that the religion specialist is often uniquely qualified to cover the religion story. Even though much of the papal coverage was quite straightforward, there were angles to the story, particularly having to do with relations between the Vatican and the American Catholic Church, that required the sense of history only a specialist writer would have.[22]

This leads to the second question, that of the *relationship* between the religion desk and other reporters. In an ideal situation, a religion writer/reporter would act as a consultant to colleagues working on stories that involve religion. The religion writer would thus provide important information but also serve as a sort of "institutional memory" regarding religion, playing a key role in establishing and maintaining policy and practice vis-à-vis religion.

## ■ Voices of Experience

But how does religion journalism work at the country's leading newspapers and broadcast outlets? What is the actual experience of the working reporters and editors who cover it? Although no "slice of time" can adequately describe a situation in the media industries where change is the order of the day, it is nonetheless critical to the discussions here to understand the challenge these people face. More important, perhaps—and to address persistent criticisms of the beat—is to understand how they *think* about what they do. That is, what are the implicit, normative ideas that define their approach to their work? Their experiences provide valuable insight into both the *practice* and the *theory* of religion journalism.

Some of the most strident criticism of the press regarding its relationship to religion has focused on the sensitivity and ability of secular journalists to understand the "substantive" side of religion. That is, religion is not only politics, economics, social events, and structures. It also makes transcendent claims and affirmations. Implicit in the idea that newspapers cannot/will not cover religion well because news *people* are not themselves religious is the assumption that this substantive dimension of religion cannot be understood in the totally rationalistic terms of conventional journalistic criteria and practice.[23]

Much of the popular criticism of press coverage of religion also begins with this idea. Although there is more understanding and sophistication about the news business among readers than is often assumed (as will be seen in Chapter 6), there is a clear sentiment abroad that newspapers do not do a good job of dealing with matters of spirituality, faith, and motivation. As one denominational press officer put it, there is relatively little coverage that "defines who we are and why we are doing all of this."[24]

This is an issue that concerns nearly all religion writers and editors. They are both aware of this criticism and aware that religion is not like other "beats." Most journalists we have spoken with agree that the way substantive belief relates to most stories is that it must be taken as a "given." It is a precursor of the behaviors and attitudes they write about, and can be taken "on faith" without sacrificing the conventional news judgment of the reporter. If the attitudes and behavior justify coverage, then it is covered. This is, of course, an unsatisfactory approximation of the "whole story" for some of the people who become the subjects of stories. Says Jeanne Pugh, veteran former religion editor of the *St. Petersburg Times,*

> "Faith" and things like people's spirituality come out in interviews. We don't need to inspire or try to inspire. That would be against the mission of the paper. Sometimes we'll get into that stuff in covering a Graham crusade or something. But still, I take a reporter's view of those things— to the extent that I have been declared unwelcome by some of them.[25]

Writing about faith is not an easy task. It goes with the territory, and most reporters seem to accept that it will always be controversial. The only standard they have is whether there is a "story" there:

> Faith issues can be covered as long as they are appropriately provocative on a personal basis. It has to be done carefully. That is, I would write differently for a denominational publication because they are not a general audience.[26]

There are some commonplace concessions to the public expectation that newspapers can and should deal in matters of "faith." The Associated Press has for years prepared a series of stories of faith and inspiration for distribution during the Christmas and Easter holidays. Many local papers run inspirational columns by local pastors or from syndicated sources. Many papers regularly run prayers in their religion sections. One religion editor reveals some misgivings about the practice but accepts that it may be a necessary concession to community sentiment:

> You'll notice that we carry prayers on the front of the section. A woman in Virginia does them and syndicates them. That is a decision that was made higher up. They thought this would be important. I've had my doubts, but people like them. They put them on the refrigerator. I don't really think that is the role of a newspaper, but in this community, people sort of expect that kind of thing, so we do it.[27]

The question of press coverage of substantive issues is one of the reasons why religion has traditionally been problematic in the news business. The suspicion on the part of their colleagues that religion reporters actually have some sort of axe to grind would be confirmed if faith and inspiration were more a part of their output. The question of how to deal with these issues becomes a major determinant of credibility with coworkers. Most writers feel they have overcome such suspicion. The following anecdote illustrates this:

> I'll never forget the time that one of the editors walked by when I was working on the syndicated prayers for the religion section, looked over my shoulder, and asked "Did you make these up or are they *real?*" I think that is a measure of the extent to which I'm seen as just another reporter here.[28]

The general sentiment among religion writers and editors seems to be that the intangible and substantive aspects of religion stories—issues of faith, inspiration, and motivation—should not be ignored entirely. But they need not always be evaluated or validated. There is so much else to write about that the substantive, while obviously important, need not necessarily be covered. The *tangible* or *material* reality of religion—its behaviors, social attitudes, politics, social life, and institutions—is the appropriate turf for secular religion writers to tread.

Another important issue is whether or not religion news is, by definition, *local* news. As was noted in Chapters 1 and 3, the idea that it *is* has deep roots in the history of journalism. And there still appears to be widespread agreement with this idea. Most reporters we have spoken with stress the idea that religion stories must usually be *local* stories. "As far as papers are concerned, religion is still primarily a *local* story, one that is based in its local impact," says Clark Morphew of the *St. Paul Dispatch.* This means that even *important* nonlocal stories in most cases must first be localized if they are to be considered for space in the paper.

This perception holds even for papers that give a particular priority to religion coverage. There is a general sentiment that such localization of coverage "softens" it. The requirement that religion be seen as a local issue seems for many to be based in the tradition of the "church page" approach even for papers that have eschewed that strict compartmentalization.

A paper that is in many ways unique vis-à-vis religion is the *Nashville Tennessean,* which has a significant commitment to coverage of religion as a "hard news" beat. For the religion editor there, however, this does not mean that the *Tennessean* considers religion to not also be a "local" beat:

> Religion can be a local beat here, and still be "hard news" largely because Nashville is a "company town." Religion here is a big employer, a big business. I try to get a good story a day, and I'm aiming primarily for hard news.[29]

The city editor at the *Tennessean* confirmed the paper's perspective of the localism of religion, suggesting that improved local coverage, not improved national or international coverage, would be the area for expansion of the beat:

> Right now our coverage is pretty much about the city and what is happening here. I would like us to do more suburban and/or county coverage. There is definitely a lot more going on right around here that we could be covering.[30]

In sharp contrast to many other papers on this point, the *Los Angeles Times* has at times not considered the issue of localism to be as important. During his tenure there, Russell Chandler told an interviewer,

> We don't have any particular need to localize our stories. I would say we try not to *ignore* local stories. In general, we favor local *hard* news over national *soft* news, but it's the *news value* that is the issue. We don't go out of our way to "localize" a story.[31]

The issue of localism thus seems to be an important way in which coverage differs from paper to paper and an important way for the beat to be defined. Even those reporters who do work within a definition of localism seem to recognize that some nonlocal stories *should* be justified by their news value but nonetheless must meet the expectation of localism.

Even if the questions of localism and substance can be solved, religion reporters still seem to face expectations and understandings that discount the beat. This is the case even among those writers who work at major papers where religion has been given more emphasis. Extensive coverage of religion is still considered the exception rather than the rule. It must be explained, even to colleagues at major religion-emphasizing papers:

There is a problem with skepticism from other reporters. Who the hell would want to *do* religion? A lot of their ideas are backlash. They went to Catholic schools, or to Sunday School, and hated it. I would say that most of them are believers, but that they are not doctrinaire.[32]

Most working journalists agree that the answer to the problem of marginalization of religion is "professionalism." That is, they are convinced that the best way to counteract entrenched attitudes about the importance and newsworthiness of the religion beat is for them to do their best to cover religion according to the standards and criteria of performance that newspapers apply to all beats:

How do we relate the elements we have to deal with? The bottom line is *trust*. We have to get the editors, readers, public, etc., to trust us. We have to *sell* a story to *all* of these contexts. A decade ago, there may have been a lot of *mistrust*—editors mistrusted and devalued religion. We have to be skilled as journalists and knowledgeable about our sources beyond the *obvious* stories.[33]

Teresa Wasson, the *Tennessean*'s city editor, ties a diagnosis of the roots of anti-religion-beat bias to a prescription for changing these attitudes by demonstrating quality religion coverage that qualifies—in conventional terms—as "news":

One explanation is, in fact, this issue of personal attitude. Religion is simply not important to many reporters or editors, *personally,* and thus they don't understand how personally important it is to readers. Since it is *not* to them, they think it must not be to readers, either.

The second, and this is even more important, I think . . . they don't understand the richness of coverage available in religion. It's not just socials and churchy things. Religion is very rich turf, in news value, and many editors don't know that. That is because *they have not seen it demonstrated.* The models of the kind of religion coverage as "hard news" that we do, are few and far between, and most editors and reporters have not seen it done like this before.[34]

As will be seen in Chapter 6, readers tend to agree with this point. For both readers and journalists, the perception of what religion news is is largely shaped through experience. If they are to think of religion news as something beyond church announcements on a church page, they have to have seen that demonstrated.

More than one reporter has come to see the skepticism with which editors typically react to their stories as a positive thing. One put it this way in an interview:

> I don't look on editors as obstacles. They are helpful. If you don't understand the story, they won't either. They are also the perfect reader—they *demand* clarity. Their demands will help you get the story done and in the paper. You have to make them understand it, or the readership won't, either.[35]

As was said earlier, everyone seems to agree that the religion beat is now held in higher regard than it was in the past. The most concrete measure of this improved status is the fact that religion is no longer relegated to only one section of the paper. "Religion used to be in the back of the paper," says one religion editor. "But that has all changed. Religion is now R.O.P. from the front page to the truss ads."[36]

There are many examples of the kinds of news that have thrust religion onto the front page in the past decades, but most reporters we have interviewed agree on a core of such stories. Most of them further agree that this ferment in the world of religion is probably the most important reason why many papers are now covering religion more and in a better way than they have in the past:

> Religion reporting has definitely improved. The papers are paying more attention to religion altogether. Why? Because of two people: Reagan and Khomeini. Because of the rise of the religious right here and abroad, editors suddenly woke up and recognized the importance and power of religion.[37]

> It seems to me that in the last 10 years, some of the types of stories that have come out have been bigger, and have been justified as religion [hard] "news." Like, John Paul II, like the new religious right and politics, there've been a lot of good news stories in religion. Whether you can call that better religion reporting, I don't know. Things like those have put religion more in the news than was the case in the previous decade or so.[38]

For some reporters, this emergence of blockbuster religion stories reveals the extent to which the religion beat itself can still be derogated:

A lot of papers appreciated the importance of religion when the TV preacher scandals all coincided. That did not necessarily translate into the religion writers *covering* those stories. For example, when Jerry Falwell gave his first press conference after taking over PTL, I was there, and the *Chicago Tribune* religion writer was there, and maybe one other, but everyone else was general-assignment because it was seen as a page 1 story.[39]

This new emphasis on religion spawned by the major national story did not necessarily mean that the idea of localism discussed earlier has fallen by the wayside. One reporter feels that the local angle is the *reason* why his paper has moved to upgrade coverage of *national* issues and controversies:

This paper had kissed off religion coverage for a number of years before I came. They just didn't think it was important. But because of the interest in religion in recent years, the new right in Protestantism, the new Pope, Khomeini, etc., suddenly religion is important again. I think the motivation was mostly local. Bakersfield is a microcosm of the nation in terms of religiosity and religious diversity, and religion became more and more prominent locally. The paper just had to respond.[40]

One editor who supervises religion reporting ties the improvement in the status of the religion beat to a change in attitudes at papers about what qualifies as religion coverage. This change in attitude in turn is based on the fact that more and more religion is "forcing itself" onto the news pages of papers. A subtler and more profound reason for changes in the religion beat than the mere number of religion stories that currently present themselves is hinted at here: the idea that religion *itself* has changed fundamentally in the past quarter century. In the so-called establishment era of American religion, there was a clearly defined and relatively powerful religious establishment. Coverage of its *institutions,* their activities and positions, could qualify as religion coverage and could be easily accomplished through such means as canned coverage of sermons by its most prominent spokespeople.

Religion news became more difficult to do and the beat more difficult to define, which seems to have accounted in some measure for the decline in religion coverage during the 1960s and 1970s. As the beat became more complex, its relatively low status meant that it fell out of favor. It is also possible, as was said earlier, that the fading of the establishment also was misread by some as the fading of religion itself.

There is yet another implication of all this. A number of observers have noted that religion becomes news when it resembles other beats. Thus, when it exhibits behaviors that can also be described as "political," "fiscal," or "scandalous" it begins to fit better with journalistic preconceptions and categories. In the establishment era, there was still an inhibition against too much of such news getting into print. Some reporters feel that with the fading of the establishment, this inhibition has also faded.

At the same time that the deference with which religion might have bee covered in the past has faded, the potenital for religion news to involve controversy persists. Indeed, the received view is that the religion beat is a particularly controversial post. Religion is thought to be something about which people feel quite deeply, and thus they are more likely to respond to religion stories than to other types of coverage in the paper. It is also a beat that has a "constituency" in the sense that religious institutions seem to be particularly attuned to the way they are treated by the "secular press."

How do working religion writers respond to the criticism that this controversy is rooted in "biases" on the part of the media? As was already noted, members of the evangelical community have been particularly vocal in their criticisms of the press. Former *Los Angeles Times* religion reporter Russell Chandler, who knows this community well, told an interviewer that the charge of "bias" is unfounded:

> I think that whatever the press does that is wrong with regard to that movement is a result of ignorance more than anything else. They sometimes deal in stereotypes or caricatures that they are unable to sort out. I don't see deliberate *targeting*.[41]

Most reporters are convinced that the criticisms they do get are largely self-serving, in that readers fail to understand the range of issues that the paper has to contend with in covering religion. Their impression is that readers are somewhat myopic and self-preoccupied in their consumption of religion coverage:

> I don't hear from people saying "you should not have covered such-and-such." Instead, they are pointing out things they think I *should* have covered. From Mainline Protestants, I mostly hear that I spend too much

time covering Catholics and Jews. . . . I've been accused of being a
Catholic who doesn't understand Protestantism, a Protestant who
doesn't understand Catholicism and an atheist or humanist who is
hostile to or ignorant of religion. Usually it's over some fine issue of
jargon or nomenclature that would be lost on the general readership
anyway.[42]

Where readers seem to be somewhat myopic in their responses to coverage,
churches themselves seem to some writers to be absolutely self-absorbed in
their desires for coverage. This places these groups in a curious position. On
the one hand, they want coverage and the credibility that coverage would
confer, but on the other hand, they want that coverage on their own terms,
their own way:

Churches seem to love publicity. Most churches would be happier if we
abandoned "religion news" and restored the "church page." That way
they could have some control by virtue of what they paid for in advertising, and they could be assured of coverage of their congregational
activities. I think that is particularly true of the Protestants. They don't
want coverage the way *we* cover it. Churches want to set the ground
rules. That is fine, but if they constrain us too much, then we can't do
our job, and we don't have a story.[43]

Most writers seem convinced that, at the least, local churches do not
understand that much of what they do simply has little "hard" news value:

When we started up, after not having religion coverage at all, people
were thrilled to get coverage for things that *never* got coverage before.
Now the honeymoon is over, and many of them have gotten savvy about
how to get coverage, and that begins to complicate things for me. Some
have hired PR men, or have volunteer publicity committees. I now get
lots of contacts from such sources, and that is definitely a pressure.
Sometimes these things bring ideas that are genuine *stories,* and that is
OK, but sometimes it is just PR.[44]

However, not all of them feel that the readership is entirely self-conscious in
its interests and desires:

They [readers] don't always agree with me. That is clear. I think that
what they want, though, is news about religion *in general.* News about
groups other than themselves—other religions. Congregations want
publicity, certainly, but we give them that in our regional tabloids. No,
religion here is something different than that.[45]

But most would affirm the idea that readers (and churches) could stand to
be far more sophisticated than they are in their understanding of the news
process. This involves their understanding of both what "news" is and how
they should behave in the public environment that is the turf of journalism:

Face it, hard news is usually bad news. In the religion beat, hard news
usually involves either scandals or appointments (or personnel problems) of some kind. The problem is that people are naturally reluctant
to share their "news gems" with us. Even Protestants don't want to talk
about "in-house" stuff with us. . . . For instance, at the UCC Synod in
this region this year, a group of conservative pastors wanted to push for
a resolution on traditional family values. It became very controversial,
and no one wanted to talk with us about it, not the pastors' group, not
the Synod staff, no one.[46]

One of these reporters, Michael Schaeffer, saw as particularly troubling
the tendency for religious organizations to want publicity and at the same
time want to *control* when and where that publicity can take place. Although
not all would agree with Schaeffer's view, he feels strongly that most
religious organizations do not, in fact, have a right to control public access
to information about themselves:

I think they do not have a right to secrecy. Most religions, but particularly Christianity, are evangelical. Christians have a doctrinal proclivity
to proselytize. They are thus going out into the public environment,
attempting to "sell" themselves to the public. You can't go out into the
public like that, seeking members, and then say "we won't talk." They
want to go out, but not have the responsibility to let the rest of the public,
that they haven't reached yet, know what they're about. If you don't
want to talk about it, don't evangelize.[47]

Does the controversial nature of religion lead to its being handled differently from other beats? Most of the reporters we have interviewed eschew

any suggestion that they steer their handling of religion defensively so as to not get caught in controversy. They feel strongly that the professionalism with which all reporters approach their jobs places them in the position to be able to look clearly and dispassionately at controversy. Editorial supervisors agree. Here is how editors at the *St. Petersburg Times* and the *Los Angeles Times,* respectively, see it:

> Controversy is not a problem for us. We get criticisms of bias for all of our coverage. Religion is just no different. You get the same letters, and concerns, and comments that " . . . why'd you cover that cult because now young people will follow them, etc. . . . " that you get about the "A" section. People there say " . . . why do you hype Ronald Reagan so much?" It's just the same bizarre twist in things. You develop a thick skin and do the best you can and fix it tomorrow if you make a mistake.[48]

> If it *were* controversial, that would not be a justification for backing off of coverage. That is one of the reasons we have our specialists. When there is something controversial, to bring in a specialist to analyze, to go to the sources, etc. [and] bring the story in its proper context is our insurance of balance.[49]

The consensus is that religion coverage has experienced a resurgence in recent years. The news value of religion has changed, and much religion has found its way into the news section of many papers. If it should ever seem that less religion "hard news" is finding its way into newspapers, will there be other justifications for the continuance of the emphasis it has found at these papers?

A managing editor addresses the question of how religion coverage is justified at his paper. Was it on the basis of its impact on circulation or advertising, or on the basis of its role in the total mission of his paper?

> We don't think of religion paying for itself any more than we think of editorials paying for themselves. I don't think of business paying for itself. I don't think the *sports* section pays for itself, not by a long shot. There's a lot of ads in there, but they don't pay for it. But you can't have a newspaper without a sports section. You can't have a newspaper without a business section. And I think we've proved that you can't have a *good* newspaper without a *religion* section. Everyone does a certain amount of religion. But traditionally it's driven by a desire to produce

revenue from church ads. I think it is absolutely necessary to have religion as a viable part of the paper's public service.[50]

In some ways, the consensus expressed by the religion writers we've heard from so far is not too surprising. Most of them work at newspapers where religion has either traditionally or recently come into its own. As a way of perhaps understanding the situation with more definition, we might turn to papers where religion has received less emphasis.

## Where Religion Doesn't Appear

It may be a measure of the times that it is fairly difficult to locate a major newspaper that does not devote at least some specialist time to the religion beat. At one point in time, two rather significant papers could be said to fit this definition: the *Oakland Tribune,* which for many years did not have a religion reporter at all, and the *Arizona Republic,* which downgraded the beat when a long-time religion editor transferred to a political assignment.[51]

Experiences at both papers reveal the extent to which the culture of the newsroom shapes the nature of religion coverage. Both the *Tribune* and *Arizona Republic* became for a time places where religion coverage was a matter of newsroom discussion, and each of them therefore provides interesting insights into a more public discourse about its role.

Belinda Taylor is a former managing editor and columnist at the *Tribune.* Religion had always seemed to her to be a gap at the paper, and she had been a keen observer of its fortunes over her nine years there. She concurs with others in the judgment that a major justification for improved coverage would be to address the gap that exists between the public and the media. She attributes much of the newsroom's reluctance to deal with religion to a misguided interpretation of the First Amendment:

Newspapers think of themselves as a branch of government. It's built into the Constitution, into how we are governed. And so I think that along with the separation of church and state, the media have adopted the notion that if they are a branch of government they somehow feel they can't have too much religiosity going on in their pages because that is not their role. I think this situation got more extreme with the Supreme Court's school prayer decision. I think that there came a much greater consciousness of "whoa, we've really got to separate this out."[52]

She also sees the institutional culture of the newsroom as one that is fundamentally resistant to religion:

> I think that newsrooms tend to be very masculine places, and the women who find themselves a role there adopt that manner. So you basically become hard-boiled and cynical, and it becomes, you know, " . . . What's this religious crap? It doesn't have a place in what we do."[53]

She suggests that the prospects of the religion beat are very clearly tied up in dominant notions of status. Religion is just not perceived as something "important." This perception of religion played an important role in religion coverage at the *Tribune*. It loomed large on those occasions when the senior staff of the paper pushed the newsroom to cover religion:

> Bob Maynard [the late former publisher of the *Tribune*] was a religious man, and so was the executive editor. Both of them recognized the problem, and both wanted to get better, improved religion coverage in the paper. And there they ran up against some existing problems that they never figured out how to overcome. Whenever they'd push the issue, the newsroom thought, "Oh God, here we're trying to cover the latest drive-by shooting and the corruption at City Hall, and they want me to take my limited manpower [and cover religion]."[54]

According to Taylor, this sort of resistance was felt often enough to keep the issue off the front burner. However, sometimes Maynard pushed further and faced even more resistance at the line level:

> Occasionally [they] were able to force, on direct order, "I want the metro editor in here and we're going to have this series." Then it became, when the metro editor would have to come out to the newsroom and sell it to this cynical bunch, "Oh God, more nonsense from the front office." And then they're forced to do it and they resent it even more and it becomes a big joke.[55]

There is a lot of religion news to be covered in Oakland. A socially conscious and activist city, churches are prominent in many causes and movements, black churches particularly so, so there was a real sense that there is much on the religion beat that was being missed, according to Taylor:

But the way that played itself out in the newsroom was a feeling on the part of the metro editor or the city editor . . . and these guys were always "hard as nails," I mean that was the culture of the *Tribune.* I know most papers have it to one degree or another, but it was particularly apparent at the *Tribune.* So there was this sense that there was "hard news" breaking all the time, and little time for "soft news" like religion.[56]

To add to that perception, says Taylor, there was also the sense that religion often presented itself as a "pressure" on the paper:

So this editor's awareness of the churches was when a particularly prominent and powerful minister would come to see the publisher, put some pressure on the publisher that we would translate it back to the newsroom. . . . It always seemed to come back to the editor as a reproach, or undue pressure on the part of that community. So they were seen as a pressure group, not as a source of news. That reinforces the notion that the people you are covering are not free of point-of-view or prejudice. And if you're not careful, you're going to end up slanting the news to please them, and you don't want to do that.[57]

From this rather restricted viewpoint of the demands of the religion beat, only *reaction* seems possible, says Taylor:

It's like you don't want to come down on any side, you don't want to say "God exists." We don't know that. So it's that constant search for neutrality with the press and also the constant wanting to stay away from the men in the high collars who are going to get mad at you and the ladies in hats who are going to want you to write about their rummage sales.[58]

If the fortunes of the *Tribune* had not turned sour and more time had been possible to explore religion coverage, Taylor is convinced that things would gradually have changed for the better. Unlike some of our other informants, though, she does not base this speculation on a sense that the beat itself is changing but that the culture of the newsroom is being transformed. Whereas news judgment was once premised on the notion of strict, unbiased objectivity, now that is understood to be less desirable as a goal, she notes:

In life you are many things that are not supposed to affect your role as a journalist. You are supposed to be impartial. But that is changing. Now it is OK to be a human being who has feelings and thoughts and values and you don't have to hide them quite the way you once did. I think there's kind of a humanization that's slowly taking place in the news operation, partly as a result of changes in men in the population in general.[59]

She also relates this to the nature of contemporary social discourse, which is dominated by the "politics of meaning" and a search for ways to bring moral discourse into public discourse. People are looking for meaning, and "the more that gets discussed in the public domain, it will find its way into the papers."

Kim Sue Lia Perkes, who has been religion editor at the *Arizona Republic* both before and after a stint as a state capitol correspondent for the paper, agrees that the culture of the newsroom traditionally has determined the prospects of the religion beat. However, she contends that the approach taken by the religion writer herself can play a role in conditioning the responses of colleagues and readers:

Religion needs to look at what is happening right now, not at obscure theological issues. That way the typical reader, who might not be religious, or think much about religion, might pick up the paper and begin to see how what happens in the world of religion is important. That is a very "hard news" way of looking at things.[60]

She feels that the reporter's approach to their own religiosity, if any, is important:

It seems there are two kinds of religion writers, those like me who are interested from an intellectual standpoint, and those who are motivated by their own beliefs or personal interests. I think the latter people can run the risk of being more biased in their coverage, less able to separate out the real issues from the beliefs, etc. As a political writer, I cannot become active in politics or run for office. It is a constitutional right, but journalists need to hold to different standards.[61]

Thus, what has worked for her has been to treat the religion beat like any other, with parallel standards and practices. This sort of self-assurance about the beat is important to stability in coverage, she contends. This became apparent to her as she moved out of religion and saw how it was covered in her absence. Religion was divided into a feature side and a "hard news" side. The latter was turned over to the news desk, where she found herself still called on for advice and contacts:

> They are frightened to death of religion stories. I find myself holding their hands, and saying " . . . Just think of it as 'any other news story.' " They feel they don't know anything about religion, or they don't like religion, so they are scared of it. They say they are not experts or theologians. I say, "Why would a religion writer need to be a theologian? A former cop is not a very good candidate to be a police reporter. The medical reporter is not a doctor."[62]

In her view, the major thing missing with religion assigned to the news desk is continuity: "We need to monitor things, there are things they miss or they don't have a sense of their significance. We need to have policy discussions." The paper is clearly more comfortable with religion being done from less of a "front line" mode, says Perkes.

When asked to reflect on the sources of the newsroom culture's discomfort with the beat, she replies that she can attribute it to two primary causes. First, religion is not a "neutral" subject for most people in the newsroom:

> It is a deep-seated personal problem for many of them. People have "closeted" their *own* religion. They have closeted it in their own *professional* lives. They keep it from their colleagues. For example, when the Pope would come to town, we'd have editorial meetings where editors and others would say " . . . Why the hell is the Pope coming to town? Who cares? Why should we cover this? etc. . . . " Then, more than one of these *very same people* would stop me in the hall and say " . . . Hey, while you are in Rome, could you bring me a rosary blessed by the Pope, or some holy water?" And then there was this one editor who was one of the most crass in those conversations, who, when the Pope came by in the parade, was the first one to run out into the street, saying " . . . the *Pope* is coming." I think for many of these people it is a kind of denial thing that makes them so resistant to religion coverage.[63]

This idea, that there may be a kind of fundamental religiosity underlying newsroom discomfort with the beat, is consistent with the experience of another of our informants, a young woman new to the beat at a major paper. Within a few days of her hiring, one of the senior editorial staff, someone who had until that time not participated in any discussions about the beat, handed her a note, saying "Here's my pastor's name and number. I think he'd be a great interview."

The second cause of discomfort about religion relates fundamentally to the way decision making is structured, says Perkes. Editors make the decisions about coverage and about placement of stories. Their attitudes regarding the beat then come to be very important. In Perkes's experience, people at that level have had a problem with religion because of the potential for controversy. But it is a fear of a very specific kind:

> It is a fear of offending the "religious types." Nobody wants "the wrath of God." The real problem is, that no one knows what to say to people when they call in. Religion is a "great mystery"—or the common perception is that it is. Journalists deal in "facts" and are used to evidence of that kind. So, they say, "How do we answer these people?"[64]

This is a very revealing point. It gets at the heart of the editorial process in the newsroom. Professional judgment provides a defense against the complaints of irate readers from other fields. If an outraged politician calls in to complain about coverage, the editor's response typically is, "Read the First Amendment." Why should it be any different, or any more difficult, if it is an outraged religionist who calls? It shouldn't, and for many editors it is not. However, in Perkes's experience this remains a factor:

> We've had a recent case of a politician who was padding his expense account. Everyone knew he was doing this, but the editors wouldn't let us publish it until we had *records*. With religion—at least as they see it—there are no "records" to show to editors.[65]

There are two telling issues in Perkes's reflections. First, to understand the prospects of religion news, we must appreciate the structure of the news business. Religion reporters, or anyone else pursuing coverage, work within an institutional and collegial context that can be as determinative of the final outcome as their own individual efforts. That context can be openly hostile to religion, indifferent, uneasy, or accepting.

Second, it would appear that the religiosity of newsroom colleagues can be a problem on its own. Contrary to the implication of such critiques as

Olasky's, Rothman's, and the Lichters', there may not be a necessary correlation between newsroom religiosity and coverage. If Perkes's (and others')
experiences are any guide, highly religious colleagues may be no more
dependable supporters of the beat than anyone else.

Younger religion reporters, like Perkes, also are beginning to redefine the
beat in a way they see as distinct from the past. For Perkes, the difference is
one of seeing religion from the perspective of subjective belief, as opposed
to a more "intellectual" focus on the functioning of religion in contemporary
life:

> Before I came, the beat was written from a "theological" viewpoint. The
> Dead Sea Scrolls would be a good example of an ideal story from that
> era. Not the political controversy over them, but something on the
> archeology or history. . . . My perspective is that it needs to look at the
> "impact right now" and why that impact is important. I worked off the
> assumption that people don't think it is necessarily important, [so] I
> have to make them *care*.[66]

Writers at the *Orange County Register,* a paper that has repeatedly up-
graded its religion beat's status, concur with Perkes. Tracy Weber, a former
religion writer there, reports that the *Register*'s interest in religion resulted
from their own readership surveys that indicated religion was second only to
crime in reader interest. However, they were committed to a "hard news"
approach to the beat.

Writing within the constraint that most stories need a "local angle," Weber
and her successor, Vanise Wagner, have nonetheless been able to do a variety
of stories about a religious scene that is rapidly changing due to immigration
and other trends. Weber echoes Perkes's notion that the beat has to be about
making things understandable to readers:

> There is so much going on in the county, religiously, that the public has
> to struggle to keep up with it all. My role is to help them with that, and
> I feel it because I have to *cram* for every subject. A lot of it is new to
> me, too.[67]

Vanise Wagner agrees that the challenge is to find a "middle ground" where
stories are informative without being too abstract and yet are intelligent
enough to actually help readers' understanding of issues:

The problem with most religion stories is that they are either too "nicey-nicey" or they're way too critical. We've got to try to strike a balance in there somewhere.[68]

Weber and Wagner both agree that the most satisfactory approach, at least in Orange County, is to treat religion as something that is primarily local but that is also *newsworthy* on its own terms. The diversity of their market area helps. "It is true all over California now," says Wagner, "[that] religion is very diverse." Orange County, for example, boasts a significant South Asian population and therefore quite a few Buddhists, Hindus, and Sikhs. "They all deserve to be covered and better understood by readers," says Weber.

These accounts reveal much about the current practice of religion journalism, but reveal even more about how the discourse within the news business itself—its own self-definitions and self-understandings—come to condition the religion beat. Religion is a bit too close to home for some. It raises threatening questions about the limits of professionalism when something that is constructed as *authentic* when it is private and (in a way) *inauthentic* when it is public suddenly presents itself for treatment in the public sphere.

Resistance need not be the result of an antireligious conspiracy, at least according to these accounts. In fact, some of the participants in this process might be very religious, personally. What they are not able to do is to see religion as a valuable element of news output. In our many conversations with working journalists, we have been struck by the sense that religion is a very real definitional problem for them, whether or not they are themselves personally religious. The canons of journalism disallow personal sentiments entering one's "news judgment." Nothing else in American discourse is constructed as being so radically personal as is religion.

Journalism may simply lack the experience with religion necessary to comfortably overcome this problem. It has, over the years, made an uneasy peace with politics. It has struggled with its coverage of race and may be finding its way. It is beginning to address morality and ethics. An accommodation that allows religion to be authentically "public" will also need to be worked out.

## Notes

1. Marty, Martin and Scott Appleby. 1992. *The glory and the power: The fundamentalist challenge to the modern world.* Boston: Beacon.

    2. Hunter, James Davidson. 1991. *Culture wars: The struggle to define America.* New York: Basic Books.

    3. Roof, Wade Clark. 1993. *A generation of seekers.* New York: HarperCollins.

    4. For a powerful account of this situation, see Marty, Martin. 1993. Where the energies go. *Annals of the American Academy of Social and Political Science* 527:11-26.

    5. For a complete discussion of new modes of spirituality as well as new approaches to the study of religious practice, see Warner, R. Stephen. 1993. Work in progress toward a new paradigm for the sociological study of religion in the United States. *American Journal of Sociology* 98:1044-93.

    6. Duin, Julia. Guest column, *Newsletter of the Religion Newswriters' Association,* Fall 1992.

    7. Steinfels, Peter. 1994. The news media and religion: A changing mood that bodes well for the nation's believers. *New York Times,* April 30, p. A4.

    8. The *Morning News* was ready to announce the launch of a new, revitalized Saturday Religion section, which within a short time achieved substantial success both in readership and in critical commentary. Newhouse News Service was at that moment in the process of acquiring Religious News Service, the long-time nonprofit news agency focused on the religious community.

    9. Cornell, George. 1994. Religion reporting is rarely taught. *Boulder Daily Camera,* April 2, p. B4.

    10. Dart, John and Jimmy Allen. 1993. *Bridging the gap: Religion and the news media.* Nashville, TN: Freedom Forum First Amendment Center.

    11. Pew was later joined in supporting NPR by the Lilly Endowment.

    12. Shupe, Anson. 1994. [Review of] *Bridging the Gap. Journal for the Scientific Study of Religion* 33:87-9.

    13. Dart and Allen, *Bridging the gap,* p. 22.

    14. Greenhalgh, Jane. Personal interview, Washington, DC, April 21, 1994.

    15. Mattingly, Terry. 1993. Religion in the news: Are we short-changing readers and ourselves with biases that filter news? *Quill,* July/August, p. 13.

    16. Allen, Jimmy. 1994. Informal remarks to the winter meeting of the National Council of Churches Communication Commission, Chicago, February 10.

    17. See, for example, Hoover, Stewart M., Barbara N. Hanley, and Martin Radelfinger. 1989. *The RNS-Lilly study of religion reporting and readership in the daily press.* Philadelphia: Temple University, and New York: Religious News Service.

    18. Ibid., p. 127.

    19. Ibid., pp. 111-3.

    20. Ibid., p. 112.

    21. Dart, John. Personal interview, March 6, 1989.

    22. A spirited dialogue ensued after the Pope's visit. Gustav Niebuhr, writing in the *Washington Post,* detailed criticisms directed at media coverage by Archbishop William Keeler, president of the U.S. Bishops' Conference. Although opinions were mixed on the quality of coverage of that event, most observers contacted by Niebuhr thought the coverage could have benefited from more specialist insight. John Dart, for example, noted that television reporters, in particular, seemed to lack the time or insight to really provide context to the story. See Niebuhr, Gustav. 1994. Media said to ignore, misreport the spiritual; academic study, prelate, TV producer agree. *Washington Post,* January 1, p. D9.

    23. This is the critique implicit in the work of Marvin Okasky and many who identify with the Rothman/Lichter work discussed in Chapter 4: that the critical defining characteristic of religion treatment is the treatment of religion's core ideas and values, and further, that the totally

secularized and rationalized world of the media cannot hope to do an acceptable job of covering something it simply does not understand.

24. Hoover et al., *RNS-Lilly study,* p. 90.

25. Pugh, Jeanne. Personal interview, January 12, 1989.

26. Pratt, Beth. Telephone interview, June 3, 1989.

27. Brisson, Tom. Personal interview, December 18, 1988.

28. Ibid.

29. Waddle, Ray. Personal interview, February 17, 1989.

30. Wasson, Teresa. Personal interview, February 17, 1989.

31. Chandler, Russell. Personal interview, March 6, 1989.

32. Brisson, interview, December 18, 1988.

33. Schaeffer, Pam. 1988. Speech to the roundtable "Religion: A New/s Story," held in conjunction with the annual meeting of the American Academy of Religion, Chicago, December.

34. Wasson, interview, February 17, 1989.

35. Briggs, Ed. 1988. Speech to the roundtable "Religion: A New/s Story," held in conjunction with the annual meeting of the American Academy of Religion, Chicago, December.

36. Ibid.

37. Niebuhr, Gustav. 1988. Speech to the roundtable "Religion: A New/s Story," held in conjunction with the annual meeting of the American Academy of Religion, Chicago, December.

38. Dart, John. Personal interview, February 12, 1992.

39. Pugh, interview, January 12, 1989.

40. Brisson, interview, December 18, 1988.

41. Chandler, interview, March 6, 1989.

42. Schaeffer, Michael. Personal interview, April 12, 1989.

43. Ibid.

44. Brisson, interview, December 18, 1988.

45. Pugh, interview, January 12, 1989.

46. Schaeffer, interview, April 12, 1989.

47. Ibid.

48. Foley, Michael. Personal interview, January 12, 1989.

49. Sotomayor, Frank. Personal interview, March 7, 1989.

50. Foley, interview, January 12, 1989.

51. Caveats are in order in both cases. Interviews revealed that efforts had been made repeatedly by the former management at the *Tribune* to upgrade the religion beat, efforts that were stalled by the sale of the paper to new owners, resulting in a major repositioning of the paper and putting any such plans "on hold." In the case of the *Arizona Republic,* at the time of our interviews in the winter of 1993, the widely respected religion writer Kim Sue Lia Perkes had been promoted to the capitol beat. However, she later returned to the religion assignment.

52. Taylor, Belinda. Personal interview, August 10, 1993.

53. Ibid.

54. Ibid.

55. Ibid.

56. Ibid.

57. Ibid.

58. Ibid.

59. Ibid.

60. Perkes, Kim Sue Lia. Personal interview, January 8, 1993.

61. Ibid.

62. Ibid.

63. Ibid.

64. Ibid.
65. Ibid.
66. Ibid.
67. Wagner, Vanise. Personal interview, October 22, 1993.
68. Ibid.

# READING AND
# WATCHING RELIGION

To this point, we have been considering the points of view of people in the media industries and expert observers of the scene. This leaves out a major part of the religion and the media equation: audiences of readers, viewers, and listeners. There are two ways of understanding news audiences (or audiences for any media, for that matter): first, there are those particularly attuned to and motivated toward a given topic, and second, there are those less attuned and more generally oriented. Media theory has long held that the former can be seen as "opinion leaders," that is, as people who have a high degree of interest in a given topic, seek out information on that topic, and then pass that information on to others.[1]

Members of the general public or the general audience—to the extent they exist—thus receive information, insight, and symbols from the media not only directly but through the experiences of others. In the case of religion news, opinion leaders can come from a variety of sources. They might be formal religious leaders, they may be the more involved laity, or they may simply be particularly interested individuals who have no formal role in formal religion but nonetheless are interested in religion news.

The more formally involved are obviously easier to locate. And they possess an understandable degree of interest and concern about media treatment, evident in comments presented in this chapter by a number of them from a variety of points along the religious spectrum. Then, in Chapter 7, the results of surveys of the general population are discussed. Taken together, these two views of the situation can provide valuable insights into the way religion news is received when it reaches its audiences and into how audiences feel about some of the issues and questions raised in previous chapters.

## ■ What Is Religion News?

Readers seem to have as much difficulty as journalists do in giving a formal definition of religion news. Not surprisingly, it seems easiest to begin with a definition that centers on institutional indicators (i.e., news about specific religious *organizations*) but that holds that religion news should also include a *broader* range of issues. Here are three examples from a group of lay leaders at a suburban Catholic parish:[2]

> Any news that is related to an organized religion because that is where we seem to identify religious things happening. Also some issues wind up being tagged "religious" issues, like abortion, but really it is a human rights issue. It's not really religious news, but the media seems to focus on it that way.

> Any issues that wind up being moral issues or touch the spirit of a people. . . . It's a little bit different from organized religion. Sometimes even with the organized religion, we kind of tend to go to our own religion and look to see if there's anything about the Pope, about the Bishop, things like that. And maybe not really worry too much about what the neighboring Protestant religions are doing.

> Cults are a religious issue, sure. It has to do with moral values and touching the spiritual part of the person.

There is broad agreement that, at the very least, religion news has to mean something beyond just the interests and activities of *organized* religion.

Some groups, such as the Assemblies of God (hereafter shortened to Assemblies), object to the use of the term "religion" itself because of the connotation of organization and structure. But even the Catholic laity we spoke with (who were otherwise the most supportive of the idea of structure in religion) accepted the idea that religion news could be news about noninstitutional activities and phenomena.

## Attitudes About Press Coverage

It is no surprise that many people in churches are critical of the way the secular press covers religion. Even when interviewers present the question as neutrally as possible, there is nearly universal concern expressed. The idea that the press has some sort of a "bias" against religion is, of course, common. One Assemblies member put it this way:

> I notice in secular press coverage of religious issues it's not unopinionated. I was taught in high school that it [journalism] is supposed to be unopinionated. I find in *Newsweek* and *Time* that the writer of the article reveals a lot of personal opinion.

There is disagreement, however, over whether this bias is brought about by some sort of a conspiracy that targets only certain religions or whether it is the result of ignorance or indifference to religion in general on the part of the people in charge of the press.

Most people we have spoken with agree that religion gets less coverage than it deserves as a matter of course. The more conservative voices (in this case, members of several Assemblies of God congregations) seem to be the most interested in the idea that a conspiracy somehow targets evangelicalism and Pentecostalism for particular scorn in the media. Interestingly, in every Assemblies interview (five such groups were interviewed for this effort) at least one person referenced (directly or indirectly) the Rothman-Lichter studies of the journalistic elites discussed earlier.

Here, an Assemblies layperson reflects on the coverage received by a "Washington for Jesus" rally he had recently seen:

> The small interests march and demonstrate and get top coverage—there can be maybe only 50 people involved—whereas here you're talking about a million people and . . . very orderly and a thing lasted all day,

people from all over the nation coming. And I wouldn't expect that to go in the religion section and I wouldn't expect that to go in the *middle* of the paper. It should be on the front page, and it wasn't. I'm looking at it now from a very commonsense point of view, I think an objective point of view here, and that's a glaring thing.

There was a sense from these more conservative readers that this state of affairs is based in the preconceptions and biases of the people involved in the media—reporters *and* editors. Here is an Assemblies pastor:

I believe there is first of all many times not a fuller understanding or comprehension or enough background of the reporters to dive into it or give objective reporting. . . . The second thing that I believe is key . . . [is] that the secular press, which is humanistically shot through and through—a product of Columbia University, 98 percent are socialistic— humanistically a product of that and that they [are] reporting from their slant, from a nonexperiential point of view from God, form a disbelieving point of view. Then we become a sect who sometimes even looks like almost half a cult who believes in the display of the divine power of God or the power of the Holy Spirit. So they don't want to touch that even with a 10-foot pole.

Because of the televangelism scandals, the Assemblies themselves went through a series of direct experiences with press coverage in the 1980s and 1990s. Their members understandably drew on these experiences as they reflected on the issue of religion coverage.

One Assemblies interviewee observed, sagely, that "with a scandal like Jim Bakker, just telling the *truth* is 'bad news.' It's not the newspaper's fault that was bad news." Most of his colleagues, however, thought that even though these scandals were, indeed, "bad news" and thus *were* newsworthy, they often were handled in a biased way:

They [journalists] can't help the humanism in them, and [they] will institute their own views on another person's Christianity. When the thing hit the paper with Jimmy Swaggart, I was actually afraid to pick up the paper and read it because you didn't know which writer wrote the article. Okay, so sometimes I would read the article and it would be facts of what happened, how it happened, and who said what. There would be no innuendo or sarcasms, and the very next day I would read an article with maybe one sentence changed but the innuendos and the dark shadows and the putdowns are so enormous. How could 24 hours make such a difference in the same set of circumstances? That's what upsets people.

Members of a mainline church seemed to focus less on the idea that journalists are "out to get" religion in general or any specific religion. Instead, in a distinctly Weberian[3] (in that it demonstrated a more intellectual or rational approach) turn, they stressed that the source of their dissatisfaction was with the seriousness and competence with which religion is handled at most papers:

What you tend to get in the secular press [is] Falwell because he's an attention-getter. He's not thought-provoking, particularly. It's just like here is this spokesman, [and therefore] he becomes an ad hoc spokesman for religion. . . . The religion desk is either an entry-level job or Jack gives it to Uncle Joe who needs something to do. And they're not incisive, they're not well researched, and they tend not to deal with controversial issues from another perspective. It's almost like the policies of those publications do not allow or at least encourage real dialogue or comment.

African-American Baptists we spoke with tended to agree more with the idea that a major precondition for sensitive coverage of religion would be whether the reporter is, in fact, a religious person:

I think when you're reading anything, you're looking at the slant of the article and the author that's doing the writing. I don't know but I can tell sometimes by the slant, the question comes to my mind, I don't think this person is a Christian, or I wonder. Sometimes it is only a line in there or something maybe that would have been written a different way from a different viewpoint.

Say when a black person is dealing with a white person and the person who is writing is white, their prejudice can come up. So if you have a writer who is not a Christian, writing about a Christian article, this person could have an affect on what he brings forth.

The Catholics we spoke with were, overall, less concerned with the way the press cover religion than were others. They felt much less reliant on secular sources for religious information than did the Protestants. They were, however, concerned about the way social issues of concern to them, particularly abortion, are dealt with:

> The only area that I see the lack of objectivity is in the life issue: abortion and euthanasia. I don't think that television is objective enough. I do think the [Philadelphia] *Inquirer* is. Claude Lewis [a member of the editorial board of the *Inquirer*] is pro-life and takes a stand. I think there is enough on both sides in the written press. On television, there's not.

The Catholics also seemed to be more concerned than others with the church as an institution and how press coverage might undermine the institutional authority of churches:

> I think with all of the dirty laundry on the lawn, the scandal and the horrible things . . . I think they have taken away some of the security of people's lives, the reverence for the church, the respect for religious people. I feel sometimes they have a tendency to identify [that] this is what is happening to all religions and they don't highlight enough those who have been extraordinarily good and have been models of greatness in their lives.

## Focusing on Faith?

As stated earlier, there are two "sides" to religion as it might be covered by the press. On the one hand, religion is made up of *tangible* institutions, behaviors, practices, and activities. On the other hand, religion has a side that is *transcendent* and *intangible*. Religion is also about "faith" and "belief." Interestingly, Assemblies members, who should be among the most "spiritual" or "spirit filled" of groups, expressed no particular expectation that the secular press would understand this substantive dimension of religion, much less somehow "promote" it:

> I don't expect them to understand "spiritual" things, but remember we are talking about *religion*. "Religion" is man-made and we don't practice "man-made religion," we practice the living word of God. So when

you say "religion" to me, that deeply hurts me. I don't have a "religion," I don't practice anything man-made, I'm a spiritual person and I practice God's word, and you have to think of another word.

For others, this spiritual, or transcendent, or motivational dimension is the essential missing ingredient of coverage. For the Catholic laity, in particular, this seemed to be what they saw as the major failing of secular religion writing:

I don't think it is vindictiveness, I think it's just the lack of knowledge. . . . They see only the surface of the story and they may not go into the depths of why a person did that. I don't think that it is their intent to cover the reasons behind things, the values behind things. But a lot of times I think in Catholic newspapers *that* [is presented as] such a part of people. It automatically comes out, even if their intention is not to share the values.

This of course echos sentiments heard earlier. Defects in religion coverage may be as much about ignorance as they are about prejudice.

## Faith Groups and the Press

There was a general sentiment that religious people and groups are misunderstood by the press and that they themselves have reason to feel that they have been particularly misunderstood by some coverage. It would be extreme to describe this as a "siege mentality," but there is a note in some of these stories that their own faith group or beliefs have been particularly disadvantaged at one time or another. A typical example of this is from a Catholic interview group commenting on press coverage of the U.S. Catholic Bishops' pastoral letter on AIDS:

The document contained something like 700,000 words and pages and pages and pages, and it had one line that said "condone the education of use of prophylactic devices to prevent AIDS" . . . and the media jumped on that one and said " . . . Catholics cave in on birth control."

There was also the common sentiment that *other* groups are sometimes *advantaged* when they are not. Here are two examples:

The press reflects the simple-mindedness that's in the church like making such a big issue over the fall of those gentlemen [Swaggart, etc.] and stuff like that, I mean that's stupid . . . that's simple-minded. They're laughing at us (when I say "us" we're not a part of that group but *they're* still thought to be the church). . . . They [the press] ignore us and give all the press to the other guys.

I think the secular press always covers the Pope and he seems to be traveling all over the place . . . but I mean that, to me, is always on the front page kind of thing, where he's going, what he's doing. . . . I'd like to see coverage of all the denominations rather than just centering on that all the time. There's other things happening, you know, and they just seem to center on just that one person all the time. . . . I think it's kind of biased.

This perception that religious people, or specifically Christians, or more specifically, people of their particular faith group, might well be disadvantaged vis-à-vis religion coverage also extends to perceptions of what it is like for people who *work* at secular newspapers. An African-American Baptist deacon put it this way:

I would think that a Christian working at a secular newspaper would definitely be constrained. Definitely, definitely. Limitations. The newspaper wants excitement, . . . [but] he has certain guidelines he has to stay in because he can be sued as can the paper and get flack from the Chief Editor, so they try to remain neutral on religious issues without getting a million letters from their readers.

This ties in with a fairly widespread perception that reporters who *do* cover religion often lack the skill or experience to do so. In the words of a Catholic deacon,

When I read the stories in the [Philadelphia] *Inquirer,* I many times think that this person either hasn't been to church in 20 years, does not know that the church has changed since Vatican II, or else just is on the fringes. It's not a person who's really involved enough in the church to know what the church is doing.

## ◼ Audiences Understand

Given what many inside and outside the news industry seem to believe, there is a remarkable level of sophistication about the realities of religion in the news among readers and viewers, if these interviews are any indication. Where much of the criticism arising from the religious community both locally and nationally has been taken to be ill-informed and based on unrealistic expectations, a different picture emerges here.

For example, there is understanding here about the differences between the "religious" and the "secular" press. These laity are well aware of the difference between the "church page" and the "front page" and have a fairly informed idea of what kind of material is appropriate for each section. They understand the concept of "hard news" and understand, by and large, that their local church or their denomination rarely makes "hard news" unless there is some sort of crisis or scandal.

Most seemed to understand the hard realities of news, as put by one leader of an African-American Baptist parish:

> The bottom line is the papers have to be sold. So I would think the restriction would lie in what is going to invite the reader's interest and not what's going to make *us* angry or offended.

To state matters simply, none expected that news of their church's activities or work projects would ever qualify for the front (news) section of the paper. In fact, in both the Assemblies and Catholic parishes there was a good deal of satisfaction with the "church page"-type coverage of such activities.

As the most modernist and rationalist of the traditions represented in these interviews, the mainline members did not differ in their attitude about the press per se. They tended to be as critical as the others, but they were unique in the view that the press, or indeed any other source of cultural insight, could be "inspirational," regardless of whether it self-consciously intended to be so. The following statement illustrates this view:

> My feeling right now is that part of some specific sort of theological direction of people, the major inspirational stuff, even nonsystematic theological stuff, is written by contemporary playwrights and novelists as much as by theologians. I think they're more in tune with the human struggles and are less constrained by whatever their assumptions might be and therefore tend to stretch, for me, the horizons. I think a person

like, in my mind, Peter Shafer probably is writing more "religious stuff" than a lot of "religious" writers.

In contrast to sentiments such as this, the interest of the Assemblies members in specifically "religious" media seems almost like a type of "prophylaxis." One member's response to the discussion was, "If you want religious news, read the Bible" [and, by extension, religious publications].

The mainline members also differed from others in an expressed desire that the secular press be infused with what they called a "deeper" or "more profound" consciousness of the religious or theological significance of major stories or major issues. Two of them gave extended discourses on this topic that illustrate that this deeper consciousness could mean, for some, a radically different *political* perspective:

There is an implied value system in the press. What makes Heidnik [a local sensational mass murderer] "bad" and dropping bombs on San Salvador or West Philly "okay"? The press tend to take a rather bland sort of middle American view of things. . . . They present dominant WASP ideology as Americanism . . . and that seems to be much more prevalent than when they are presenting Moslems or Judaism or other religions.

Take Central America as a specific issue and our involvement [the involvement of their particular congregation] in public sanctuary as part of that. I think the secular press covers just the issues, about what's happening there, and tends to be pretty clearly a reflection of the prevailing political climate of this country. They don't give big play to what I would consider a significantly different point of view. Certainly the *New York Times,* on an issue like disarmament, tends to play a very conservative role in challenging the assumptions of our Defense Department. So you get around to tinkering with how many missiles or how many bombers and that's not that it's irrelevant, but there's nobody challenging what values they reflect other than self-preservation. . . . I feel like there is a lack of dialogue going on. . . . I'm not trying to reduce the question to issues, but I suggest that truth resides elsewhere.

It is not surprising that discussion of these issues often turns to the "hard news" mission of the daily press. Many of the religiously involved people we spoke with observed that much religion news is "good news," and thus not really *news* in an "if it bleeds, it *leads*" media environment. Even the most conservative voices among them, who were otherwise the most virulently critical of the *motivations* of the media, expressed the sentiment that this role of the press—covering hard news—is understandable and acceptable.

## ▄█ The Problem of Diversity

There was also widespread recognition of the problem of *religious diversity* and its challenge to secular reporters. This sentiment did not necessarily let the media "off the hook," though. There is an expressed feeling that reporters' "biases" are part of what prevent them from better dealing with diversity. This was felt most strongly, again, by the more conservative informants, in this case Assemblies members:

> The secular press is rather reluctant to get into the religious news reporting and commenting because it is such a volatile powder keg. This community has Jews, Catholics, [and] different denominations of Protestants. For the secular press to be objective or realistic about them, it becomes an issue that one group may not like to read or to hear about the other side. That's most important to me. It can become a very hairy issue as far as the press is concerned: From what point of view should they report the religious news? Is it the biggest church?

Methodist, Baptist, and Catholic informants were more likely to think that it is simply ignorance or incompetence that keeps journalists from successfully dealing with diversity, not any absolute bias against religion in general.

Along with the general idea that religion news must be first and foremost *news* is the idea that religion should *still* play a larger part in the straight news on a day-to-day basis than it usually does. Everyone here seemed to share the opinion that much "hard news" has religious overtones but that the secular press rarely suggests that there is much religion going on in personal or community life. A Methodist lay leader said, "You could read the entire daily paper here and never know there were any people of faith living in this city." For many, this perception seemed to have been based in concrete experience with issues particularly important to them:

What about all the different areas of life that relate to religion or religion touches upon? . . . How about religion as it relates to politics and politics as it relates to religion? Recently we talked a lot about the bill dealing with the handicapped groups and homosexuals and so forth, the "civil rights" bill. That was a political issue, yet it has religious overtones and is of interest to a lot of religious groups . . . so you have a whole lot of areas that are not religious, strictly, in nature but yet touch on religion.

In the secular news, everything is immediate and oncoming. You don't see enough of the religious view or of the community news that would show the role of the church and its activity. Even if you do see a church doing something in the community, a revival or something, it doesn't follow through. You anticipate its coming, but what happened *after* that revival?

Consistent with this idea, most informants agree that newspapers have an absolute responsibility to cover religion in the same way they cover other beats, with the same level of attention and competence. This is based on the perception that, as it is commonly done, religion coverage is limited in scope. An African-American Baptist put it this way:

I think of it [secular press coverage of religion] as boring, dull, because they use a basic pattern. It doesn't have the interest or the highlights on it that the "regular" news has.

Of all these interviews, the Assemblies members were the most critical of religion coverage, and the most convinced that its deficits were linked to the biases of news organizations. The following statement by an Assemblies pastor reveals a clear-headed sentiment that, in spite of these criticisms, his desire is for a type of coverage of which he still feels newspapers are fully capable:

I don't expect them [the press] to understand "spiritual" things, but remember that we're talking about *religion* now, and I expect them to use the same type of professionalism in the area of religious news and stuff that they use in the area of political or medical or scientific or any other of those areas. . . . I'm not willing to let them off the hook for religious stuff because they don't understand. They were able to do an adequate job, a good job, of reporting the scandals, [so] they can do a good job in general if they want to.

The major difference on this point was expressed by the Catholics, who seemed less interested than the others in secular religion coverage. They tended not to think that secular papers have any particular responsibility to cover religion and tended to see these matters dualistically, with a clear division between "secular" and "sectarian" realms. Sectarian needs for information, they seemed to be saying, can be acceptably met by denominational or other specifically "religious" publications. They were much less interested in discussions about these issues than the other groups, and their ideas and concerns were far less specific and focused. This coincides with the finding from national surveys (covered in Chapter 7) that Catholics are less interested than Protestants in religion news overall.

Catholics also tended to feel much more strongly than Protestants that there is an acceptable line of demarcation between "external" concerns of religious groups, which are appropriate for the secular media to cover, and "internal" concerns, which should be off-limits to them. Even the Assemblies members who expressed frustration with press coverage of their recent scandals seemed much more accepting of this scrutiny than did the Catholics interviewed.

Consistent with this, Assemblies members (again, the most critical of the secular press of all the groups) did *not* look to the secular press for spiritual guidance or insight and did *not* expect that even if secular reporters were "born again" their responsibility was to provide inspiration. They felt that "human interest" stories can "uplift the human spirit," as one of them put it, but they do *not* think that it is the role of the secular press to do what ministers, religious institutions, and religious publishing do better:

I don't believe that anyone is expecting an exegetical interpretation of the scriptures from the secular press. That's what you get on Sunday morning, Sunday evening, Wednesday evening services, or whatever.

An African-American informant agreed:

People should zero in on the Christian magazines and issues rather than the secular people writing on Christian issues. There's a difference. Simply, it's like someone writing about ballet who has never had any background or any study in dance or ballet. You can't talk about something you don't know and give a very good outlook. So this is why Christians must stick to the writings that other Christians are writing rather than the writings of secular people writing about Christian issues.

The more conservative Protestant informants saw the *religious* press as a *supplement* to, not a substitute for, the secular press. In their view, the spiritual aspects of stories are the responsibility of the religious press. Catholics shared this view, although they saw the religious press (in particular their Diocesan paper) as embodying both coverage of spiritual matters *and* an acceptable coverage of other matters of concern "inside" the "Catholic family":

> I don't think there is any comparison between secular and religious periodicals. The religious paper [*The Standard and Times*] obviously is geared toward presenting the *truth* of the matter to Catholics who are reading it and others who are reading it.

> I don't pick up the *Inquirer* to look for religious things. If I want religious things, I automatically go to *The Standard and Times.*

Mainline members tended to differ from the others on this point:

> It's very difficult for me to think of religious journals as being a source of religious information because of my notion that religious information does not necessarily have to be predicated on the fact that it has a specifically "religious" *imprimatur* to be the kind of question that I think of as being fundamentally a religious question. So I think of a lot of the things that you read in secular journals as being more "religious" than the stuff you read in religious journals—more open-ended, more aware of mystery.

## Differences and Similarities

The most striking differences between the groups in their interest in religion news and information were these latter views. The members of the more liberal congregations seemed less interested in or likely to read self-consciously "religious" publications for religious insight or information. They tended instead to infuse *secular* publications (in a way consistent with

H. Richard Niebuhr's "Christ of Culture" paradigm[4]) with meaning. Meanwhile, the Catholics viewed religious insight and information very practically and concretely and tended not to look to the secular media for it. To their way of thinking, Catholic publications were the appropriate forum for these issues.[5]

Both of these tendencies are confirmed in the national surveys discussed in Chapter 7. Non-"born again" Protestants were much less likely to read religious periodicals than were those who were "born again." Catholics on those surveys expressed lower levels of interest in religion coverage by the press than did other groups.

In spite of the relative Catholic disinterest and the attraction of the conservative Protestant interviewees to religious publications, it did not appear that for any of these groups *religious* periodicals are a substitute for the coverage of religion as *hard news* that they wanted to see in the secular press. Even those who reported being the heaviest readers of religious periodicals saw these only as *supplementing* what they should be able to expect from the secular press (and were not getting): not coverage of religion as a proprietary activity of *their* sect but of religion *in general* as a significant aspect of daily life for most Americans.

Consistent with the notion of "opinion leadership" with which this chapter began, everyone here expresses a strong general interest in coverage of *religions besides their own.* They are "religion interested." Although there was some competitive sentiment that other religions get preferential coverage, most interviewees want to know more about other faiths, faith groups, and the full range of issues that might fall into the category "religion."

This interest extends, for some, to include information *outside the borders* of the United States. Mainline members, in particular, were quite global in their interest, wanting much more information about the "religious dimension" of other major news stories.

All groups seemed to understand that *"good news" stories,* or stories of faith and inspiration, do not necessarily fit in the normal range of newspaper coverage. Although some groups expressed more interest in "inspiration" than did the others, all seem to accept the dictum that "bad news sells papers."

Most seemed to be knowledgeable about current issues in *their own denominations.* These formed the background of their assessment of how well the press covered them. It was less clear that they understood *other religions* very well. This lack of knowledge and their self-consciousness about it seemed to be part of the explanation for their interest in broadened, improved and mainstreamed religion press coverage. One person in fact stated that his *only* source of information about the world of religion is mass media.

Everyone here shared a fairly sophisticated understanding of *how journalism works,* and of what they can reasonably expect newspapers to do in the way of religion coverage. They know what sells newspapers. Some of them—the more conservative—tended to support a "media elite" view of press bias. Other Protestants saw this bias as cutting in both directions and being based in indifference rather than animosity toward religion. The Catholics were particularly concerned that the social issues coverage of the daily press exhibits a "liberal" bias.

At the same time, there was remarkable consistency on the question of *where* people get their *information about religion.* Most people here described a "two-step" flow of religious information, where leaders or interested laypeople read and passed on articles and information to others. This was particularly the case with information about their own groups or denominations. For information about other religious groups, most of them depended *directly* on mass media, both *secular* and *religious.*

Nearly everyone felt that press coverage *could be improved.* What they tended to want for their own group is more exposure in a less "biased" or "stereotyped" way (felt most strongly by the conservative Protestant and Catholic groups). In terms of general religion coverage, most were not expecting secular newspapers to be fora for "faith" or "inspiration" other than in a very restricted sense.

There were also mixed feelings about whether *religious media* are an *acceptable substitute* for the coverage the secular media do not provide. Assemblies and Catholic members seemed to feel that they are. Methodists and African-American Baptists felt this less strongly.

There seemed to be few significant differences between the *leadership* and *laity* groups. Although professional parish leadership exhibits more technical knowledge of religion in general than does the laity, it is not significantly out of step with members in terms of attitudes, desires, and opinions about press coverage.

Finally, it was clear from these interviews that most informants understood the structure and function of the various *genres* of news. Although the concept of "religion news" may still defy a consensus definition, there was strong sentiment that much that goes on in the world of religion is "newsworthy" but not likely to be covered in the front section where it belongs alongside other aspects of the culture. This was not a call for the material that traditionally ran on the "church page" to find its way onto the front page.

Instead, it was a call for the front page to reflect the religious life of the community and culture more than it does.

This desire to have religion be "run of paper" reveals a desire that it be *mainstreamed* in the conceptual and structural world of the newspaper. This runs counter to conventional received practice in the newspaper industry, where religion has been compartmentalized in a section, as a feature beat only, or confined to opinion or commentary.

## Notes

1. See, for example, Katz, Elihu and Paul Lazarsfeld. 1955. *Personal influence*. New York: Free Press.

2. All informant comments in this chapter are taken from a set of interviews conducted with members of five different congregations in the Philadelphia area. The congregations were chosen to represent a range of demographic and faith perspectives. For a technical description, see Hoover, Stewart M., Barbara N. Hanley, and Martin Radelfinger. 1989. *The RNS-Lilly study of religion reporting and readership in the daily press*. Philadelphia: Temple University, and New York: Religious News Service.

3. Max Weber predicted that religions of the Establishment, such as the Protestant mainline groups, would be typified by a more intellectual, less emotional understanding of faith and its place in culture.

4. Niebuhr, H. Richard. 1956. *Christ and culture*. New York: Harper Torchbooks.

5. The findings here were consistent with other recent studies of denominational and faith-group differences in understandings of the relationship between religion and the media. See, in particular, the following chapters in *Religion and mass media: Audiences and adaptations*, edited by Daniel Stout and Judith Buddenbaum. Thousand Oaks, CA: Sage, 1996: The passionate audience: Community inscriptions of "The Last Temptation of Christ" (by Thomas Lindlof); Mainline Protestants and the media (by Judith Buddenbaum), Catholicism, conscience, and censorship (by Ted Jelen); Evangelicals' uneasy alliance with the media (by Quentin Schultze); Fundamentalism and the media, 1930-1990 (by Margaret Lamberts Bendroth); and Protecting the family: Mormon teachings about mass media (by Daniel Stout).

# THE AUDIENCE FOR
# RELIGION

The readers and viewers of religion news heard from in Chapter 6 provide some definition to our understanding of religion and the press. The most important finding from that chapter is that the assumed localism and parochialism of the "religion audience" is not well founded in fact. Those voices—clergy and laity in a number of congregations and parishes—shared some remarkable things in common, not least of which was their interest in seeing a different, more sophisticated approach to religion taken by the media.

But those voices also could be said to have been "too special" in some important ways. The fact that they are leaders in their parishes and congregations means that they probably differ from the audience in general. Residual secularization theory, for example, suggests that the public in general might well have lower levels of basic religion interest than these leaders and that the audience in general might also therefore find the idea of improved coverage (or, indeed, *any* coverage) less important.

114

The purpose of this chapter is to look at the audience for religion news in more depth, breadth, and detail. Along with these ideas about localism and parochialism, the "received" view of religion and the press holds that audiences in general should have little interest in religion. Further, our traditional ideas about contemporary religious practice predict that levels of religiosity among newspaper readers will be lower than in the population as a whole.

These and other preconceptions begin to falter when we look at data from national surveys.[1] Although it should come as no surprise, the majority of daily newspaper readers are religious people, with nearly 70 percent of those for whom religion is "very important," "fairly important," or "not very important" in their lives reporting that they read a newspaper every day. This clearly suggests that those interested in religion read news as frequently as others in the population do.[2]

At the same time, there is some difference in reported newspaper reading between members of various denominations. Members of the traditionally evangelical churches[3] report daily newspaper reading in slightly lower levels (64 percent report doing so) than do other Protestants (73 percent) and Catholics (75 percent). Again, these levels of reported reading are higher than expected.

However, denominational membership is not the only factor that defines variation in American Protestantism. There is as much variation in belief *within* some denominations as between them. This tendency, which Martin Marty[4] has called the "two-party system of American Protestantism," has been a major factor in Protestant churches. The rise of the evangelical movement over the past 15 years has had effects that are quite distinct from church membership; there are evangelicals within non-evangelical churches and vice versa, a matter returned to later.[5]

As a measure of the factor of evangelicalism per se, it has become common to use the survey question of whether one considers oneself " 'born again' or evangelical" (30 percent of all respondents answered "yes"). Although there is some difference in daily newspaper readership between those who consider themselves born again and those who do not, the difference is again small: 67 percent versus 73 percent, respectively.

Those who consider themselves born again are less likely to read newspapers every day, but they are much more likely to regularly read *religious* newspapers (including local, regional, and sectarian papers): 57 percent (only 42 percent of non-born-again respondents reported reading them regularly).

**TABLE 7.1**   Newspaper Readership Compared With Importance of Coverage
of Religion

|                      | Percentage Importance of Religion Coverage | | | |
|----------------------|--------|--------|----------|------------|
| Reading Frequency    | Very   | Fairly | Not Very | Not at All |
| Every day            | 66.1   | 72.0   | 78.2     | 69.8       |
| A few times a week   | 24.7   | 21.7   | 19.9     | 25.4       |
| Once a week or less  | 8.8    | 5.9    | 1.6      | 4.8        |

This suggests that for some evangelicals, who are slightly less oriented to the daily press than are others overall, religious newspapers might be a supplement. The relatively small number of such publications may mean that they can be a supplement only for a portion of the overall religion-interested readership (slightly less than a third of all respondents reported having access to such papers).

Religion-oriented magazines are, of course, much more commonly available, and most respondents appear to have access to them. Yet they are regularly read by a minority of respondents. Even among the born-again evangelicals for whom religion is "very important," only 37 percent regularly read religious magazines. Among those (evangelical or not) for whom religion is "very important," 33 percent report reading religious magazines regularly.

This leaves one with the sense that the general readership for daily newspapers is both fairly religious (much more so than is the case in other countries, for instance) *and* not generally as exposed to the religious press as would be the case if they were relying on that source alone for information. But do they expect to see religion in the daily newspapers they read? Table 7.1 reports responses to the question "How important is it to you, personally, that the newspapers you read cover religion?" Overall, 66 percent of respondents felt it was at least fairly important to them that newspapers cover religion. The majority of those who consider this coverage important are, in fact, frequent readers of newspapers.

Taken with the generally low reported levels of readership of religious periodicals, these findings suggest that the majority of religious and religion-news-oriented readers have only secular sources for information about religion. They do not, by and large, turn to the religious media. Much larger percentages of them are readers of the secular press.

## ◼ Religiosity and the "Secular" Press

Is this surprising? Should we expect religious people to *prima facie* reject secular sources? Interestingly, data from another source indicate that respondents who are more religious are no less likely than others to report having confidence in the press. The General Social Survey of the National Opinion Research Center (NORC) regularly asks this question. In one of its surveys focused on religion, only 18 percent overall reported having a great deal of confidence in the press, whereas 53 percent reported having "only some" confidence and 25 percent reported "hardly any." When respondents of various levels of religiosity and types of religious preference are looked at separately, no statistically significant differences appear.

The high level of interest in religion news in these data and the earlier finding of high levels of religiosity among regular newspaper readers run counter to popular wisdom, at least in the news business, about who reads newspapers. The association between religiosity and newspaper reading also holds up across most demographic categories. Thus, the "third variables" that might mitigate this relationship (education, gender, income) seem not to.

Table 7.2 tests the hypothesis that the association between religion and newspaper readership might be a function of history. The years 1970-1990 saw a tremendous upsurge in religious activism, particularly on the part of communities that traditionally eschewed such behaviors.

The rise of the New Right, Catholic politicization around the abortion issue, textbook controversies, and other such public debates saw more and more involvement and interest on the part of religious groups. As a result, it might be that for *some* religious people, public involvement and interest in public issues (such as would lead them to read secular newspapers regularly) has, over time, made them regular newspaper readers.

Table 7.2 compares respondents' levels of church attendance (one measure of religiosity) against their reported daily reading of newspapers from 1972 to 1988, a key period in the development of this new consciousness. For each year, the percentage of daily readers among those who attend church less frequently (less than once a month) and those who attend more frequently is presented.

Both the reported levels of church attendance and reported frequency of newspaper readership declined steadily across these years. However, the relationship between attendance and readership remained constant throughout, with frequent attenders roughly 10 percent more likely than infrequent attenders to also read newspapers daily.

**TABLE 7.2**  Percentage of Frequent and Infrequent Church Attenders Who Read
Newspapers Daily, 1972–1988[a]

|        | Percentage Frequency of Attendance | |
|--------|------|------|
| Year   | Low  | High |
| 1972   | 63.4 | 74.2 |
| 1975   | 61.0 | 69.9 |
| 1977   | 57.1 | 68.2 |
| 1978   | 51.7 | 61.8 |
| 1982   | 46.4 | 56.9 |
| 1983   | 52.0 | 57.6 |
| 1985   | 47.6 | 58.5 |
| 1986   | 47.4 | 60.3 |
| 1987   | 50.3 | 57.0 |
| 1988   | 45.0 | 58.4 |

a. The source of these data is the General Social Survey of the National Opinion Research Corporation
(NORC). Percentages between the Gallup surveys reported here and the NORC surveys are not directly
comparable due to slightly different instrumentation (questions) used.

## ▓ Readers' Interest in Religion Coverage

It seemed from the interviews in Chapter 6 that readers have a clear appreciation for the structure of the typical newspaper. That is, they may understand the difference between the "front" and "back" matter in the newspaper
and understand the difference between the "hard news" sections of the paper
and the sections devoted to features and softer news. It also seemed that there
was little confusion in the minds of the participants in the qualitative
interviews about the status and importance of the traditional "church page"
with its ads and announcements. They clearly had a broader understanding
and expectation of what might qualify as religion coverage than the "church
page." Although defining newspaper coverage of religion as only a feature
or "soft" beat is a limited vision of its place in the paper, nonetheless the
major way it is defined and can be measured is as a stand-alone identifiable
department or section.

This is the basis on which much qualitative analysis of religion coverage
is done, both within and outside the industry. How religion stacks up against
"sports" or "food" or "entertainment" as a beat is one way that newspaers
and their readers try to evaluate the priority it gets.

With that in mind, one of our national surveys presented respondents with
a list of nine "special interest" newspaper topics,[6] which they were to rate,

**TABLE 7.3** Importance to Readers of Nine "Special Interest" Newspaper Topics

| Topic | Score |
|---|---|
| Education | 5.69 |
| Health | 5.60 |
| Business | 4.85 |
| Food | 4.54 |
| Religion | 4.50 |
| Entertainment | 4.40 |
| Personal Advice | 3.72 |
| The Arts | 3.78 |
| Sports | 3.46 |

on a scale from one to seven, how important it was to them personally that the newspapers they read cover each of these topics. Table 7.3 presents the overall score of each item, ranked highest to lowest.[7]

Religion was neither the highest nor the lowest ranked, although it did rank ahead of sports in overall interest. It is important to remember that rankings are an expression of readers' *perceptions* of importance, not necessarily measures of their *habits,* and that the differences, while statistically significant, are quite small. Those who call themselves born again rated religion as much more important than did others.

Region of residence also made a difference. Table 7.4 presents rankings and scores for the same religion coverage item by respondents' region of residence. This determined where religion ranked against the other "special interest" categories in that particular region.

**TABLE 7.4** Regional Differences in Importance of Religion as a "Special Interest" Topic

| Region | Rank | Score |
|---|---|---|
| New England | 8 | 3.63 |
| Middle Atlantic | 6 | 4.35 |
| East Central | 5 | 4.37 |
| West Central | 4 | 4.71 |
| Southeast | 3 | 5.12 |
| Southwest | 3 | 4.99 |
| Rocky Mountains | 5 | 4.15 |
| Pacific | 8 | 3.90 |

**TABLE 7.5**   Likelihood of Reading "Special Interest" Topics

| Topic | Score |
|---|---|
| Education | 6.65 |
| Business | 5.82 |
| Health | 5.60 |
| Entertainment | 5.04 |
| Food | 4.81 |
| Religion | 4.56 |
| Sports | 4.22 |
| The Arts | 3.99 |
| Personal Advice | 3.88 |

The highest levels of interest are in those regions where religiosity is highest, such as the traditional Bible Belt in the South and Southwest. Interest is lowest in the Pacific Northwest.

Readers were also asked to be more specific. They ranked these nine topics themselves, this time according to which they would be "most likely to read." This was a forced choice; they could only choose one "most important" (seven on the scale), one "next most important," and so on. It was expected that this question would more accurately reflect actual behavior than would the earlier item, which was only a rating scale, if it forced respondents to rank their likelihood of reading a given category. Table 7.5 presents the overall results.

It is perhaps not surprising that the order here came out nearly the same as with the earlier item where respondents scored topics by their perceived importance. Readers seemed to be reporting behaving in ways consistent with their beliefs about what is important for newspapers to cover.

For both men and women, religion was neither the most nor the least likely to be read. Women seemed slightly more likely than men to read such stories, but the differences in scores and ranking were small. A notable difference was in the likelihood of reading sports, where men were far more interested than women (not surprisingly), and business, where the difference was less striking.

A stark difference in the likelihood of reading religion appeared when evangelicals and non-evangelicals were compared. Those who consider themselves born again reported being much more likely to read religion than did others. Again, as was the case with the rating of *importance* of religion coverage, readers in the South and West were more likely to read religion stories, with those in the Pacific Northwest least likely to do so.

**TABLE 7.6**  Percentage Likelihood of Denominational Groups Reading "Special Interest" Topics

| Topic | Evangelical Protestants | Other Protestants | Catholics | Other/None |
|---|---|---|---|---|
| Education | 6.55 | 6.68 | 6.79 | 6.54 |
| Health | 6.25 | 6.31 | 6.52 | 6.92 |
| Business | 5.87 | 5.62 | 6.12 | 5.37 |
| Religion | **5.66** | **4.88** | **4.16** | **5.28** |
| Food | 4.66 | 4.88 | 4.73 | 5.21 |
| Entertainment | 5.04 | 4.91 | 4.90 | 5.09 |
| Sports | 4.46 | 4.22 | 4.26 | 2.59 |
| The Arts | 3.62 | 3.77 | 4.01 | 4.19 |
| Personal Advice | 3.60 | 3.94 | 3.92 | 3.81 |

Table 7.6 shows that there were also some differences between denominational groups in likelihood of reading religion coverage.

Like those who consider themselves born again, members of evangelical churches also reported a higher likelihood of reading religion coverage than did other preference groups. For the two groups of Protestants, religion ranked fourth and fifth in likelihood; for Catholics, it was seventh. This confirms the sense from the interviewees in Chapter 6 that Catholics are less interested than others in secular coverage of religion.

Respondents were also asked to rate on a seven-point scale the paper they "most often read" for the quality of its coverage of these nine non-news topics. The results appear in Table 7.7.

Again, the score represents relative position on a seven point scale, where seven is the highest score and one the lowest. What is remarkable here is the sharp reversal of position of both sports and religion. Although religion generally ranked close to sports in the various ratings of importance of religion coverage, when readers were asked to rate actual coverage, the divergence was striking. The message is clear: The newspapers they read do not do a very good job of covering religion.

Interestingly, this finding of dissatisfaction generally held up regardless of the circulation size of the newspaper in question. This means that dissatisfaction is high both in small towns, where the newspaper is presumably closer to the community *and* in large cities, where the metropolitan dailies have traditionally employed specialists to cover religion.

Respondents were next asked *directly* how frequently they read *religion news* when it appears in the newspaper. Some interesting differences were

**TABLE 7.7**   Respondents' Satisfaction With Coverage by Newspaper "Most Often Read"

| Topic | Score |
|---|---|
| Sports | 5.74 |
| Business | 5.29 |
| Entertainment | 5.18 |
| Education | 5.00 |
| Food | 4.99 |
| Health | 4.76 |
| The Arts | 4.67 |
| Personal Advice | 4.39 |
| Religion | 4.32 |

found among readers. Table 7.8 presents the male-female results, and Table 7.9 lists the results for those who say they are born-again evangelicals and others.

Women and evangelicals seem much *less* likely than men or nonevangelicals to read religion news when it does appear in the newspaper. This is not consistent with other aspects of religiosity and religious behaviors, where women and evangelicals generally express higher levels of religious interest than do their cohorts. However, it *is* consistent with overall newspaper reading behavior, where men are, for instance, much more likely than women to report regular newspaper reading. In the case of gender, it seems that women are more likely to report preference for, or interest in, religion news, but men are more likely to actually read it. The same tendency holds for born-again versus non-born-again respondents. This is consistent with a definition of religion news as directed at religion interest, rather than to religiosity per se, an issue returned to later.

**TABLE 7.8**   Male–Female Differences in Frequency of Reading Religion News

| Question: How frequently do you read religion news when it appears in the newspaper? | Percentage Women | Percentage Men |
|---|---|---|
| Whenever it appears | 19.6 | 28.6 |
| Frequently | 12.3 | 18.6 |
| Occasionally | 22.9 | 21.5 |
| Infrequently | 18.4 | 17.3 |
| Just about never | 25.7 | 13.9 |
| Don't know | 1.0 | 0.2 |

**TABLE 7.9**  Evangelical and Non-Evangelical Differences in Frequency of
Reading Religion News

| Question: How frequently do you read religion news when it appears in the newspaper? | %<br>Born Again | %<br>Non-Born Again |
|---|---|---|
| Whenever it appears | 11.3 | 30.7 |
| Frequently | 8.3 | 19.0 |
| Occasionally | 20.1 | 23.3 |
| Infrequently | 25.5 | 13.9 |
| Just about never | 34.3 | 12.4 |
| Don't know | 0.4 | 0.7 |

## ■ Definitions of Religion Coverage

Defining what constitutes religion news is a major challenge for practitioners
and observers alike. On one survey, respondents were shown a list of 16
"types" of religion story. To test the hypothesis that religion-news interest is
a *local* and *parochial* affair, the list was presented to respondents so that local
and parochial concerns were first, with the scope of coverage moving
outward conceptually and physically from their home locations. Table 7.10
presents the complete list of response "types" in the order in which they were
administered.

Respondents were asked to score each of these on a scale from one to
seven, with seven being "very important" and one being "not important at
all" for newspapers to cover. The overall results for this item are shown in
Table 7.11, with the categories ranked from highest (most important) to
lowest (least important).

This is a surprising result. Far from being oriented *only* toward local and
parochial interests or issues of faith experience, respondents seem also to
have a *translocal* and *universal* interest in religion news. When looked at
slightly differently, in terms of the percentage of respondents who said that
a given category is "most important" to cover, the order was nearly the same,
although the local items slipped lower in the rankings. This finding clearly
challenges journalism to more directly infuse its output with attention to the
religious side of local, national, and international life, society, and politics
as well as covering religion per se in certain ways. Further, the fact that high
percentages of newspaper readers are interested in religion, that they expect
religion coverage, that most of them do not turn to "religious" sources for
news that fits this interest, and that they are generally not very satisfied with

**TABLE 7.10** Sixteen Categories of Religion Coverage

1. Stories of individual faith experiences
2. Local church news and announcements
3. Local religious issues besides church news and announcements
4. National religious groups and denominations
5. Ecumenical movement and cooperation between religious groups
6. Beliefs of various religions besides your own
7. Major American religious movements (fundamentalism, evangelicalism, the charismatic movement, etc.)
8. Alternative or "new" religious movements (New Age movement, cults, etc.)
9. National religious issues and controversies (scandals, textbook controversies, etc.)
10. Role of religion in American politics
11. Role of religion in foreign or international politics (Middle East, Iran, Northern Ireland, etc.)
12. Ethical and social issues
13. Social and ethical positions and pronouncements by major faith groups (as on abortion, nuclear policy, the economy, etc.)
14. Presentation of opinion and commentary (e.g., columns or editorials by major religious leaders)
15. Presentation of humor or cartoons relating to religion
16. Results of surveys or polls on religious topics

the coverage religion gets from the daily press paints a picture of religion news that is far removed from the traditional or "received" definition of it.

Table 7.12 lists the rankings of these topics (in order only—without the scores) given by men and women. As shown, to the extent there is support here for it, the localism/parochialism hypothesis holds more strongly for women than for men. Women ranked local church news and local religious issues higher than men did. However, interest in social and ethical issues and the positions and pronouncements of faith groups on social issues was higher for both men and women than expected.

This was also the case for those demographic classes labeled traditionally "religious": born-again evangelicals, older people, residents of smaller communities, residents of the South, and respondents having lower education and income were more interested than others in the local issues, yet reported lower levels of news readership. Those groups reporting higher levels of news readership (men, for instance) were the ones least interested in local and parochial religion coverage.

**TABLE 7.11** Mean Scores of Religion Coverage "Types"

| Type of Coverage | Score |
| --- | --- |
| Positions and pronouncements | 4.77 |
| Ethical and social issues | 4.63 |
| Local church news and announcements | 4.34 |
| Local religious issues | 4.29 |
| Religion in American politics | 4.26 |
| Foreign or international politics | 4.25 |
| National issues and controversies | 4.22 |
| National groups and denominations | 4.11 |
| Other religions besides your own | 4.01 |
| Ecumenism and cooperation | 3.96 |
| Opinion and commentary | 3.96 |
| Faith experiences | 3.83 |
| Surveys or polls | 3.66 |
| American religious movements | 3.61 |
| Alternative or "new" movements | 3.49 |
| Humor or cartoons | 2.91 |

**TABLE 7.12** Male-Female Rankings of Religion Coverage "Types"

| Males | Females |
| --- | --- |
| Positions and pronouncements | Positions and pronouncements |
| Ethical and social issues | Ethical and social issues |
| Foreign or international politics | Local church news |
| National issues and controversies | Local religious issues |
| Religion in American politics | Religion in American politics |
| Local religion issues | Foreign or international politics |
| Local church news | National issues and controversies |
| National groups and denominations | National groups and denominations |
| Other religions besides your own | Other religions besides your own |
| Ecumenism and cooperation | Opinion and commentary |
| Opinion and commentary | Ecumenism and cooperation |
| Surveys or polls | Faith experiences |
| Faith experiences | American religious movements |
| American religious movements | Surveys or polls |
| Alternative or "new" movements | Alternative or "new" movements |
| Humor or cartoons | Humor or cartoons |

We can begin to build a comprehensive statement of the nature of reader interest, based on material from Chapter 6 and from these survey results. We are able to say, with some assurance, that readers (and, by extension, listeners and viewers) are more sophisticated and knowledgeable about the news business and about the coverage of religion in the news than they are often given credit for. People heard from in Chapter 6 understood how journalism works and what they could reasonably expect newspapers to do. Although some were prone to accept the "media elite" argument as a way of explanation, not all held this view.

There was a general consensus that religion coverage could use some improvement. Some were somewhat group-centered in their views of what that "improvement" might entail, with Pentecostals and Catholics particularly wanting their own faith to be presented in a less "stereotyped" way. At the same time, there was a strong interest in *general* religion coverage, and no real expectation that newspapers or television will become forums for "faith" or "inspiration" more than for information.

And that is what seems—almost universally—wanted: *information.* Most people quoted in Chapter 6 described their *own* sources of information about religion as flowing in two ways. Consistent with long-standing theories of the flow of information and influence, they rely on clergy or lay leaders for information about their own group or its traditions. However, for information about religion in general or about other groups, they turn overwhelmingly to the secular media and want to see more of it presented there.

The implication of this for journalistic practice is that what audiences expect from the secular media is merely that religion be more represented in news output. They have a need for information about religions besides their own and about religion's role in national and international affairs. They thus do not carry the narrow or parochial bias assumed by the "received view."

We submitted the data in Table 7.11 to a statistical procedure called a *factor analysis.* This is a somewhat esoteric procedure designed to identify commonalities among the responses to question batteries such as this one to see if there are sentiments or responses that tend to cluster together. This would tell us, for instance, if there is a tendency for the same people to be interested in both "local news," and "national" issues, or whether different respondents are attracted to those different realms of interest. Table 7.13 presents the results of this analysis.

These results indicate that there are two somewhat independent dimensions underlying these responses,[8] which we labeled *localism/traditionalism* and *translocalism/universalism.* As the loadings indicate, interest in items

**TABLE 7.13** Factor Analysis of Religion Coverage "Types"
(factor loadings: all items)

| Type of Coverage | Translocalism/Universalism | Localism/Traditionalism |
|---|---|---|
| Faith experiences | .15 | .79 |
| Ethical and social issues | .18 | .85 |
| Local religious issues | .38 | .78 |
| National groups and denominations | .52 | .67 |
| Ecumenism and cooperation | .54 | .61 |
| Other religions besides your own | .55 | .57 |
| American religious movements | .62 | .52 |
| Alternative or "new" movements | .64 | .31 |
| National issues and controversies | .73 | .26 |
| Religion in American politics | .73 | .32 |
| Foreign or international politics | .78 | .19 |
| Ethical and social issues | .72 | .26 |
| Positions and pronouncements | .70 | .30 |
| Opinion and commentary | .58 | .51 |
| Humor or cartoons | .57 | .12 |
| Surveys or polls | .60 | .43 |
| Variance explained | 54.2 | 7.5 |
| Total variance explained | 61.7 | |

like faith experiences, local religious issues, and denominations loaded heavily together and on the *localism* dimension. The less local and less parochial items loaded together on the *translocalism* dimension. These items are grouped into their relevant factors in Table 7.14.

This means, in the simplest terms, that two sentiments regarding religion coverage are present here. One sentiment sees religion coverage pretty much in the traditional, "received" way. The church page, or religion section, dominated by stories of faith and by concern with local religious issues, is of primary interest, along with a dose of interest in the traditional denominations and in social and ethical issues. The other sentiment sees religion in more universalistic terms and is more interested in religion news focused on the role of religion in public life.

This also means that, for certain purposes, we can typify these two factors as "ideal types" of interest. To do this, we created what are called factor scores, where a given respondent receives a score based on his or her relative strength of interest in one of the two factors.

**TABLE 7.14** Explication of Localism/Traditionalism and
Translocalism/Universalism Factors (factor loadings greater than .5)

| Factor | Factor Loading |
|---|---|
| *Localism/Traditionalism* | |
| Faith experiences | .79 |
| Ethical and social issues | .85 |
| Local religious issues | .78 |
| Naitonal groups and denominations | .67 |
| Ecumenism and cooperation | .61 |
| Other religions besides your own | .57 |
| American religious movements | .52 |
| Opinion and commentary | .51 |
| *Translocalism/Universalism* | |
| Foreign or international politics | .78 |
| Religion in American politics | .73 |
| National issues and controversies | .73 |
| Ethical and social issues | .72 |
| Positions and pronouncements | .70 |
| Alternative or "new" movements | .64 |
| American religious movements | .62 |
| Surveys or polls | .60 |
| Opinion and commentary | .58 |
| Humor or cartoons | .57 |
| Other religions besides your own | .55 |
| Ecumenism and cooperation | .54 |
| National groups and denominations | .52 |

Although analysis using these scores is less than precise, we were able to use the scores in one way to establish relationships with demographic characteristics. The results of this analysis are presented in Table 7.15.[9] Although few of the coefficients are very strong, many are statistically significant and give a general picture of the characteristics of those respondents who express preferences for these two types of religion-news interest. Women tend to be more drawn to localism/traditionalism. Localists/ traditionalists also are more likely to say that religion is very important in their own lives, to attend regularly, and to report having been born again. Evangelical denomination membership is more strongly associated with localism than is mainline membership. Not surprising is the fact that education and income are positively associated with translocalism, meaning that higher-income and better-educated respondents are more likely to choose that package of interest "types."

This confirms that there is a clear and independent interest in religion news among the readership that does not fall into the traditional categories. Rather

**TABLE 7.15** Demographic Characteristics of Localists and Translocalists (Pearson correlation coefficients)

| Characteristic | Localists | Translocalists |
|---|---|---|
| Female gender | .14** | .06* |
| Importance of religion | .51** | .09** |
| Income | −.15** | .13** |
| Education | −.17** | .20** |
| Religious attendance | .44** | .09** |
| Born again | .43** | .09** |
| Evangelical denomination | .21** | −.02 |
| "Seven-Sisters" denomination | .05* | .02 |
| Catholics | .01 | .04 |

*$p < .05$; **$p < .01$.

than being primarily interested in "bake sales," their own faith groups, or religion in their own communities, many readers have a broader approach.

One way to understand these findings is to compare them with the "ideal reader" for whom most journalists feel they are writing. That reader is typically someone who is literate, broad-minded, and interested in a variety of issues. What the traditional view of religion coverage has failed to appreciate (and what these data tend to show) is that such "ideal readers" might *also* be interested in religion.

It also must be remembered that both "types" of reader are present in the audience. These data do not allow us to quantify their relative numbers, and it would be a mistake to stereotype these readers in any case. Looking again at the factor loadings in Table 7.15, those readers who cluster primarily around the localism/traditionalism item *also* express a significant interest in larger issues and in religions besides their own. They are interested in broader ethical and social issues and in national groups and denominations. This means that, all other things being equal, religion journalism could look beyond the local and parochial for its understanding of readership interest, provided it began in these directions.

## Religion and the "Culture Wars"

Data such as these can also be used to probe the audience for religion in terms of its religious sensibilities. In one survey, questions were included that enabled respondents to be classified according to current religious/political

**TABLE 7.16** Religious Liberalism and Conservatism Within Denominational
            Categories

|  | All | Catholics | Seven-Sisters | Evangelical Protestants | Other Protestants | Other Religions |
|---|---|---|---|---|---|---|
| Conservative | 46.1 | 38.9 | 47.4 | 51.0 | 47.8 | 52.3 |
| Liberal | 48.2 | 52.4 | 48.4 | 43.5 | 47.8 | 44.7 |
| Don't know/ not applicable | 5.7 | 8.7 | 4.1 | 5.6 | 4.3 | 3.1 |
| n | 980 | 262 | 213 | 155 | 125 | 112 |

and institutional trends. Most such research has taken particular pains to look
at evangelicalism both in terms of belief and in denominational identification. To more fully consider the religious demographics of the current
situation, we can specify, among Protestants, both *evangelical* and *mainline*
members.[10]

We can also specify sentiments in the population related to religious
restructuring. Denominational identification is only part of the current story,
as Wuthnow[11] has shown. To address respondents' positions independent of
denomination, one survey asked each of them to typify themselves along a
continuum of religious liberalism and conservatism. Specifically, they were
asked to rate themselves on a six-point scale from "very liberal" to "very
conservative." Table 7.16 presents the relationship between these two items.
To deal more efficiently with the "liberalism/conservatism" item, we divided
respondents into two categories, splitting responses at the midpoint.

This is a striking finding and a confirmation of the idea that American
religion *is* being restructured. Where we might have expected to find a clear
relationship between, for instance, evangelical denomination and likelihood
to typify oneself as "conservative," there was less of that tendency. Evangelical members are more likely to be religiously conservative and mainline
members more likely to be liberal religiously, but the tendencies are not as
large as predicted.

In a way, this confirms *both* the notion of restructuring and the rise of
personal autonomy in matters of faith.[12] Although we might have expected
respondents who are more conservative to gravitate to evangelical groups
and those who are more liberal to gravitate in the other direction, people tend
to stay where they are. This is part of the continuing "war in the churches"

**TABLE 7.17** Demographic Characteristics of Religious Liberals and Conservatives

| Characteristic | Liberals | Conservatives | n | Significance |
|---|---|---|---|---|
| Education | | | | ** |
|   Less than high school | 45.8 | 40.4 | 178 | |
|   High school diploma | 47.0 | 48.0 | 302 | |
|   Some college | 52.9 | 43.6 | 523 | |
| Gender | | | | ns |
|   Males | 49.8 | 42.1 | 592 | |
|   Females | 49.4 | 44.2 | 501 | |
| Race | | | | * |
|   Whites | 50.6 | 42.6 | 810 | |
|   Nonwhites | 44.8 | 46.6 | 193 | |
| Income | | | | ** |
|   <$20,000 | 36.2 | 37.9 | 595 | |
|   $20,000–$40,000 | 30.8 | 31.7 | 512 | |
|   >$40,000 | 33.0 | 30.4 | 485 | |
| Size of place | | | | ** |
|   Over 250,000 | 51.8 | 39.7 | 200 | |
|   Other urban | 48.6 | 45.0 | 455 | |
|   Non-urban | 49.4 | 43.1 | 348 | |

$*p < .05$; $**p < .01$; $ns$ = not significant.

where liberal-conservative differences are as likely to hold *within* denominations as *between* them. This of course underlies the sociopolitical dynamic that has come to be called the "culture wars."[13]

Tables 7.17 and 17.8 confirm that this liberalism/conservatism measure taps some predictable dimensions. College graduates are more likely to be liberal than are those without a high school diploma. Whites are more likely than nonwhites to be religiously liberal. Those from the larger cities are also more likely than those from rural areas to call themselves liberal. Women are more likely than men to call themselves conservative as are nonwhites.

In general, those who call themselves conservative are more conventionally religious in their behaviors than those who call themselves liberal. Fifty-five percent of the conservatives attend services regularly, whereas only 33 percent of liberals do. Fifty-seven percent of the conservatives think religion is "very important," whereas only 28 percent of the liberals do. Further, the conservatives are classically conservative on belief measures: 45 percent take the literalist position on the Bible, compared with 27 percent

**TABLE 7.18** Religious Liberalism/Conservatism Differences in Belief and
            Behavior Measures

| Percentage who: | Conservative | Liberal | Significance |
|---|---|---|---|
| Volunteer in religion | 32.9 | 15.3 | ** |
| Volunteer in human services | 10.1 | 13.3 | ns |
| Volunteer in other roles | 2.8 | 7.0 | * |
| Have same religious preference as at age 16 | 76.0 | 73.6 | ns |
| Attend religious group other than church | 28.1 | 13.7 | ** |
| Attend church regularly | 55.1 | 33.0 | ** |
| Consider religion "very important" | 57.3 | 28.5 | ** |
| Have had a religious experience | 33.5 | 19.1 | ** |
| Consider oneself born again | 34.1 | 17.4 | ** |
| Believe Bible is literal | 47.2 | 27.3 | ** |
| Have a literal view of creation | 58.1 | 36.9 | ** |

$*p < .05$; $**p < .01$; $ns$ = not significant.

of the liberals, and 58 percent take the literal, biblical view of creation, whereas only 37 percent of the liberals feel that way.

## ◼ Media and Religiosity

We are also able to both typify the media *use* of various religious groups and subgroups and measure their reactions and preferences regarding media treatment of religion. Television viewing and newspaper reading differ in their respective relationships to religiosity. Frequent attenders (in this case, those who attend "a few times a month" or more) are also more likely than less frequent attenders to be daily news readers. The reverse is the case for television viewing. Frequent attenders are *less* likely to be heavy television viewers, and this relationship is one that has held remarkably steady for the past two decades.

This is consistent with what we know of the demographic characteristics of news reading and television viewing. Better-educated people read newspapers more and do not watch as much television as people with lower levels of education. What needs to be underscored, once again, is the religious character of these respective audiences. Very unlike what the received wisdom would predict, the better-educated news-reading audience is also reli-

**TABLE 7.19** Religiosity and Media Use Trends (in percentages)

| Percentage Who | Overall | Attend Once a Week or More | Attend Less Than Once a Week | Once a Year or Less | Significance |
|---|---|---|---|---|---|
| Read newspaper daily | 53.6 | 63.5 | 48.5 | 49.1 | ** |
| Read Sunday paper weekly | 74.0 | 78.5 | 71.3 | 72.3 | * |
| Read local paper daily | 19.9 | 22.8 | 20.4 | 16.4 | * |
| Read magazine weekly | 47.6 | 54.3 | 46.2 | 42.6 | ** |
| Read religious magazine weekly | 14.8 | 32.1 | 9.1 | 3.6 | ** |
| Watch religious TV weekly | 15.3 | 28.7 | 12.5 | 5.0 | ** |
| Attend a movie weekly | 7.9 | 4.8 | 8.1 | 10.7 | ** |
| Rent a video weekly | 26.2 | 20.8 | 32.6 | 24.9 | ** |
| Watch cable TV weekly | 47.1 | 42.3 | 48.8 | 50.0 | * |
| Watch TV 4+ hours daily | 33.5 | 29.9 | 33.4 | 37.1 | ** |

*$p < .05$; **$p < .01$.

gious. Religion is *not* necessarily associated with the sort of ignorance and narrowness previously assumed.

Table 7.19 looks in detail at religiosity and a range of media behaviors. What emerge here are some clear differences in media use among respondents of various levels of religiosity. Frequent attenders reveal, first of all, a bias toward reading. They read daily newspapers, Sunday papers, and magazines in significantly higher percentages than do less frequent attenders. The latter are more likely to watch television, attend films, or rent videos. This means that there is a tendency for the audience for nonprint media to be less religious than the readers of magazines and newspapers. We have no data on whether this holds for television *news* as well as *entertainment*. However, age is a factor here, for younger people are both more likely to be drawn to nonprint media *and* less likely to be frequent attenders.

Table 7.20 presents the same behaviors, this time comparing religious liberals and conservatives. Both are similar in their media behaviors, with nearly the same percentages reporting frequent reading of newspapers and magazines. Conservatives are more likely to watch religious television and read religious magazines. Liberals are significantly more likely to be involved with nonprint media. They are twice as likely to attend films as conservatives, about half again as likely to rent videos, and more likely to watch cable television. The difference between liberal and conservative levels of television viewing is not statistically significant.

**TABLE 7.20** Media Use by Religious Liberals and Conservatives

| Percentage who: | Conservatives | Liberals | Significance |
|---|---|---|---|
| Read newspaper daily | 55.0 | 54.7 | ns |
| Read Sunday paper weekly | 74.6 | 75.9 | ns |
| Read local paper weekly | 63.9 | 54.8 | ** |
| Read magazine weekly | 49.2 | 46.8 | ns |
| Read religious magazine weekly | 21.4 | 10.0 | ** |
| Watch religious TV weekly | 21.8 | 9.9 | ** |
| Attend a movie weekly | 5.1 | 9.7 | ** |
| Rent a video weekly | 21.6 | 29.7 | ** |
| Watch cable TV weekly | 42.5 | 50.4 | ** |
| Watch TV 4+ hours daily | 30.3 | 34.9 | ns |

$*p < .05; **p < .01; ns$ = not significant.

## ▮ Interest in and Satisfaction With Television's Treatment of Religion

The question of audience interest in and reaction to *television's* treatment of religion is next addressed. Table 7.21 presents the level of agreement with a set of four statements regarding the way religion is treated for each of six *genres* of television. As can be seen, the responses were not very intense, tending not to move very far off the midpoint of "4." There are, however, significant differences that deserve some discussion.

The *highest* level of agreement was with the notion that network news and talk shows need to carry more religion. It does appear, though, that when network news does carry religion it does *not* do so too negatively (in the opinion of viewers). The response option that network news treats religion too negatively received the *lowest* level of agreement. Responses on the point that there should be more religion in television were the highest across the board. Apparently, these respondents think there should be more religion, period.

The most negative treatment of religion appears to be in public television programs, according to these respondents, which they see as also being the most unfair to both traditional and "new" or alternative religions. Religious television, interestingly, is perceived as being more unfair to mainstream than to new groups, whereas network news is seen as fairest to mainstream groups.

**TABLE 7.21** Respondent Satisfaction With Television Treatment of Religion (mean scores, seven-point scale, 7 = "agree")

| | Network News | Local News | Prime-Time Entertainment | Talk Shows | Religious TV Programs | Public TV Programs |
|---|---|---|---|---|---|---|
| Should be more religion content | 4.01 | 3.99 | 3.92 | 4.04 | — | 3.77 |
| Religion too often treated negatively | 2.92 | 3.31 | 3.24 | 3.08 | — | 3.54 |
| Unfair to traditional or mainstream religious groups | 3.19 | 3.43 | 3.42 | 3.34 | 3.44 | 3.55 |
| Unfair to new, unusual, or minority religious groups | 3.27 | 3.46 | 3.45 | 3.31 | 3.15 | 3.57 |

Differences greater than .14 are significant.

## ■ Some Conclusions

Religion continues to be important to most Americans. They express their religious interests in private beliefs and public behaviors, and both have persisted in American society in spite of long-anticipated secularization. On a basic level, most media audiences are religious audiences. Religion is not (obviously) their primary motivation for reading and viewing, but it can be said that within any audience group there will be a significant, if not preponderant, religious interest present.

When that interest does self-consciously turn toward religion, readers (and, by extension, listeners and viewers) have a broader view of the limits of the religion beat than many in the media industries have. There are significant segments of the media audience that see religion as an important element of the broad range of news coverage and not as something that can or should be confined to the private sphere of belief alone.

Religion and religious practice are changing to a great degree. Not only is there more diversity of religious belief now than in the past, the way people are expressing their religion is also changing. There are important differences in American religiosity that are not confined to the structures of denomination or historic faith. There are, for example, religious liberals and religious conservatives within most faith groupings, and these identities tie people together across those groupings. There is thus a "pan-denominational religiosity" that connects those on the various sides of the "culture war" almost irrespective of their "root" religious identity in the various denominations and groups. Universalized or "broad truths" religion is discussed in a later chapter.

Comparisons with media use measures reveal some interesting relationships between belief, behavior, and media. Those who are the most outwardly religious are more embedded in print culture than those who are less involved. However, religious liberals and conservatives differ far less in terms of their reported media use. Both liberals and conservatives are embedded in the media audience, with a slight tendency for liberals to watch more nonprint media. This is, of course, a possible effect of age, where older people tend both to be lighter viewers of media and to be more conservative in general.

Audiences for the most prominent of the nonprint media, television, are not terribly opinionated about its treatment of religion. This may be related to their relative lack of experience with a range of types of treatment. In general, viewers want more religion coverage in television news and on other programs. Network news fared best in assessments of its coverage when religion appears, and public television was considered to be the most negative in its treatment.

Media audiences continue to expect more and better treatment of religion, particularly in news programs. Their definition of religion is a broad one. They do not expect religion news to focus on their own particular beliefs or communities or groups so much as they expect the media to represent the underlying contributions of religion to daily life in the culture and the nation. The data, then, confirm the sense that media decision makers should understand an important distinction: the difference between "religion interest" and "religiosity." There is much evidence here that interest in religion, in information about religion, and in coverage that reveals the religious dimensions of other stories transcends questions of religious belief per se. It is no longer adequate to think of the religion audience as made up of people who are intensely religious. The issue and the need are of a different character than that.

# Notes

1. Results here come from three national surveys conducted by the Gallup Organization. For each, national probability samples of 1,100 adults were surveyed in the spring of 1988, spring 1989, and spring 1993. The first survey was intended to establish baseline relationships between various measures of religiosity and religious interest and newspaper readership. The second survey contained more refined measures of qualitative interest in religion coverage, based on pilot testing and the results of the qualitative interviews (see Chapter 6) that took place between the administration of the first two national surveys. The third survey included similar items to the first two but extended the analysis by adding questions dealing with nonprint media. For technical reports of these surveys, see Hoover, S., B. Hanley, and M. Radelfinger. 1989. *The RNS-Lilly study of religion reporting and readership in the daily press.* Philadelphia: Temple University, and New York: Religious News Service; and Hoover, S., S. Venturelli, and D. Wagner. 1994. *Religion in public discourse: The role of the media.* Boulder: University of Colorado School of Journalism and Mass Communication.

2. This finding has been confirmed by other recent studies. See, in particular, (a) The role of religion in newspaper trust, subscribing, and use for political information (by Judith M. Buddenbaum) and (b) The role of religion in public attitudes toward religion news (by Judith M. Buddenbaum and Stewart M. Hoover), both in *Religion and mass media: Audiences and adaptations,* edited by Daniel Stout and Judith Buddenbaum. Thousand Oaks, CA: Sage, 1996.

3. As has been conventional practice in such surveys, those denominations considered "traditionally evangelical" were Southern Baptists, "other Baptists," and the Missouri Synod Lutheran Church.

4. Marty, Martin. 1970. *Righteous empire.* New York: Dial Press.

5. Hunter, James Davidson. 1991. *Culture wars: The struggle to define America.* New York: Basic Books.

6. This list was derived intuitively from the categories of de partments and standing features most often used in industry research, with additional categories that are commonly compared with religion in industry considerations of these issues. For the precise wording, and other technical details, see the technical report by Hoover et al., *The RNS-Lilly study.*

7. The questionnaire did not, at this point, indicate to respondents that the survey was particularly interested in religion.

8. The factor scores are equivalent to correlation coefficients that measure the relationship between a given item and a given underlying dimension, or factor. These items are said to load on a given factor, and these factor loadings give an idea of the relative relationship between the various items and the two factors.

9. These figures are Pearson correlation coefficients. They essentially measure the strength of association between two items and can take a value anywhere from −1 to +1. The further the value varies from zero, the stronger it is. Negative values are negatively associated, meaning that when one of the variables increases, the other decreases. An example is the common association between education and income. They are positively correlated, meaning that their coefficient would take a positive value, and its distance from zero would be a measure of the strength of that association. By contrast, education and television viewing are negatively associated. The higher one's level of education, the less likely one is to watch television. The coefficient between television viewing and education would thus be negative, and the distance below zero would be a measure of that relationship. A coefficient of −1 or +1 is rare, for it means that things are perfectly correlated—that they vary together at exactly the same rate.

A note of explanation is necessary about the demographic and religious items used in these tables. The gender item is a variable that uses female as the positive value. Therefore, a positive coefficient means that women are more likely to choose a given response. The item marked "7-Sisters" pulls out those Protestants who belong to the seven largest mainline groups (American Baptist, Evangelical Lutheran Church in America, Episcopal Church, United Methodist Church, United Church of Christ, Disciples of Christ, and United Presbyterian Church) and groups them together. The "evangelical denomination" item does the same thing for those denominations traditionally called evangelical.

10. For the evangelical specification, we included members of those denominations commonly understood to be primarily conservative-evangelical in orientation. For the mainline specification, we included members of the seven most prominent mainline groups, using the label "7-Sisters" after the use originally employed by *Newsweek* religion editor Ken Woodward.

11. Wuthnow, Robert. 1988. *The restructuring of American religion.* Princeton, NJ: Princeton University Press.

12. See complete discussion in Chapter 3.

13. Hunter, *Culture wars.*

# RELIGION AND THE
# MEDIA IN CONFLICT

Previous chapters considered the conditions that surround the religion story. Religion writers and editors work within a set of received understandings that continues to have an impact on coverage, even as the situation seems to be changing. Readers and viewers both within and outside the religious community have their own views, generally expecting a greater amount and quality of coverage than has traditionally been offered.

At the same time, there has been change in at least the *quantity* of coverage. ABC News has been regularly covering religion in its flagship news program for several years. The *Fresh Air* program and activities at NPR have contributed significantly to the representation of religion on public radio. An increasing number of documentaries and related programs have appeared on public television, and there has been some movement in commercial broadcasting in the area of news. There have been big changes in the print media as well. Most notably, perhaps, was the founding of a major religion section by the *Dallas Morning News* in 1995.

Although the issue of *quantity* of coverage has—to an extent—been addressed, the *quality* of coverage is another matter. It is important to consider both dimensions because there is evidence that quantity alone will never suffice to quell the criticism of media treatment.

Many examples could be chosen to illustrate this point, but none is perhaps more typical than the controversy that arose in 1993 and 1994 surrounding the coverage of the visit of the Pope to World Youth Day in Denver (Colorado) and coverage of what turned out ultimately to be groundless allegations of sexual misconduct lodged against Archbishop Bernardin of Chicago. Occurring when they did, at a time when there was already an increased level of public scrutiny of press coverage of religion, these incidents provided the occasion for a good deal of comment and reflection.

Most observers agreed that the Youth Day coverage was generally quite positive, serving up lots of images of earnest Catholic youths and providing a powerful platform for the Pope's visit. Even though there was some unevenness, particularly between the national print and local broadcast coverage, overall it was the most positive press the American Catholic Church had received in quite some time.

Coverage of World Youth Day, however, became the occasion for public discussion of religion coverage in general as a result of a postconference press conference held by the U.S. Catholic Bishops. At that event, Archbishop William Keeler of Baltimore, president of the bishops' conference, decried what he called the "preprogrammed" nature of most coverage of Catholicism and singled out the Youth Day reportage for particular criticism. Although he agreed that most stories "were fair, even glowing," he went on to say that these stories were too often accompanied by a "preprogrammed 'Catholic Story' " focusing on dissent and disarray in the church.[1]

During the same period, the bishops were also dealing with the controversy over Cardinal Bernardin, and in much of the discussion the two incidents became conflated. At the November press conference, Archbishop Keeler took the press to task for its focus on the controversy in both of these events, losing track of the "real story" of American Catholicism:

"In this story the church in the United States is in disarray, rife with dissent," he said, while developments like the church's growth by a million members last year or the wide demand for Catholic schooling and the services provided through Catholic hospitals and charities are neglected.[2]

The archbishop also spoke from personal experience with the constraints of journalistic convention, particularly in broadcasting. For example, he objected to an interview on NBC's *Today* show during the Denver event. *Today,* he said,

> had given him only 30 seconds . . . to explain the Catholic Church's position on abortion, birth control, celibacy and the male priesthood. Said the archbishop, "The glib answers they seek to important questions leave no room for detail and nuance, no room for the whole universe of concerns on which the Holy Father challenges all humanity."[3]

In an analysis of coverage of these controversies, Frank Somerville of the *Baltimore Sun* drew the lines of demarcation between the church and the press rather starkly. Somerville quoted journalism professor Richard Schwarzlose, who had told the Associated Press that

> in his opinion, the reporters' handling of the allegations against Cardinal Bernardin was generally fair. "Only a decade or two ago," the professor said, "a lawsuit like this would probably never have been filed, and if it were it probably wouldn't be covered. Back then, there was what would have been called a 'gentlemen's agreement.' Maybe we'd call it a 'cover-up' today."[4]

Somerville continued his assessment by observing that a good deal of the controversy, particularly over allegations of sexual abuse, could also be laid at the door of the Church's own approach to press and publicity over the years:

> The fact is that the climate of cynicism and suspicion in which Cardinal Bernardin was forced to defend his innocence was created by the church authorities themselves through their years of denial, cover-up and inaction in the face of clear evidence of priests' abuse of children.[5]

Somerville's account came before the allegations against Cardinal Bernardin were withdrawn for lack of evidence, but he nonetheless speculated that the charges might well prove to be unfounded and the controversy (and the Church's past history of dealing with such matters) then all the more tragic.

In this one incident, we can see the nub of the problem of religion coverage. The conventions of journalism—its interests in revelation and exposure of wrongdoing—clash directly with the concerns of the Church—to avoid controversy certainly but more fundamentally to arrogate to itself the power to interpret its own story. Archbishop Keeler's words could be echoed by many, if not most, religious leaders.

Such feelings are, of course, not unique to the religious community. Journalist Cokie Roberts observed at a symposium on religion coverage,

> I must say, it is exactly the same as the way any other trade sees the media. . . . The people inside the media think we are, by and large, being fair and balanced and just telling the facts as they are, ma'am. And the people—who are in the, whatever the trade is or profession, in rare cases—are convinced that we are all out to get them, a bunch of biased, awful people who always get it wrong. There is truth to both sides, but part of the problem . . . is the nature of journalism.[6]

But there are ways in which the situation with religion is unique. Unlike other beats, it has traditionally been afforded a good deal of deference by the media and only recently come under more intense scrutiny. Religious leaders also have a unique understanding of their own prerogatives. The idea that religion might submit itself to the vagaries of the public sphere is still a controversial one, and religion and religious institutions continue to feel a special sense of control over their version of their own stories.[7] To use Archbishop Keeler's words, the media do not have the same sense of the nuance and the "universe of concerns" important to the Church.

On the other side of the controversy is the journalist, suggesting that the essence of credibility and responsibility in contemporary public life is a level of candor that makes the Church uncomfortable. Regardless of the sensitivity and embarrassment involved, the Church should have been forthcoming long before now (they would say), and the drumbeat of coverage of Church dissent is the result of years during which the institution stonewalled the media.

### ■ The Inevitability of Conflict

In assessing the gap that exists between religion and the media on these issues, it is important to keep in mind that a certain amount of this conflict is inevitable. Just as it is inevitable for business or the military or the university to at times be uncomfortable with its treatment by the media, it is inevitable that churches and religion will feel the same way. But there are ways that the situation is different for religion, because to invoke the gulf between religion and the media is to invoke a conflict that goes back centuries to the beginning of modern religion and the modern media in the West.

One of the most important causes of this conflict is a characteristic of the media as we know them in the Anglo-American tradition that is fundamental to their very being. The so-called liberal-pluralist philosophy of the press, given its form and shape by a legal record in Britain and the United States and articulated by social theorists such as John Milton, holds a particular role for the press in the establishment and maintenance of democratic society. In the vernacular, this role has been variously called the "watchdog" or the "fourth estate." The special protection afforded the press by the First Amendment (ironically the same place that addresses religious freedom) is founded on the notion that a free and responsible press is the most important check on the excesses of government.

This idea rests on a more fundamental function of the media. The "power of publication" is rooted in the capacity of the press to act in particular ways in civil discourse. In a classic work of early media theory, the sociologists Paul Lazarsfeld and Robert Merton[8] theorized that one of the most basic functions of the media is what they called "the enforcement of social norms." By this they meant that the media have a nearly unique ability to sanction private behavior by making it public. Thus, they are able to expose that which would ordinarily be kept secret, and by so doing, they can bring the norms of society to bear. The ability of a local newspaper in a small town to reveal that paving contracts are being granted without competitive bids to the brother-in-law of the county commissioner acts as an important check on that type of behavior. And it is not only the actions of the local paper to do so but its *potential* or its *capacity* to do so that gives it its power in public discourse. Thus, according to Lazarsfeld and Merton, norms are enforced, and private action is affected even when no critical incidents occur.

More sensational examples abound. Until recently, a "gentlemen's agreement" kept the press from delving too deeply into the private lives of public figures. National political leaders of the 1960s had much more freedom in private than do those of the 1990s, due to a shift in this ethos. Now, times have changed, and very different standards of private conduct are applied in Washington. This is a direct result of the mechanism of the press.

## ▓ The Power of the Press

This power of the press thus cannot be underestimated and is nearly impossible to circumvent, particularly in the age of global media. Chinese authorities, for example, may have wished to keep the events of Tiananmen Square private (and were able to do so in the protected space of their own media), but global airing of them was inevitable.

This is the first component of the set of historical conditions underlaying religion-press relations. Two other interrelated components are also critical to our understanding: *the rise of the modern public sphere* and *the development of printing.*

Before the early modern period, European discourse was largely the province of the Church and the State. What public discussion took place was controlled by these two entities. This power over discourse was both a measure and a reinforcement of their legitimacy. With the rise of the new bourgeois class, mass democracy, the modern state, and the corporation came a new type of—and a new set of contexts for—discourse.

The most influential thought on this topic has been the work of German sociologist Jürgen Habermas.[9] Habermas holds that what made the public sphere in the modern period different from that of earlier times, such as in ancient Greece or Rome, was that the emergence of a *public* depended on the development of a new notion of the *private.* The social, political, and economic changes of the period supported the emergence of a new conception of private life, where private individuals had the autonomy to engage in public debate over issues including the limits of state authority.[10]

This process depended on the emergence of a new kind of society that resulted from an intermixture of aristocratic and bourgeois classes:

> Habermas does not mean to suggest that what made the public sphere bourgeois was simply the class composition of its members. Rather, it was *society* that was bourgeois, and bourgeois society produced a certain form of public sphere. The new sociability, together with the rational-critical discourse that grew in the salons (and coffee houses and other places), depended on the rise of national and territorial power states on the basis of early capitalist commercial economy. This process led to an idea of society separate from the ruler (or the state) and of a private realm separate from the public.[11]

The role of the media in these developments was critical, according to Habermas. This role had two valences. One was that the print media were intimately involved in the extension of trade, playing an important role in the mercantile economy. Newsletters that provided market price information were among the earliest publications, and they soon began carrying news along with financial data. Second, the print media became intimately involved in the development of the broader public discourse that evolved along with the economy.

This discourse gradually came to see itself as fundamentally about opposition to state authority:

A certain educated elite came to think of itself as constituting the public and thereby transformed the abstract notion of the publicum as a counterpart to public authority into a much more concrete set of practices. The members of this elite public began to see themselves through this category not just as the object of state actions but as the opponent of public authority.[12]

Further, the press began to play a role in this as a rational-critical reasoning emerged in the discourse and began to be represented in the press as well. Other genres of written work also emerged, forging a new relationship between producers and readers:

The relations between author, work, and public changed. They became intimate mutual relationships between privatized individuals who were psychologically interested in what was 'human,' in self-knowledge, and in empathy.[13]

The emergence of this new discourse and new classes of participants in it was not the whole story, however. Equally important were the physical and structural relations that made this kind of discourse possible. Key to these were the institutional sites where discourse flourished. The best known of these were the coffeehouses found in London and other cities from the mid-17th century onward. These are remembered as the places where *literati* such as Milton, Marvell, Pepys, Addison, and Steele held forth, but "critical debate ignited by works of literature and art was soon extended to include economic and political disputes."[14] By the first decade of the 18th century,

Habermas reports, there were over 3,000 coffeehouses in London alone. Similar developments occurred in France and Germany.

Several characteristics of this development were crucial. This new discourse disregarded social status, it was "in principle" inclusive, it made rational argument the sole arbiter of any issue, and it opened up for debate areas that "until then had not been questioned":[15]

All sorts of topics over which church and state authorities had hitherto exercised a virtual monopoly of interpretation were opened to discussion, inasmuch as the public defined its discourse as focusing on all matters of common concern.[16]

The characteristics of this new sphere of public discourse underlay the dimensions of what we know as the media sphere today. The power of the press to make matters public (literally "to publish") derives from the heterogeneity of access to the public sphere that emerged in the period Habermas describes. What makes a private conversation into a public one is, after all, this very question—whether participants in the conversation are part of a private collective or a more heterogeneous public.[17]

It is further significant to consider the consequences Habermas outlines: that the public sphere became an important challenger to church and state authority and that conversations previously suppressed were now possible. Habermas tends to focus his attention on the consequences of this situation for the state and for other institutions, including the modern corporation. By extension, however, we could make a parallel argument that the Church, long accustomed to nearly unchallenged control over discourse about itself, now found itself facing an entirely different situation.

The role of the development of *printing* in these matters cannot be overstated. Habermas and other commentators point to the development of printing and publishing as playing a key role in supporting the institutions and practices of the public sphere. It was integrated into both the rise of mercantile economics and the development of the intellectual climate necessary for the support of the liberal notion of the "marketplace of ideas" so basic to Miltonian press theory. And printing has long been assumed to have had important implications for the Church during the Reformation. The Lutheran reforms could not have taken place without printing, and it supported both the theological effects of the reformation and important social effects, such as the spread of literacy in Northern Europe.

Following the line of argument laid out by Habermas, however, and pursuing our interest in the sources of conflict between religion and the press, leads us to another implication of printing. Elizabeth Eisenstein[18] has demonstrated in her important work on the consequences of printing that along with the development of the printing press came the establishment of a new, entirely "secular" guarantor of public discourse: the publisher. This new class, arising in conjunction with the development of the marketplace economics of the mercantile class and the emergent public sphere, achieved a remarkable prominence in a very short period of time, often as managers of coffeehouses as well as publishing operations.[19] This means that the primary impact of Gutenberg's[20] invention was not in the spread of books or literacy so much as it was in the spread of *presses* themselves and through them the creation of an entirely new class of public authority—again, the publisher. Printing enterprises, Eisenstein found,

> served as a kind of institute or activity . . . which rivaled the older university, court, and academy and which provided preachers and teachers with opportunities to pursue alternate careers.[21]

Publishing thus quickly achieved a social, cultural, and political prominence, and its modes and methods of practice began to spread:

> [The] point of departure . . . is not the invention of one device in one Mainz shop but the establishment of many printshops in many urban centers throughout Europe over the course of two decades or so. This entailed the appearance of a new occupational culture associated with the printing trades. New publicity techniques and new communication networks also appeared.[22]

Within a century, printing and publishing came to help define the new approaches to political discourse spreading across Europe. Suppressed in some places and tolerated in others, publishers eventually became important political figures in England, a legacy carried by English colonists in the New World and ensconced in the Constitution by its founders.

The realm of "publishing" has now developed far beyond the limited context of the printing of tracts, newsletters, and newspapers. Publishing today involves not only the daily press but a whole panoply of mediated texts and products, all of which collectively define an entirely new context of public discourse. Today, in an era dominated by such discourse and in which people spend unprecedented time and resources on media products, the public sphere is a *mediated* one.

## ▉ Prospects for the Church

This has had some rather profound implications for the pre-Reformation controllers of discourse, the Church and the State (as well as for the university and the trades). They and indeed all social institutions must now submit themselves to the demands and definitions of the media in order to have access to the public sphere. Thus, the process of "publicity," with all of its conditions and contradictions, is necessary if the Church is to exist in public, as the mediated realm now dominates the terms of access and attention.

There is a lively debate about the extent, nature, and implications of this challenge. If the Church is to accept these new conditions, does it sell its soul for the sake of publicity? Can mediated communication ever approximate the true communication of authentic religious experience? Are the modes of communication in which the media engage (visual and experiential) authentic?

It is clear that there are variations across religious traditions in their concerns about the media. Although it is beyond the scope of this book to fully explore these issues, there are some facts worthy of consideration here. First, some religious traditions, most notably conservative Judaism and Islam, are profoundly "aniconic," meaning that they have, as a matter of doctrine, prohibitions against anthropomorphic representation, particularly of the godhead and the prophets.[23] This leads to a particularism in their understanding of media representations, especially those that are the most "iconic" or visual. Second, there are some religious traditions that seem particularly comfortable with the media, most notably American evangelicalism and its various offshoots.[24] Third, there are those traditions, including mainline Protestantism and Catholicism, that have taken a more tentative view of the media, not necessarily informed by aniconism nor by the more aggressive posture of the evangelicals.[25]

But it is the evangelical model that is the most germane to our argument here because evangelicalism has so deftly found itself a place of prominence in American media discourse over the past 25 years. The phenomenon of televangelism represents, for example, a coming to terms with the demands, limitations, and potentialities of the media sphere.[26] Evangelical broadcasting is but one small part of a much larger and more significant religious media enterprise, including book publishing, and a wide range of other cultural and communication commodities.

One implication of all of this that has often escaped attention is the role of such commodified religious expression in the support and maintenance of popular piety. In an address to a conference of religion scholars in 1995, Barbara Wheeler of Auburn Seminary reported on her several-years-long study of evangelical culture. One aspect of that culture that stood out for her was its investment in commodities, in things:

> Evangelicals turn out stuff: thousands of Christian recordings, even more books—a new Christian gothic novel, I was told by an avid reader of them, is published every week—along with almost every other kind of fiction, poetry, Bible translations and paraphrases, advice, celebrity biography, and countless devotional volumes; magazines pamphlets, newspapers, broadsides, leaflets; plaques, posters, greeting and note cards, bumper stickers, ceramics, jewelry.[27]

Wheeler compared this situation with the condition of mainline Protestantism, which takes a far different view of such cultural commodities, and raised a note of concern about the implications of this situation:

> Mainline Protestantism does not have enough of a culture. By comparison with the prolix popular culture of the evangelicals, mainline Protestantism inventory of symbols, manners, iconic leaders, images of leadership, distinctive language, decorations, and sounds is very low indeed. . . . Without these elements of culture, mainline Protestantism cannot create something a religious tradition must have to survive: a piety.[28]

There is evidence that this orientation to the commodities and the practices of the mediated public sphere is not unique to evangelicalism nor to this century.[29] Much contemporary religious and quasi-religious practice is gradually moving toward a more fungible boundary between the world of religion and the world of the media on the level of *actual practices* of audiences and adherents. What all of this points to, however, is a situation where the conditions of the mediated public sphere place certain demands on individuals and institutions that might wish to be present there. It is not just that religious institutions and individuals must submit themselves to the demands of the media, but that to *exist at all* in contemporary culture is to exist in the media. This places a burden on any and all pretenders to inclusion to either move to a posture of more or less aggressive promotion or to be marginalized in public discourse.

In all of this, at the same time, is an expectation that to be present in public discourse is not enough by itself. One must be there with *credibility,* and that is a difficult thing to engineer. Televangelists achieved a good deal of political and other prominence by—in a sense—*buying* their way into the public realm. They constructed networks that were fundamentally private. Studies done in the early 1980s at the height of their prominence demonstrated that they attracted small audiences of the already convinced. They preached to the choir more than they achieved a purchase on the public mind through the public sphere.[30] Their public face was instead based on their coverage by the secular press, a factor that figures such as Pat Robertson and Jerry Falwell used to great advantage.

To be in the public sphere with credibility demands that the conditions of that space be satisfied, as we have said, and it places a challenge before religious institutions and leaders that goes something like this:

> Suppose you had only a certain amount of money to spend on media. Which of the following would you choose? To produce a 10-part series of hour-long documentaries on the history of your tradition or faith group over which you would have complete control, but which would appear intermixed with the program-length advertisements on cable, or to be interviewed on PBS by Bill Moyers (with obviously no control over the agenda) for five minutes? Which would you choose?

The choice is, at the very least, a contested one because the platform, the forum, and the credibility afforded by Bill Moyers and PBS are of priceless value in contemporary public debate, a fact known almost viscerally by leaders of all public institutions. This means that, regardless of the resources available to them, most religious organizations desire presence in the credibility-rich public medium of the secular press more than they do access to closed and private networks.

## ▉ Stresses and Strains

Secular journalists are then on the "front line" of this process, and the fact that some religious groups are particularly aggressive in pressing the point gives support to the premise that religion is only interested in its own, narrow concerns. Dart and Allen provide this description of a common sentiment in *Bridging the Gap:*

> Religious leaders expect "publicity" in the form of news stories, said Mike Cosgrove, an editor at the *Fairfield (CA) Daily Republic.* He added that the same is true of business people. "Unfortunately for these people, when a story does not come out which explains all sides of an issue objectively, they get upset because some negative aspects of their group were revealed," said Cosgrove. "The news media's job is to report facts—not serve as a public relations firm."[31]

The sum and substance of the situation is that religious institutions are in the position of having to surrender control over their own symbols in exchange for access to the public sphere and are unlikely to be entirely comfortable with this exchange. In concrete terms, this predicts that religious groups and religious figures will never be entirely satisfied with the constructions of themselves they will see in media "stories." For the profession of religion journalism, this means that it may be too much to expect that the objects of a given story will be entirely satisfied with their portrayal. Were they to tell their own stories, they would naturally tell them differently.

As journalists construct their narratives, they are writing for a different audience than the object group or individual. They are attempting to make that group "make sense" to a more general audience. They are working at the level of generality and sensibility that exists somewhere outside the boundaries of the objects under study. This is an important function of journalism and one that has broader implications, as will be seen.

But this task is made doubly difficult by the fact that the landscape of religion is shifting. Interpreting the world of religion to a general public discourse might have been easier in an earlier era, but today, observers from all perspectives see a religious landscape far different in some ways that have serious implications for its coverage by the media.

## Notes

1. Niebuhr, Gustav. 1994. Media said to ignore, misreport the spiritual. *Washington Post,* January 1.

2. Steinfels, Peter. 1993. Bishops assail press on sex charges. *New York Times,* November 16, p. A24.

3. Somerville, Frank. 1994. When a cardinal is accused of sex abuse. *Baltimore Sun,* March 6, p. 4E.

4. Ibid.

5. Ibid.

6. Roberts, Cokie. 1995. Comments to the Commonweal Forum on religion and the media. *Commonweal,* February 24, p. 33.

7. This is perhaps nowhere more obvious than with the Vatican. A 1996 incident regarding the health of Pope John Paul II raised speculation that the Vatican might be withholding information. In a report on the incident on National Public Radio, reporter Sylvia Pojoli observed, "Analysts say that Vatican reluctance to reveal that the Pope might be seriously ill is dictated by a centuries-old custom of being in total control of what information gets out." *See* Sylvia Pojoli. 1996. *Morning Edition,* National Public Radio, October 4, 1996.

8. Lazarsfeld, Paul and Robert Merton. 1974. Mass communication, popular taste, and organized social action. In *The processes and effects of mass communication,* edited by Wilbur Schramm and Donald Roberts. Urbana: University of Illinois Press, pp. 554-78.

9. Habermas's most definitive work on the topic is *The structural transformation of the public sphere: An inquiry into a category of bourgeois society.* Cambridge: MIT Press, 1989.

10. For a complete discussion, see Calhoun, Craig. 1992. Introduction: Habermas and the public sphere. In *Habermas and the public sphere,* edited by Craig Calhoun. Cambridge: MIT Press, pp. 1-48.

11. Ibid., p. 7.

12. Ibid., p. 9.

13. Habermas, *Structural transformation,* p. 50.

14. Ibid., p. 33.

15. Ibid., p. 36.

16. Calhoun, introduction in *Habermas,* p. 13.

17. Admittedly, Habermas's conception of the inclusivity and heterogeneity of the bourgeois public sphere is too broadly drawn. Much comment has been focused on the conditional nature of access to this sphere. See, in particular, Fraser, Nancy. 1992. Rethinking the public sphere: A contribution to the critique of actually existing democracy. In Calhoun, ed., *Habermas,* pp. 109-42. It is probably most precise to understand the emergent public sphere as *relatively* heterogeneous and inclusive, an argument that could still be made about it today.

18. Eisenstein, Elizabeth. 1978. In the wake of the printing press. *Quarterly Journal of the Library of Congress* 35:183-97.

19. For a more complete history of the coffeehouse as a center of publicity, see Emery, Michael and Edwin Emery. 1992. *The press and America.* Englewood Cliffs, NJ: Prentice Hall.

20. Recent scholarship has accepted that movable type originated in Asia long before Gutenberg, and the technology may well have been carried to Europe by Asian traders in the centuries before his work in Mainz came to fruition. See Crowley, David and Paul Heyer. 1991. *Communication history: Technology, culture, society.* New York: Longman, pp. 80-81.

21. Eisenstein, "In the wake," p. 191.

22. Ibid., p. 194.

23. Although much scholarship remains to be done in exploring these issues in the visual culture of religion, an interesting and helpful first step can be found in Coleman, Simon. 1996. Words as things: Language, aesthetics and the objectification of protestant evangelicalism. *Journal of Material Culture* 1:107-28.

24. Ibid. See also the following: The millenium and the media (by James Moorhead) and Communication and change in American religious history: A historiographical probe (by

Leonard Sweet), both in *Communication and change in American religious history,* edited by Leonard Sweet. Grand Rapids, MI: Eerdmans, 1993, pp. 1-90; Schultze, Quentin. 1987. The mythos of the electronic church. *Critical Studies in Mass Communication* 4:245-61; and Schultze, Quentin. 1995. Evangelicals' uneasy alliance with the media. In *Religion and mass media: Audiences and adaptations,* edited by Daniel Stout and Judith Buddenbaum. Thousand Oaks, CA: Sage, pp. 61-73.

25. No comprehensive recent account of these issues exists. For discussions of the early years of Protestant and Catholic broadcasting, see Ellens, J. Harold. 1974. *Models of religious broadcasting.* Grand Rapids, MI: Eerdmans; and Fore, William F. 1967. A short history of religious broadcasting in the United States, 1933-53. Unpublished report for the National Council of Churches, New York. A more recent account with regard to Protestantism can be found in Michele Rosenthal. 1996. "Turn it off": Television in the *Christian Century,* 1945-1960. Paper presented at the Conference on Media, Religion and Culture, Boulder, Colorado, January 14.

26. This is not to say that evangelical experience with the media has been uniform. Janice Peck, for example, has argued that televangelism represents two separate and contradictory turns: religion adapted to television and television adapted to religion. Far from a unified or unitary phenomenon, she argues, religious television has radical differences within it. See Peck, Janice. 1993. *The gods of televangelism.* Creskill, NJ: Hampton Press. This does not, however, obviate the overall point that certain evangelicals have taken the media sphere quite seriously and have eagerly engaged it, regardless of the outcome.

27. Wheeler, Barbara. 1995. We who were far off: Religious divisions and the role of religious research. Address to the Religious Research Association, St. Louis, October 27.

28. Ibid.

29. Moore, Laurence. 1994. *Selling God.* New York: Oxford University Press.

30. See, for example, Gerbner, George, Larry Gross, Stewart Hoover, Michael Morgan, Nancy Signorielli, Robert Wuthnow, and Harry Cotugno. 1984. *Religion and television.* Philadelphia: Annenberg School of Communications; and Hoover, Stewart M. 1988. *Mass media religion: The social sources of the electronic church.* London: Sage.

31. Dart, John and Jimmy Allen. 1993. *Bridging the gap: Religion and the news media.* Nashville, TN: Freedom Forum First Amendment Center, p. 23.

# RELIGION AND BROADCASTING

*U*ntil now, relatively little attention has been given to the treatment of religion by the most public, pervasive, and "democratic" of all the media: broadcasting. Our concern here is news, but broader questions have been repeatedly raised about the role and place of religion in broadcast entertainment content as well. Stephen Carter, for example, points to prime-time television as a major context in which religion is constructed in American public life in his book *The Culture of Disbelief.*[1]

By assessing the status of religion in broadcast news we can address two separate but related issues. First, we can look at broadcast practice vis-à-vis religion as a *measure* of the broader public construction of religion. Second, we can use this analysis to describe the limits of and potentials for more focused coverage of religion. The history of broadcast religion actually proves to be a very revealing case of *policy making* about religion coverage, something that is harder to observe in the print media where few formal contexts of policy exist.[2]

We have each of these tasks in mind as we look at the history and present practice of religion treatment by broadcasting and broadcast news. It is valuable, at the outset, to note that broadcasting shares some things in common with the print media. First, the entire controversy over media "bias" regarding religion can be generally (and reasonably) applied to all media. In fact, broadcasting is *particularly* implied in these discussions because it is the dominant medium in American public culture as measured both by its audience exposure and by its general profile in debates about the media. The Rothman-Lichter research discussed earlier, for instance, combined its data on the print media with data on the three commercial television networks and PBS, calling them collectively "the media elite."

Second, practice in broadcast news rather consciously refers to practice in the print media. What is "news" for the major national dailies is also "news" for the major networks. In the same vein, what we have said about journalism being articulated into broader public discourse applies as readily to broadcasting as it does to the print media. Although there might be some generalized and naive sense in which broadcasting is less contemplative about itself, it is no less involved than print media in its own discourses about its treatment of such things as religion, as demonstrated by the recent developments in broadcast news.

What we can say in general about broadcasting is that it has been much less likely than the print media to give any attention to religion at all. Conservative critics[3] have laid out assessments of broadcasting's failings in this regard as have such observers as Dart and Allen.[4] Even prominent voices within the industry have spoken to the issue. Dan Rather of CBS News told *TV Guide,*

> Religion was consistently underreported [in 1993]. That's especially unfortunate when you remember how many of the worst conflicts today are born of religious misunderstanding. . . . There isn't a news organization that wouldn't benefit from greater attention to the coverage of religion.[5]

For our purposes, it is enough to suggest that the recent addition of religion reporters or "desks" at some national broadcast media are significant because before that there had been *no* such positions in the entire history of American broadcasting. However, the situation is quite a bit more complex because there had been, from the very earliest days of American broadcasting, very prominent and significant religious broadcasting.

### ■ Religion and Broadcasting in America

Until recently, none of the major commercial networks had religion reporters in their daily news operations. Stories dealing with religion in these programs were also rare, tending to focus on institutions (Rome correspondents traditionally covered the Vatican when major news was made there, for example) or on controversies and scandals. Peter Jennings, in explaining the decision by ABC to add a religion reporter in 1994, expressed the same sort of dissatisfaction found among critics and observers of network practices in the area. "I came to the conclusion that we simply weren't doing a very good job in the area of religion."[6]

The same held for local television markets. Until recently, of the approximately 600 network-affiliated and independent VHF stations in the country (those most likely to have local news operations), only two, WFAA in Dallas and KSL in Salt Lake City, had religion reporters. WFAA's was Peggy Wehmeyer, who moved to ABC News in early 1994. A third station, KOTV in Tulsa, added a religion reporter in 1993. By 1997, stations WTHR in Indianapolis, WREG in Memphis, and WKRC in Cincinnati had joined these ranks, and it was clear that the numbers would gradually increase.

On one level of analysis, this should be even more surprising than the situation with the networks. If, as Rothman and the Lichters have claimed, the major networks evidence an institutional culture that does not understand religion, it is more understandable that they would leave religion "off the news agenda" than it is that local television stations would. The latter should be more closely articulated into their local cultures and reflect the religiosity of their regions.[7] Why, then, haven't stations in, say, Atlanta, Nashville, Birmingham, or Bakersfield taken religion into their news purview?

*Radio* has a somewhat different story. Several network news programs have, over the years, dealt with religion as part of the news. The longest-lived of these, *The World of Religion* on the CBS Radio Network, is still in production at KMOX in St. Louis and airs over CBS-owned-and-operated radio stations several times a week.[8] UPI Radio Network has employed a religion editor for the past 10 years, according to published accounts, and provides a religion newsfeed for stations wishing to purchase this specialized service. Other radio wire services also offer specialized religion packages.[9]

Some local radio stations in major markets have devoted attention to religion. WINS in New York, for instance, has for many years included regular religion commentaries in its weekend news cycles.[10] There are similar examples that, although not exactly the same as religion reportage, represent a commitment to the topic.

Saying that there has been a paucity of attention to religion in broadcast *news* is not to say, of course, that there has been no religion on the air at all. There is actually a great deal there, but it differs substantially from the "ideal" of religion reportage represented in recent developments. First, there is the long and significant tradition of independent quasi-commercial religious broadcasting, beginning with the fundamentalist "radio preachers" of the 1920s and stretching to the programs known as "televangelism" today. Second, there is nearly as long a tradition of religious programming presented on a "public service" basis by commercial broadcasters, usually in cooperation with one or more of the major faith groups in ecumenical alliance.

Broadcasting has thus had no tradition of religion news to parallel that which has long held sway at the nation's newspapers. Instead, there is a situation that seems to describe in its own structure the particular construction of religion in public discourse we have observed as the general case. The "radio preachers" and televangelists represent the intensity and privatism of religion that have traditionally been encouraged to flourish away from the public stage. The "public service" model of programming represents a mode of broadcasting based on a limited ascendancy of religion in public culture—able to exercise a certain autonomy but within socially and culturally defined limits.

There is reason to think that these two interrelated activities have functioned, in part, to establish standards and expectations for broadcast treatment of religion. By their mere existence, they have conditioned audiences and producers to certain understandings of what happens when religion appears in broadcasting and may have served to reinforce in the minds of media decision makers certain perceptions of its "natural" role and place.

It is further possible to see religious broadcasting as a particular site of struggle over the cultural ascendancy of religion in modernity. It is significant that the first "radio preachers" and the subsequent televangelists represent one side of the great religious-cultural divide that defines American religion in the late 20th century and that the "ecumenical" or "establishment" broadcasts represent the other side.

## ▪ A History of Struggle for Definition

It is often not recognized that the emergence and development of religious broadcasting was actually *integrated into* rather than being a mere *reflection of* the broader modernism-fundamentalism conflict of the early 20th century. Although it might seem obvious that this was a coincidence—that the development of the technology of radio communication coincided with the rise of fundamentalism and naturally became one among many sites of its expression—there is reason to suggest a deeper connection between religion and religion's use of broadcasting.

Joel Carpenter, in a fascinating study of early fundamentalist radio, describes the integral connection between the medium and its early fundamentalist users. Far from seeing it as merely another means of evangelism, these preachers saw a powerful, cultural, almost mystical instrument in broadcasting, one that had the power to confer social and cultural status and power:

> The evangelical coalition's mastery of mass communications, claims one observer, has been the matrix of its survival and success. I don't see it exactly that way. Rather, in an age of sight and sound, evangelicals have used the reality-establishing force of mass communications to convince themselves—and many others, apparently—that they are a real presence in American public life. They have transmitted their images into the "show windows of modern publicity."[11]

Quentin Schultze concurs, noting that broadcasting stimulated a powerful ambivalence in these early users: on the one hand, drawn to its power and, on the other, fearful of its implications. But Schultze suggests that a "mythos" of broadcasting—that it has implications far beyond its "informational" or "publicity" capacities—has taken hold in the minds of conservative Christians.[12]

For whatever reasons, fundamentalist Christians were among the earliest users of broadcasting, beginning in the era before uniform federal regulation began. By 1925, more than 10 percent of all stations were licensed to religious organizations. Jeffrey Hadden and Charles Swann note that among these religious licensees, "for every [mainline broadcaster] there were a dozen evangelicals."[13]

This first phase in the history of religious broadcasting ended in 1927 with the creation of the Federal Radio Commission (FRC). Because of increased scrutiny of broadcast licensee performance by the FRC combined with the developing commercialization of radio (and the effects of the Depression), the majority of religious stations on the air in the 1920s were no longer there at the end of the decade. By the mid-1940s only about a dozen remained.[14]

The activism of the FRC had two rationales. First, if radio were to develop to its potential, broadcast licensees would have to be held to technical and fiscal standards that would regularize and organize the radio marketplace. Second, and more important to our purposes here, attempts at regulating religious broadcasting during the 1920s proved to be particularly vexsome for the FRC and its predecessor, the Commerce Department. To put it simply, religious broadcasters had provided more than their share of controversy and challenge to government regulators.

Aimee Semple MacPherson was only one among many such controversial figures, according to broadcast historian Eric Barnouw. When Commerce Secretary Herbert Hoover moved to withdraw MacPherson's license due to technical irregularities in her transmissions, she resorted to an otherworldly defense. She wired Hoover,

PLEASE ORDER YOUR MINIONS OF SATAN TO LEAVE MY STATION ALONE STOP YOU CANNOT EXPECT THE ALMIGHTY TO ABIDE BY YOUR WAVE LENGTH NONSENSE STOP WHEN I OFFER MY PRAYERS TO HIM I MUST FIT INTO HIS WAVE RECEPTION STOP OPEN THIS STATION AT ONCE.[15]

Such figures as MacPherson, Billy Sunday, and "Fighting Bob" Shuler thus very early on set the terms of debate over the proper nature and scope of religious broadcasting. This debate had, from the beginning, two related elements. First, there was the issue of *controversy* itself. Religious use of broadcasting seemed somehow always to involve nettlesome practices that did not easily fit into the businesslike expectations of regulators, commercial operators, and mainstream audiences. Second, there was the question of religious *factionalism*, which was joined by the more mainstream religious community. A 1927 article in *Christian Century* titled "Should Churches Be Shut Off the Air?" observed that the airwaves were rapidly being taken over by a multiplicity of—often conservative—religious voices and concluded that "there is a serious question whether religion, as now carried on the air, is a community friend or nuisance."[16]

The mainstream alternative was articulated by S. Parkes Cadman, a progenitor of the mainline/ecumenical broadcasts of succeeding decades:

If one uses the radio merely to preach doctrinal views, he will fail. On the other hand, if he uses radio to broadcast the great basic principles of religion and of the welfare of the world, we find in it an agency of unprecedented value.[17]

This approach, which has been called "broad truths," thus contrasted sharply with the virulent appeal of the evangelical radio preachers. Due in no small part to a desire for the avoidance of controversy, the radio industry itself soon began expressing its preference for this mainstream approach represented by Cadman. A passage from a 1923 issue of an industry publication is indicative:

> It becomes apparent that we have not to consider the question shall radio be utilized for broadcasting religion, but rather should radio be used by this particular church for broadcasting the particular form of worship used by this church?[18]

As a result of what quickly became the common interests of broadcast stations and broadcast presenters from the mainstream churches, an arrangement was worked out that gave speakers such as Cadman, Harry Emerson Fosdick, Ralph Sockman, and David H. C. Read airtime on what were then the major radio outlets: the General Electric and Westinghouse stations in New York.

This proved to be the model for what occurred after the introduction of omnibus regulation of broadcasting in 1927 and 1934. In both the Radio Act of 1927 and the Communications Act of 1934 (which remained in force for over 60 years) provision was made for the regulatory body to oversee communication services to local communities that served the "public interest, convenience, and necessity." The FRC and the subsequent Federal Communications Commission (FCC) took steps under this doctrine to ensure that a wide range of community interests would be served by broadcasting, religion being prominent among them.[19]

Thus the newly regulated and regularized broadcasting that evolved in the period 1927-1935 had an important incentive to give an account of religion as part of its overall service obligations and to ensure, based on the experience of the period before 1927, that the religion aired was of a variety that involved "broad truths" and was noncontroversial. Broadcasting in this era quickly became dominated by radio networks that soon achieved a national scope and came to determine much of industry practice vis-à-vis specialty topics such as religion. However, this practice was to evolve without a great deal of direct involvement from the regulatory authorities. Aside from general expectations, they gave few guidelines.

NBC's approach became determinative of the network philosophy that developed regarding religion. "NBC will serve only the central or national agencies of great religious faiths . . . as distinguished from individual churches or small group movements," said a 1928 NBC statement of principles.[20] NBC was the dominant network in the early years. Its major rival, CBS (founded in 1927), struggled financially and, as a result, was open to selling airtime for religion.

Independent religious broadcasters thus gravitated to CBS, and one of them, Father Charles Coughlin, precipitated yet another crisis over religious controversy. Coughlin began appearing on CBS in 1930 and rapidly built a following through his mixture of populism and ardent nationalism. His program took on more and more of a "political" stance, as he attacked both "unregulated capitalism" and "international bankers." A confrontation ensued with CBS management, which insisted that Coughlin "desist from these subjects and to submit advance scripts."[21] Coughlin appealed directly to listeners, who sent 1,250,000 letters of protest to the network.

CBS decided to take a different approach and replicate the NBC model. It moved to replace all paid religious broadcasts (including Coughlin's) with a program called *Church of the Air* that offered free airtime to speakers from the three "major" faiths on a rotating basis. This donation of airtime, called "sustaining time," thus became the dominant model for network treatment of religion.

Coughlin continued his program by creating his own network of individual stations (based at WOR in New York) linked by leased telephone lines. He became more and more overtly "political" in his broadcasts, first supporting Roosevelt and then teetering toward fascism. He suggested that communist countries were more oppressive of Christians than the Third Reich was of Jews, that Nazi actions elicited publicity because of Jewish influence in government and the arts, and that Jews were leaders in communism against which Nazi Germany had to fight in self-protection.[22] He also objected to attempts to censor him on radio, characterizing them as "Jewish Terrrism." [23] His anti-Semitism and pro-Nazism eventually led to his being discredited in the wake of national consensus forged by the United States' entry into the war.

The Coughlin affair had far-reaching consequences for broadcast policy and practice regarding religion. The National Association of Broadcasters (NAB), the industry trade association, moved in 1939 to adopt its first

industry code, and it included provisions covering religion that were widely
perceived to have resulted from the still-fresh memories of the Coughlin
controversy. The *New York Times* reported that the code "was seen in some
quarters as designed to bar Father Charles E. Coughlin from buying time on
stations belonging to the Association," for the code was explicit regarding
religion:

> Radio . . . may not be used to convey attacks upon another's race or
> religion. Rather it should be the purpose of the religious broadcast to
> promote the spiritual harmony and understanding of mankind and to
> administer broadly to the varied religious needs of the community.[24]

In its discussion of appropriate approaches to controversy, the code set an
important precedent and provides a telling account of the developing self-
understanding of broadcasters regarding their role as guardians of public
discourse. The code directed that potential controversy in broadcasts should
be dealt with by integrating controversial spokespeople into "public-forum-
type" broadcasts, where the "control of the fairness of the program rests
wholly with the broadcasting station or network."

The notion of "fairness" remains controversial to this day. Its direct impact
on the issue of network practices regarding religion was that it came to be
interpreted in a specific way. That is, broadcasters took full responsibility
*themselves* for the character and nature of religion on their airwaves. This in
turn led them to move toward a kind of religious broadcasting that represented consensus, promoted "spiritual harmony and understanding of man-
kind," and spoke to broad, varied interests.

They chose to pursue this through an extension of the NBC model,
whereby major ecumenical and faith groups were given sustaining time for
national broadcasts. Ironically, this meant that at the same time these broadcasters moved to assert control over potentially thorny issues in the area of
religion they were quickly absolving themselves of this responsibility. Henry
Bellows of CBS spoke to the issue during congressional debate over the 1934
Communications Act:

> We have uppermost in mind freeing ourselves from the responsibility
> which we are not qualified to assume of allotting time on a commercial
> basis to different religions. . . . So long as we view this question solely
> in the light of business practice, we are likely to fail to give the radio
> audience the balanced religious broadcasting it is entitled to.[25]

These deliberations are significant to our concerns here because of an important difference between American broadcasting and print media: broadcasting is regulated. As a result, it has had to engage in policy discussions that have been both more open and more deliberative than is the case with print journalism. Thus, decisions made at the time of the 1934 Communications Act together with the companion *NAB Code* (written expressly to guide industry practices under the Act) were determinative of later practice in many areas, not least of which was religion.

What was the general doctrine that developed? Clearly, the broadcasting industry chose, for understandable reasons, to dodge the issue of religion rather than meet it head-on as an affirmative obligation that would find its way readily into such things as news broadcasts. This history reveals a construction of religion as potentially controversial and as something that rightly exists outside the purview of the broadcaster engaged in a rationalist pursuit of business opportunity. As a result, religion developed in national broadcasting in a specific way.

First, industry doctrine regarded religion as something that needed to be pursued in the most *general* rather than *specific* terms. One way to avoid the sort of controversies encountered in the 1920s and 1930s was to construct religious interest as something that could be engaged on a general level of "spiritual harmony."

Second, industry doctrine *eschewed professional responsibility or judgment* regarding the character and nature of religion content. Unlike in areas such as business, agriculture, the arts, or the "hard news," where broadcasters moved aggressively to establish a place of parity with the print media (the epigram of the industry's publication *Broadcasting Magazine* refers to the "fifth estate"), broadcasters chose to defer their professional judgment in religion to the faith groups they invited to participate in the sustaining-time system.

This is a delicate point. Broadcast licensees are, of course, ultimately responsible and accountable for all the content they air. The networks continued to exercise control and influence to a certain extent in their working relationships with their sustaining-time partners over the years.[26] However, it is clear that the whole purpose of the sustaining-time system was to eliminate the necessity of the industry taking responsibility on some level for what they considered to be the internecine issues of interest within the religious community. This point can be clarified by referring to the approach to religion adopted elsewhere, such as in the United Kingdom. Both the British Broadcasting Corporation and the independent commercial networks in Britain maintain their own internal religion units and produce a wide variety of programming including news, documentaries, commentaries, and, of course, broadcast religious services.

Third, industry doctrine constructed religion as a *public service* responsibility rather than as something that would necessarily infuse entertainment offerings or—more important—*news*. This was, in part, responsive to the evolving regulatory doctrine of the time. Both the FRC and the later FCC issued guidelines for "public service" performance that until 1960 explicitly included religion. The compartmentalization of the "public service" rubric had itself resulted from debates over the crafting of the 1934 Act. In a key decision, Congress voted against requiring airtime or license set-asides for "public service" as a matter of law, leaving it instead to the responsibility of broadcasters to ascertain and serve these interests within the run of their schedules. The discourse about "public service" and subsequent industry and regulatory practice (facing obvious commercial pressures) resulted in public affairs programming being marginalized and eventually truncated to the point of near nonexistence in most television schedules. Religion has thus suffered the same fate as agriculture, education, the arts, local talent, and the myriad other offerings originally envisioned as part of the overall "public service" offered by American broadcast licensees.

This doctrine recognizes one important difference between the print and broadcast media. The print media are able to afford the luxury of compartmentalization. "News" and "feature" sections can, to an extent, stand alone. Religion writers at many papers regard the religion section as a positive thing, a place where they can craft coverage that is complete and expansive. Newspapers think of their product as being divided into "beats" and give the various beats allocations of space appropriate to their needs.

In broadcasting, compartmentalization is more problematic. Ratings pressures cause broadcasters to care very much about audience and programming flow. Thus, interrupting the schedule with programs that are significantly different is discouraged. This means that, unlike the magazine orientation of newspaper layouts, broadcast texts are constructed to be as homogeneous as possible. Rough edges, such as educational and public affairs programs, naturally get pushed to the margins.

For religion, this has meant that part of the struggle has been for it to find its way from the "margin" of the broadcast schedule to the "center." Religion's call for improved treatment in broadcasting is not for a reintroduction of sustaining-time, public affairs programs, even if scheduled at times other than early Saturday and Sunday mornings, but instead to be taken on board as an element of the central programming, both news and entertainment, controlled by the broadcaster and network and watched by what are considered the more important audiences.

With some important and significant exceptions and struggles along the way, in the years between 1939 and 1975 religion content in broadcasting was dominated by the sustaining-time system. At the same time, fundamentalist and evangelical broadcasters did not disappear. They continued to buy airtime on local stations and on the Mutual Radio Network, and they gradually built up a constituency. Hadden and Swann sum up the implications of this situation:

> The future course of nonmainline religious broadcasting in the U.S. was set: It would of necessity be entrepreneurial. Fundamentalists would have to buy time, and their audiences would have to furnish the money. This was their only avenue to radio, and they would fight to keep it open.[27]

The latter-day inheritors of this tradition are, of course, the televangelists. At the same time, the sustaining-time system has almost wholly disappeared on the national level. At the present time, none of the major networks produces a weekly sustaining-time television program, and the resources devoted to those that remain are shrinking.

Although the purpose here is not to investigate the practices of religious broadcasters themselves, two points do, however, need to be emphasized because they remain significant. First, as was noted with regard to the early days of fundamentalist radio, religious broadcasting became an important element of the emerging struggle between modernism and conservatism in that era. It played both a practical and symbolic role in those conflicts and was central to their development. This situation is a continuing one.

George Marsden has shown, for instance, that moves by moderate evangelicals in the 1940s and 1950s to craft a less socially pernicious image for conservative Christianity involved an appreciation of the role of broadcasting and the other public media in that process. Billy Graham was hailed by those forces as the person to fulfill this task, and his high-profile broadcasts were central to the project.[28]

Second, as these more moderate conservatives began to become more active through the founding of the National Association of Evangelicals (NAE), the implications of the network approach to religion came into further relief. In its policy documents, the NAE emphasized the necessity of its broadcasts being able to preach "doctrinal" sermons.[29] This was a clear challenge to the notion of "broad truths" emphasized by the NAB and the mainline churches that participated in the sustaining-time system.

A minor controversy has arisen over the role of the mainline churches in the sustaining-time system. There are charges (implicit in Hadden and Swann, for example) that mainline complicity in the public-service system had the effect of "keeping the evangelicals off the air." The implication is that there may have been a cynical manipulation of a situation that worked to the advantage of the dominant, mainline groups. As the history reviewed here shows, however, there was a fundamental reason for the lack of coop- eration, put succinctly by the NAE in its policy statement. Evangelicals wanted to preach doctrine in broadcast programs. The networks and mainline churches were committed to a "broad truths" approach. These were simply incompatible with one another. There may have been minor conspiracies or a chain of complicities along the line, and it can certainly be said that this marginalization advantaged one group over the other (at least for a time), but no more nefarious an explanation is necessary or justified.

This review of the early history of broadcast treatment of religion helps resolve one of the conundrums with which we began. How was it that broadcasting developed in the United States (the most religious of the Western industrialized countries) for over 50 years without more attention being given to religion in its news and entertainment programming? Part of the answer is that in its early history broadcasting achieved a construction of religion that allowed it to be treated at the margins rather than at the center of broadcast content. This construction can be attributed in part to tensions and pressures faced by broadcasting in its formative years. More important, though, it represents a reaffirmation of the problem religion has faced in enter- ing public discourse in general. Its construction into the private realm meant that evolving doctrine in the area of broadcasting could follow a "path of least resistance" and conveniently compartmentalize religion. It is only in recent years that this situation has come under increasing pressure and that some change has begun to occur in that most central of broadcast practices: news.

## Evolving Practice in Broadcast Treatment of Religion

A comprehensive analysis of broadcast coverage is neither practical nor possible at this point, but against the historical backdrop, a review of three cases where particular attention is now being given to the religion story should help us understand the particular challenges faced by broadcasters as they begin to place more emphasis on religion.

Two of these cases come from public broadcasting. It is an ironic feature of this field that public broadcasting has been more reluctant than commercial broadcasting to address religion. The commercial networks have at least dealt with religion through a combination of paid-time and sustaining-time programming, as flawed as those have proved to be. Public broadcasting has, in comparison, done comparatively little.

This is what makes the development of the creation of a religion desk at National Public Radio so significant. Public television news, by comparison, remains relatively quiet. The *MacNeil-Lehrer News Hour* does have one producer who deals with religion and has an arrangement whereby the veteran religion editor at *Time* magazine, Richard Ostling, does periodic pieces on religious issues for the program. And it was announced in 1997 that a new program, *Religion News Weekly,* was entering production for public broadcasting supported by foundation funds and hosted by veteran television newsman Robert Abernathy.

However, the general tenor of public television has historically been much less receptive to the topic. William Fore, former member of the Corporation for Public Broadcasting Advisory Board, recalls at least one major coproduction opportunity dealing with religion that was simply passed up "for no apparent reason, other than disinterest."[30] Bill Moyers, a prominent voice within public television, and one who has often addressed religious issues both directly and indirectly, recalls an intriguing conversation with a decision maker at a major station:

> I was talking with him about a series on religion, and he said I could develop it if I wanted to, but that they'd not put money into it. I asked "Why?" and he responded, "Who'd be interested?" I reminded him that my show on *Amazing Grace* was the second highest-rated thing they did last year, and he said, "Yes, but that wasn't *about* religion."[31]

John Santos, a producer at WNET in New York and former member of the religion unit (the staff who worked with sustaining-time productions) at CBS, attributes public television's attitude to a "carry-over" of commercial networks' "counterreligious bias":

> There was a large "cognitive gap" in my conversations with network people, looking at why there was no ongoing coverage of culture and religion, in spite of its "news value." I couldn't get them to acknowledge that this merited more ongoing coverage. Our stories need to draw on

"an information file" that acknowledges the contribution of religion and culture to other things we cover.[32]

The implicit positioning of religion is thus rooted in deeper, cultural understandings of religion's place, says Santos. "There is a 'federalism' of news culture, where religion is in the 'domain of the private.' " This also has serious implications for the professional self-understanding of the journalist, for there is an implicit challenge in covering religion, a challenge to the journalist's own worldview. "Covering beliefs implies a vulnerability on the part of the reporter," notes Santos.

Public broadcasting's reluctance to deal with religion can be attributed as well to statutory limitations. The CPB charter prohibits "denominational programming." Further, notes Ralph Jennings, general manager of the public radio station at Fordham University, construction grants awarded to public licensees specifically prohibit the facilities being used for "sectarian purposes."[33] These could be seen as either narrow or expansive in their implications, notes Jennings, but have generally been regarded as broadly discouraging explicit inclusion of religion in content.

At the same time, there are examples of change in attitude at public television. The *MacNeil-Lehrer* case is one. Programs aired within the past few years include Moyers's *Amazing Grace,* his interviews with Robert Bly and Joseph Campbell, and his *Healing and the Mind,* all of which dealt more or less explicitly with religious sensibilities and religious issues. In 1996, he aired two much more explicitly religious series, one of which was *Genesis,* a study of the book in the Bible, the other an exploration of the thought of religious historian Huston Smith. There also have been the PBS programs *Faith Under Fire, Mine Eyes Have Seen the Glory,* and *The Glory and the Power.* Other such projects are in the works, some as coproductions. Santos, who is now actively involved in developing properties that explicitly include religious dimensions, finds the atmosphere at public television changing, if slowly: "I am having less difficulty in public broadcasting than I had at CBS. There is more openness."

## ■ The Development at ABC News

In a videotaped presentation to the meeting of the Religion Newswriters' Association, Peter Jennings described the thought process that resulted in ABC hiring a full-time religion reporter:

This was an idea which was long overdue, let alone whose time had come. About three years ago I began to get the feeling that religion or spirituality was playing a much larger role in American life generally, so I began to agitate to see whether or not we could get it as a regular department on *World News Tonight*.[34]

Jennings suggested that his own awareness of this issue was related to his experience in the Middle East, which had given him a particularly keen appreciation of Islam:

I observed that we and our colleagues don't do a very good job covering Islam, and by extension, I assume we are not dealing with all of religion very well, either. You will note, for instance that we at ABC never use the term "Islamic fundamentalism" because we realize that is a misnomer. Others do use it, but all of us need more consciousness of religion in general.[35]

The first challenge that ABC faced was the specific question of the qualifications of the person being sought to fill the post. The kind of calculus that went into this question reveals much about the implicit challenge of someone who must cover religion, yet remain professionally distant from it:

At first I wasn't exactly sure what I wanted. I hope I don't offend anybody, but it seemed to me that we wouldn't be best served by someone who was of the spiritual community, so to speak. . . . I was looking really hard for just a good reporter in the first instance who would see in the multifaceted subject of religion and spirituality a tremendous challenge to a reporter.[36]

This idea that religious identification might be prima facie inconsistent with journalistic professionalism runs deep as a theme in the print media as well. Jennings's own assessment of it relates it to the parallel question of whether a reporter can be politically active and remain objective enough to do a professional job on a politics beat:

I grew up with this tradition of reporters not belonging to any organized political party, not telling people how they voted and not wishing to compare themselves to the public in any way lest they be cast in some way or another. . . . I think the news establishment, in general, has felt somewhat uncomfortable with declaring itself as individuals as being religious which, of course, is inconsistent with the national statistics in a very big way.[37]

And what of his competitors? How is this move being received by the other national news outlets?

My competitors haven't called up and said "What a wonderful idea you have." But I do notice on the other networks that there has begun to be the beginnings of more religion coverage than they have given before.[38]

The journalist chosen was Peggy Wehmeyer, a reporter at WFAA-TV (an ABC affiliate) in Dallas. According to *USA Today*,[39] she began her television career in 1980 after having served as spokeswoman for a seminary in Dallas. During her time at WFAA she had covered community and news beats as well as religion.

Press accounts of her hiring also addressed the issue raised by Jennings, that of the role of her own faith or beliefs in her coverage. *Dallas Morning News* asked her about her own religion, and she demurred,

"I'm a religious person, and it's a very important part of my life," she said. But she describes herself as nondenominational and declines to say what church she belongs to. She is, however, impatient with journalists who question whether a committed Christian can be objective in covering religion. "People say, 'How can you be a Christian and cover religion comfortably?' " Ms. Wehmeyer said. "I would ask them, 'How can you be a political reporter and then go vote?' "[40]

In her work with ABC, which began in January 1994, Wehmeyer participated in *World News Tonight*'s "American Agenda" feature. The first segment she contributed covered the role that religion played in combating a problem of anti-Semitism in Billings, Montana. Next, she secured an interview with President Bill Clinton that became the basis of a two-part report on Clinton and religion. The first of these programs dealt with his relations with the evangelical community; the second probed his own faith and prayer life. Her third major effort was an investigation of religious values in Hollywood. These all aired within the first three months of her hiring.

When asked how covering religion for television differs from doing so for the print media, she responded that there are two major areas of constraint:

It differs in two ways. One, television is a visual medium. There are certain stories that work better in print: Biblical inerrancy, abstract ideas, etc. . . . These are impossible to do on television. Two, time is a constraint. We have at most 90-120 seconds in television. I am on the American Agenda team which means that I have the "luxury" of four minutes or so, but that is about four script pages, that is about all. Oh, there is one more. Cameras intimidate people. It's not just a reporter walking in with a notepad, it is a whole crew.[41]

Television has been described as a more "personal" medium than print, but Wehmeyer doesn't feel that that is an apt way of understanding its difference:

I really don't think it's that it is more personal. I wouldn't do some individual scholar's view of the resurrection, for instance. In print, they're on the religion page, so they can be more segregated to the religious audience. We have to appeal to the non-religious audience as well. We can't be too narrow.[42]

Her output has been at the level anticipated by the structure of her assignment, but Jennings and the producers in New York agree with her that much more could be done on the beat were the person-power available. At her own request, Wehmeyer continues to be based in Dallas. She sees this as giving her more perspective on things than would be the case if she were based in New York.

She sees a role for herself in serving as a broader "institutional memory" for *World News Tonight*. She has been the "first stop" for religion stories that have come in so far:

I just got an announcement from Chuck Colson that he and Dobson and some others who claim to represent 25 million Americans have petitioned Clinton to undo an executive order regarding family planning in foreign aid programs. Now, is that news? I'm not sure.[43]

She seems comfortable with applying rather standard news judgment to the religion beat and integrating her work into the overall product of the program. For example, she reflects on her reaction to the announcement that a number of prominent evangelical groups had agreed to begin cooperating with prominent Catholics on social advocacy projects:

I thought, "Should we cover this?" but I took it to New York, and they said "Yes, but what does it *mean?*" and I think that is the right answer. We'll cover it when it makes news. Like I think I'll call Colson tomorrow and ask him if this compact [with the Catholics] is in effect, then where are the Catholics on this letter to Clinton?[44]

She thinks she can play this role rather well:

I've been doing religion since 1977, and I've got a good sense of it. That's the thing with a lot of people. They are simply not comfortable with it. Like a producer from New York told me that she went to a funeral and was so uncomfortable being in a church. I said, "That's interesting—I'm not at all uncomfortable in church." I think people in broadcasting let their discomfort about religion get in the way of covering it.[45]

The amount of attention her new post has gotten her was initially a surprise. She did not expect to become the target of so much news herself, and it has been distracting her from actually carrying out her job. She has had so many requests for interviews that Peter Jennings at one point told Terry Mattingly of Scripps-Howard News Service that he feared it might be keeping her from actually doing her work.

The newness of such an assignment and her unique position are obvious reasons for the amount of interest she has generated. "I'm a first, and I expected to just be able to do my job, but I'm a symbol of change." Her main discomfort is with interviewers who want to know about her, her own faith, and her own background. She notes that because she covers religion, people want to be assured about "who she is" and "what she knows," questions that would not naturally be put to reporters on other beats:

One kind of response you get is from heady people who want to know " . . . Do you know everything about everything?" Like there was this one religious leader who I was talking with and I asked him a question about a very small point, and he muttered, "Some religion correspondent ABC has." I was really put off by that, but then I said, "No, that is not who I am. I am not an expert, I am a reporter."[46]

Another question she is asked gets more to the heart of classic questions of journalistic professionalism:

The other question . . . is "Are you one of us?" It is of such symbolic importance that there is now this network correspondent that they want to know if I'm in the fold, because that would be so significant. . . . For example, I think they think that my own position on abortion might have something to do with the way I cover things. I don't have the luxury of even thinking about what I think about abortion. I am too busy trying to conduct an interview. What my source thinks is the issue, not what I think.[47]

What is her opinion of the reason why it has taken so long for someone to hold a position such as hers? She attributes the history to the discomfort with religion she senses among her colleagues at the network, something that is obviously changing. Asked whether the fact that religion seems to be inherently complex and controversial might also be a factor, she responds,

I think that would be such a weak argument to make against coverage. Controversy is what news is about. They [those who shy away because of controversy] should be covering things *because* they are controversial, not shying away from them. And the complexity of the beat—that is the core of what we do. We sort out complexity. We exercise our judgment and go on from there. I just don't think those excuses hold water.[48]

The picture that emerges is of the religion beat, at least at this network, being handled very much as other beats are. The inclusion of religion is trend-setting, and ABC is searching for models of coverage. The models that seem most appropriate are those that pursue religion in the same way as other areas are covered. While there might be some expectations that it would somehow be treated differently, neither Jennings nor Wehmeyer sees any reason for making distinctions between religion and other areas of coverage. Judgment of the resultant "track record" must, of course, await a decent interval.

## Developments at National Public Radio

Public discussion of the status of religion coverage reached a peak with the ABC News hiring of Wehmeyer and with the conicidental revelation by National Public Radio that it had also begun looking more seriously at the religion story. Jimmy Allen was quoted in a story on *Business Wire* wire service as commending both of these decisions.[49] Allen had learned of the NPR initiative during an interview taping for *All Things Considered.* In fact, NPR had assigned one of the senior correspondents in its Cultural Unit, Lynn Neary, to begin covering more religion in mid-1993, and by the end of the year she had contributed a number of stories to NPR's major programs on that topic. Also, in early summer 1993, NPR's *Talk of the Nation* program devoted a week-long series to religion and began a long-term series on the Ten Commandments soon after.[50]

The addition of another full-time religion correspondent to the Cultural Unit and an increased profile for religion on its flagship news programs *Morning Edition* and *All Things Considered* were being planned. Also, the producers of *Weekend All Things Considered (WATC)* secured a grant from NPR's internal News Excellence Fund to produce a series on religion for that program during 1994-1995.

These moves were significant for a number of reasons. First, NPR represents (as do ABC and public television) the northeastern "media elite," identified by critics as the most resistant to the religion story. Second, in spite of its relatively small listening audience, NPR is among the most influential of all national media. *All Things Considered* and *Morning Edition* are widely listened to by members of the political establishment and other members of the media. A wire service story described NPR's "bona fides" this way:

> Public Radio's 14.7 million listeners are only a tiny slice of the radio audience but demographic tables are not of great concern to NPR. Why? Because it is the unofficial bulletin board for tens of thousands of government officials, including President Clinton and those in Congress. Lobbyists pay attention, as do businessmen and journalists. . . . By capturing such a niche market of policymakers and shapers, NPR achieves unparalleled access and influence.[51]

Third, NPR has always been in a unique position to be able to cover topics like religion particularly well. Not constrained by commercial pressures, public radio has demonstrated the effectiveness of radio as a medium in its news and cultural programming. Why religion has not been more a part of the mix is a major question that deserves some consideration.

For Jane Greenhalgh, executive producer of *WATC,* the issue is not the absence of religion coverage but the type of coverage:

Media coverage of religion tends to be about abortion or school prayer—so we don't hear about the spiritual aspect of things. We want to do things talking about spirituality, not controversy.[52]

In further discussion, it is clear that NPR felt the *substance* of religion needed to be given some airing. Substance might include spirituality per se but things beyond as well. The *WATC* move into religion resulted from thinking about a series of special projects on topics such as the economy. Religion emerged in the discussions, and it was an "aha!" experience once the staff delved into it:

When Sara [Sara Sarasohn, then an assistant producer] found that people thought the media don't do a very good job of covering religion, and then this great statistic that 92% of Americans have at least a nominal religious affiliation, we said this is *unique* and it is something *significant.* Those figures are far different from Europe and most other countries. Most of them are not that devout, or active, but it does mean that it is something very important for people.[53]

One of the first stories that *WATC* did with its new funding dealt with people "returning to religion" as they age and their social conditions change. This was a learning experience for the production staff:

I remember talking with the reporter who did the "returning" story [Ted Clark], and we commented that among the interviewees we'd only talked with two atheists or agnostics. I said, "But that is how things are. Most people are religious. If you take the overall statistic of 92%, then in any group you are only going to find a few nonreligious people."[54]

But they have already run into some of the classic challenges—for instance, the questions of complexity and controversy:

I've got a question about covering religion that has to do with diversity. If we cover one, do we cover them all? [Sarasohn] And we *do* hear from them. A Lutheran minister called me up after we did a piece on that tornado in Alabama [that killed people in a church, including the young daughter of the church's minister]. Dan Zwerdling [the host] asked the minister how she explained something like this to her parishioners. . . .

The minister who called me was upset because he said we would never challenge a rabbi to explain the Holocaust.[55]

In a demonstration of the maxim that critics often focus on one specific aspect, ignoring others, Greenhalgh reports that when she asked this particular caller if he had heard the piece they had produced that same week dealing with Orthodox Church celebrations of Easter, "He responded that he had heard it and it was very good."

They were surprised by the response to these stories:

We wondered when we started out, "Would people talk about religion?" I was actually a bit surprised at how ready they were to do so . . . how it seemed like they were surprised and pleased that we were doing this. One woman said "I'm glad the Lord will be on NPR." I mean there were NPR listeners among those we interviewed and they were pleased about religion finally appearing. There are people out there who don't know about religion, but not many. It is something that many people are involved in and think about.[56]

As was noted earlier, all these initiatives in the area of broadcasting are taking place in a context where there is relatively little previous experience on which to base them. There are few if any models. Thus, decisions being made now are setting standards for subsequent production. They are at the same time indicative of the underlying, normative understanding of the nature of religion in contemporary culture. In the case of *WATC,* that understanding is of religion as being both personal and noninstitutional:

I did interview ministers [for the piece on returning] and chose not to use most of them. It just seemed to me that the voices of laypeople were more persuasive or more meaningful. Who should comment, an "expert" or a layperson? When a minister says something about religion, it has some status, but laity voices are more compelling, aren't they?[57]

This approach recognizes two fundamental issues. First, radio is a medium that seems particularly good at conveying "the personal." Second, the fact that lay voices are now more compelling is a measure of the decline of institutional authority and the rise of personal autonomy discussed in more detail later.

Lynn Neary, who covers religion for the Cultural Unit at NPR, concurs that a "personal" approach to religion is the most attractive. For example, here are her thoughts on the "Evangelical-Catholic Compact" announced in spring 1994:

> I haven't been able to do it yet, and I am sure I will do something on it eventually, but first I ask myself, "Do my listeners want to hear about every blip on the screen right now? It is my sense that "no, they don't." And then I would need to convince—and I could be wrong about this—the people on the news shows, I mean they might say ". . . No, I don't think so, not really." I think they are much more interested in things where you can bring people into it. That is NPR. I think print journalists can do it more readily . . . because they have more space to bring those kinds of analytical religious stories in along with the other ones.[58]

So a personal, "people oriented" approach is the most likely one taken for most religion coverage in her unit, Neary confirms. She reflects on the importance and permanence of the beat. Why cover religion in the first place?

> Well, you have life and death struggles going on over the schools and I think this is a really important thing to keep covering and be aware of. I think some people have the idea that because Robertson's campaign failed and because the '92 Republican campaign with Buchanan made these strident speeches that turned people off, I think people think, "Well, that took care of it," and it has faded from the scene. I think that the more you report on it the more you are aware of religion's importance and of the diversity within it, even within evangelicalism, which was, to be frank, a surprise to me.[59]

What have been her other "learnings" on the beat? A recent piece on the "culture wars," in which she reported on moral education styles in conservative and liberal families in Colorado Springs, gave her the opportunity to look at these families' religious activities close-up:

> You know, I've been going to a lot of religious services since I started doing this, many more services than I've been to for a long time, and I was really hit by this when I went to those two services. You go to these church services and they are inevitably moving. You are looking at

people who somehow just have such an involvement in what they are doing. Especially when they sing because singing is such a big part of it. Whatever form it takes, whether it is dancing in the aisle with the charismatics or a Garrison Keillor reading, which is what they were doing when I walked into this Unitarian Church.[60]

But there is another side to this intensity: the question oi diversity. That is, how can intensely held religious feelings from a variety of directions be brought together either in the context of a story about religious conflicts or, more generally, in a public discourse about the place of religion?

You see this wonderful thing [religion] that draws people together that's really beautiful in a lot of ways. And then you think, "How is it that this thing that is so good and has such a positive effect on people is so terrible and so divisive and has caused so many horrible conflicts?"[61]

Not all of this can be dealt with by journalism, in Neary's view. "That [the intensity] is the core mystery of it, and I don't know how journalism can penetrate that."

Journalists depend to some degree on direct feedback from readers and listeners. Audience mail and calls tend to be focused on certain stories or issues. Significant feedback is generally taken into account along with other means of self-evaluation, however. Colleagues tend to be important sources of information as do incidental contacts with people in social settings. This incidental feedback is given some credence as it is a perceived audience that is not responding to "hot buttons" so much as it is taking a longer, more general view. Such people thus can come to represent the "general audience" in the mind of the journalist. For Neary, such contacts are important in shaping her initial approach to the beat:

When I do a story on the new Christian right that doesn't make them out to be maniacal, people are very interested in that. They say, "I never thought about that." I had someone come up to me at a party one time after a piece I did on Concerned Women of America where one woman had blamed her feminist mother for her troubles. This person said, "What was this thing with her blaming her mother for everything?" But she found it interesting and thought-provoking. Another guy, a gay guy came up after [the woman] who had actual conflicts with CWA people who were demonstrating here in D.C. against gay rights. He said, "I even got in a fight on the metro with those women, and I liked learning more about what made them tick. I was really fascinated by what they said. I hate them, but I was fascinated by them."[62]

For some listeners, access to people of intense religious convictions is new and fascinating because it presents worldviews that are not readily accessible in their own milieu:

I think for most people outside of places like Colorado Springs, this is all new and interesting stuff. . . . I was at a party and this woman came up who knew I was at NPR to say that she'd heard that report [on Concerned Women of America], and knowing my work she had to ask if that was really the way I thought it was with those women. It is like a window to their world.[63]

Not all such observers envy the journalist's access, however. "I have had people come up to me and say 'How can you stand to do so much of this?' but I find it absolutely fascinating, and the more I get into it, the more fascinating it becomes."[64]

John Dinges, editorial director of NPR News, sets the position of the network regarding religion in historical context:

I think you have a prejudice in public radio—what I call a secularist presumption that applies not just to public radio but to journalism in general. There is kind of the idea that we are under the same restrictions as the government is in the establishment clause and we don't obviously want to show preference for one religion over another. That has translated into "let's not deal with it at all."[65]

This is based in a deeper context, that of the history of modernism and the Enlightenment, says Dinges:

Journalism is a creature of the Enlightenment . . . the idea that there are facts, that knowledge is power. Many of the tenets of our profession are products of the 18th century. I have realized that I have to rethink things, such as what does freedom of the press mean? What does objectivity mean? I think there has been an opening up. Now, I want to make a distinction between this and the trivialization of news that we see so much. I am talking about something completely different.[66]

In his view, the recent moves toward improved coverage of religion at NPR are rooted in a change in atmosphere that has resulted in feelings that were there all along now beginning to come out:

> A lot of us are feeling that ignoring religion is not the way of dealing with it. And they are kind of coming out of the closet—no longer feeling that they have to apologize for their interest in religion.[67]

Sean Collins, executive producer of *All Things Considered,* concurs: "I have been here 10 years and I have witnessed a willingness on the part of people here to speak up in editorial settings and this to be a reality check." However, he suggests that the new interest in religion at NPR is not only personal but is rooted in a professional judgment about the importance of religion in contemporary issues:

> I think it comes from an honest evaluation of the world at the moment and certainly of American society. . . . We can't claim to be covering American society and ignore religion.[68]

Dinges says that his awareness of the need for attention to religion emerged from observing practice on some of NPR's programs:

> One of the things that kind of woke me up to the bad job we were doing covering religion was when I realized in our own programming we were so uneven in our approach. One of our programs was heavily Jewish, and as a result we did wonderfully sensitive stuff about Judaism. But there was never a piece about the religious meaning of Christmas. There was the hypocrisy, the commercialization. That was kind of predictable, except for the fact that we were doing such a great job on the Jewish holidays. Then you had the trend that really bothered me, which was to do no stories—almost no stories about Protestantism, like they are so much a part of the background that you don't notice them. And Catholicism—reporters would always get in some reference to the miracles or saints in some piece about Catholics. They would basically convey that pre-Vatican II stereotype.[69]

What is the root cause of the change in atmosphere? Dinges sees two primary conditions:

Number one, people are getting older—people who are in decision-making positions. It is a generational thing. A certain generation grew up in the '60s and '70s and it was not cool to be religious. This group is now in their 40s and 50s and other things being equal they would be more interested in religion anyway. The other factor is the atmosphere in the country, in which you have an enormous awareness that there is a lack of direction. There is something wrong with the way we inculcate values. . . . I think a lot of people are coming back around to an examination of, an appreciation of, spiritual dimensions.[70]

But how does that relate to news? Spiritual issues can be relevant in feature or culture coverage, but is there a place for them in news?

The Koresh affair is a good example. If reporters had understood the basic language of religion and were able to ask the right questions and get the right answers, they wouldn't have had as big a problem explaining the incredible turn of events and tragedy. I think the coverage was very inadequate because of the lack of this. . . . In other words, you are going to have people that can be good reporters and specialized reporters in an area that very often comes into major stories.[71]

This is consistent with the issue raised earlier about the role of the religion specialist in helping perfect coverage in the general news area. But what kind of approach should be taken to religion per se? Dinges is not entirely satisfied with the notion that radio is somehow a more personal medium. Instead, he sees it as more generally addressing the emotions:

I think broadcasting captures more human dimensions than print does. McLuhan called it a "hotter" medium. It can deal with ideas—radio particularly. Radio can be the medium of discussion, even more so than television because you are not distracted by the pictures. It is a medium of ideas and so is print. But radio has something that print does not and that is you can convey feelings, emotions, color, human texture. Unless you are a Unitarian or a Theosophist or something, there are ideas in religion, but you can't talk about Catholicism, for instance, without some kind of emotional color to it.[72]

Sean Collins agrees that radio is qualitatively different from other media, and the root of that difference is its intimacy: "It has long been understood that radio is, of all the forms of mass communication, the most *intimate* form."[73]

But the notion that radio taps a level of emotion could also be perceived as a danger. This idea, that broadcasting somehow appeals to the "heart" more than the "head," surfaces frequently in discussions of the comparative capacities of various media. The "emotionalism" of televangelists, for instance, has frequently been cited by supporters and proponents alike as one of the key elements of the form. When talking about journalism with its presumption of objectivity, is the notion that radio is somehow more colorful a disincentive to coverage of religion?

> I don't think that is any more a danger than with anything else we do. I mean, think of the danger of broadcasting dealing with politics. The possibilities for demagoguery are infinite in broadcasting. Any mass medium has that danger. Journalism has structured itself to deal with that danger. We basically present something that is not promoting one agenda or the other in a very general way. It certainly is a long way from being a problem in the way we cover religion.[74]

And what of the problems of controversy and complexity? How is religion coverage to "choose" among competing advocates and claims?

> You do get questions like we got at the recent public radio conference, "How do you give equal time to the many, many religions?" I don't think that is much of a problem because the fact that people ask that question is an outgrowth of one of the points that James Davison Hunter made, which is that we journalists have always treated religion as politics, as if it *were* politics. It is like you take the overlay of the political system and put it under religion and then you treat them the same way, so you give equal time to the Protestants and Catholics just like you do the Democrats and Republicans. But wait, there are Jews and Muslims, and then you throw up your hands and don't do anything at all.[75]

What is the answer to this problem of complexity and diversity in the world of religion?

> You don't treat religion as politics. It is not politics. I used to treat religion just like other journalists do. You did it just like it was another political party to the extent you covered it. You covered institutional

issues and who's up, who's down, who's in, who's out. You covered ecumenism, covered the Pope. We covered all these institutional things but . . . didn't cover the ideas and values. What we didn't do was cover the religious dimensions in our other stories. By that I mean the ideas and values.[76]

Collins contends that the issue of controversy should not be a problem in the first place:

What topic do we cover that is not controversial? You know we can't do anything without being criticized for the way we have done it. I've read enough listener mail to know that almost every piece we do elicits that response from someone, so in that sense, religion is equally controversial as health reform as a topic.[77]

## ◼ A Normative Approach

Each of these informants at NPR agrees that this new approach to religion was long overdue. Agreeing with others' assessments of the situation, they came to the conclusion that on the face of it religion coverage had been inadequate in that it did not reflect the basic religiosity of the American people and did not take religion seriously as a component of many of the other stories routinely covered. What to do, however, once that conclusion had been reached is a big and complex question.

In general, the approach taken at NPR has seemed to be one of coverage at the level of personal experience rather than at the level of institutional activity. There are good reasons for this. The individual, experiential level is particularly interesting and important at this point in time. It works well on radio. And most important perhaps, it is perceived by most of these informants as the area most underreported in coverage up to this time.

But there is more to the challenge of the religion beat. John Dinges lays out the mandate in the area of religion that he sees uniquely "on the plate" of public radio:

In public radio we think we have a very strong mission, a societal democratic mission. I think people are expanding that notion to say "that doesn't mean just having 'good government' forums. That might mean having discussions with people, forums with people in which they talk about spiritual values."[78]

So there is a perceived discursive role to be played by public radio in its approach to this issue (as well as others). Lynn Neary's experience with covering the "culture wars," discussed elsewhere, is indicative. It is all well and good to grant religion more of a place and profile. That is essential. However, the complexities of the religion story dictate that a certain normative approach needs to be sought and considered. As NPR moves ahead with (what is hoped will be) a long-term commitment to a greater presence of religion there, the fact that a change in atmosphere has taken place is a necessary but not sufficient condition.

There is a desire to "finally" validate "faith and spirituality" as authentic elements of human experience. But the danger is that such a goal will ultimately lead only to subjectivity and do little to extend the idea of religion as an element of "public discourse"—the Tocquevillian ideal discussed in more detail in Chapter 3—or move it outside the private sphere. Ultimately, journalistic judgment or a normative framework of some kind must enter in.

NPR, ABC, and others in broadcasting must recognize that they face challenges unique to the practice of broadcast treatment of religion and unique to this particular moment. Among these are the following:

The continued recognition of the *underlying religiosity of the American public and the religious basis of many news stories,* both domestic and foreign. The nature of religion in these contexts will continue to evolve, and approaches to its coverage will necessarily also need to evolve.

- Religion coverage does require *special expertise.* Not just anyone can do it, anymore than "just anyone" could be a senior business correspondent overnight. Just because it is a "private" and "personal" matter does not set it outside the realm of critique and analysis, and such analysis requires specialized knowledge.
- Religion coverage needs to be "moved to another plane" where the criteria are *democratic and consensual, not merely liberatory or celebratory.* That is, it must be recognized that it will not be enough simply to give public voice to—and celebrate—diverse and authentic religious expressions, however novel and fascinating that endeavor is. Religion journalism has a responsibility to make sense of these things for the "court of public opinion," the realm of public discourse.

- Religion journalism must always *necessarily be a consensus view* of some kind. It will not be a view that any individual or group of religionists will applaud or appreciate. Like other journalism, it is for a general audience and should be directed at building general understanding.

Above all, a definition of religion is needed that fits the aspirations of journalistic practice. This involves knowing when and where the "religious dimension" of stories is called for. In a roundtable discussion of these issues, the news director of a major commercial radio station expressed some surprise at the idea that there *would be* a religion angle to environmental coverage:

> I was astonished to hear that. You [the religious community] want to talk about the environment? What do you want to tell me about the environment from the religious side of the issue? Don't castigate me for not thinking about it, because I don't put religion and the environment together. I really don't.[79]

What is needed is for religion journalists to develop and maintain a definition of religion that articulates it into stories that might, on their face, not appear to be about religion. Doing this requires journalists to replicate for themselves here what has naturally evolved in other areas of coverage: a natural reference group and an ongoing discourse about the nature and scope of coverage. Most people in the newsroom participate—formally and informally—in consideration of the politics and crime beats. A few of them even engage in dialogue about education and business. As we have seen, such discussions about religion are much more rare.

Religion journalists (like other journalists) must be in the position of exercising independent judgment. Access to the "public sphere" is a precious resource, and NPR and ABC are both flagship media. The pressures for access and the controversies that can ensue put religion coverage in a particular kind of "hot seat." As a defense against such pressures and as a way of shaping and focusing coverage, affirmative action might be taken to ensure that at least the following are accounted for:

- *An "institutional memory."* The religion beat needs to represent a continuity of approach and judgment. Viewers and listeners deserve to

have stories put into conceptual and historical context. There also needs
to be a kind of "policy" regarding religion stories, and continuity is
important there as well.

■ *Sources.* This is related to the issue of memory, obviously. Sourcing is
the lifeblood of journalism, and religion is no exception. Particularly as
it is covered in ways that move beyond the "personal" and "experiential," the religion "story" needs to refer to the sources that can make
meaningful analytic contributions to coverage.

■ *Expertise, a reference group, and "integration."* As stated earlier, religion
is not a story that can be covered by "just anyone." It requires a certain
expertise and specialization. Religion journalists do not need necessarily to be academically trained in religion. As has been said elsewhere,
good religion journalism is, simply, good journalism. What must be
recognized is that it is as specialized and as important as any other beat.
Further, those who cover it can benefit from regular contact with a
reference group with whom they can talk about story ideas and approaches to coverage and from whom they can get feedback. The beat
should not be isolated. The religion desk should also be integrated into
the overall operation. John Dinges points to the Koresh incident as an
example of the necessity of such integration. Noting that the essentially
religious nature of the crisis was missed by most coverage because of a
lack of religion expertise, he suggests that it should have been otherwise:

> Very often the term Balkanization is used to describe this place and
> that is a problem. In such an obvious case as the David Koresh thing,
> I know we would have sent the person that understood religious
> coverage down to do some stories to dig into that, no question.[80]

■ *A sense of "professional judgment."* As noted earlier, one of the problems with religion coverage is the insecurity that ensues when stories
or approaches are challenged. "What do we do if someone complains?"
seems to be the implicit question that guides editorial decision making
in some cases. The antidote to this question is not just good professionalism, in the sense that coverage that is honest and well-done is its own
best defense. The antidote also involves the journalist feeling that she
or he can justify the approach taken on the basis of sound, professional
standards. This should be no different for religion than for other beats.
The existence of an institutional memory, good sourcing, a set of

collegial relationships to which the journalist can refer, and a developing expertise can all help insulate the religion journalist against such challenges.

■ *An understanding of audience needs and interests.* A good deal of news is planned and written out of a sense of "news judgment." This is not altogether a bad thing, particularly if the journalist is working within a framework of careful analysis, good, complete sourcing, and open dialogue with selected communities of experts, colleagues, and readers. However, at some point, research into audience interests might be helpful. Some data on this were presented in Chapter 7, but much more can be done.

## ■ The *Fresh Air* Approach

Another model of religion coverage on public radio is the daily syndicated interview program *Fresh Air.* Although it is primarily about current events and popular culture, regular listeners hear its host, Terry Gross, frequently delve into religion either with guests who represent religious movements or by probing the beliefs of interviewees who are there for other reasons.

Because *Fresh Air* has been cited as an example of a format in which religion was done particularly well, excerpts from a longer discussion/ interview with its host and production staff are presented that provide some insights, even though the interview format is obviously quite different from news coverage. According to one of *Fresh Air*'s producers, programs that deal with religion come in three different kinds:

One is that someone has written a religious memoir of some kind and it is an interesting book with interesting reflections wrestling with issues that whether you're of that faith or not you will have an interest because they're human issues. Then, there's the kind of political category. Religious conflict in the news. We did an interview with an Islamic scholar right after the World Trade Center bombing, for instance. There's also interviews with religious pressure groups, like on abortion, family values, etc.[81]

The third category is cases where religion "just comes up" in an interview about something else:

It's not that we set up the interview to talk about religion but it comes up. For example, there are a lot of musicians, like when we had Al Green on.[82]

Terry Gross thinks that the reason why it is likely to come up in interviews is because of the nature of interview subject matter. When asked to reflect on why religion is so often involved, she replies,

One of our big beats tends to be identity. It seems like in America, that's one of the big issues now. Everybody is trying to figure out who they are and how their racial group or their gender or sexual orientation or religion affects who they are and where they fit into the larger culture. So, in that sense, issues like race and religion and gender and sexual orientation are just coming up all the time in first-person interviews with people. If I'm interviewing somebody in a first-person kind of way about their life as opposed to their area of expertise, if they are religious, if the spiritual life has been an important part of their life, it will likely come up in the interview.[83]

She sees the purpose of pursuing issues of faith to be that of enabling listeners to understand differences:

When we deal with religion it's often about understanding and respecting difference. Because you have your religion, . . . you don't understand or you don't really know that much about the next person's religion. So part of the reason for talking about religion is so that people understand different faiths and can respect them.[84]

But why does faith come up so frequently in her interviews? "In a very practical way. A lot of really motivated, serious, inspired people are people of faith."[85]

The prominence of religion in contemporary culture puts it on the agenda frequently. Issues that appear in the news can become topics for the show, particularly if they are complex:

Our philosophy of covering issues is if we're confused we'll cover it. . . . We're not political experts, so our attitude is if we're having trouble keeping up, our listeners must be, too, and we better find somebody who can explain what is happening.[86]

The approach to religion taken by *Fresh Air* could be described as a *naturalized* one. The topics and issues that are the natural material for the program are likely to have spiritual or religious dimensions. When these come up, it is the responsibility of the program to make them clear to listeners for whom they might otherwise be confusing. Importantly, the producers and host of *Fresh Air* expect that a certain amount of religion will surface during the program and so are prepared when it does. Their responsibility when that happens is to make it clear to a general-public level of understanding and discourse.

It is important to understand how this differs from an approach that unquestioningly accepts all religious sentiment as *personal* and therefore *valid. Fresh Air* does not let religion reside in a protected, private realm. It must come out into open discourse and explain itself:

> I guess I have this bias of liking to hear people wrestle with their faith. Ask tough questions about their faith. As opposed to people just coming on and telling you how wonderful life is or how easy it is once you've found your way.[87]

> It's more like a secular approach to faith. Like how faith impact comes up against things in the world. Whether it's politics or whether it's just things in your life that you have to deal with. Not people just talking about religion for the sake of talking about religion.[88]

What can be learned from this model that helps us understand the dilem mas of broadcast news treatment of religion? First and most important is the point that, even on this program where the objective is less "hard news" and more "feature" oriented, the approach that is taken stresses discourse and understanding, not deferential or uncritical presentation of claims, ideas, or values. The result is worth the effort.

The second thing learned from the *Fresh Air* model points to the sort of naturalism that typifies its approach to religion. Rather than being bound up with concerns about controversy or complexity, the program merely lets religion enter the discourse naturally. Once it is there, it is then carefully probed so as to increase understanding among an audience assumed to be a rather general one, not one that necessarily understands this religion or all religions well. This kind of generalism has always typified the idealized audience for journalism, and there is no reason why religion journalism should be any different on this score.

# Notes

1. Carter, Stephen. 1993. *The culture of disbelief.* New York: Basic Books.

2. Material from this chapter has also appeared in Hoover, Stewart and Douglas Wagner. 1997. History and policy in American broadcast treatment of religion. *Media, Culture, and Society* 17:7-27.

3. Olasky, Marvin. 1988. *The prodigal press: The anti-Christian bias of the American news media.* Westchester, IL: Crossway Books,

4. Dart, John and Jimmy Allen. 1993. *Bridging the gap: Religion and the news media.* Nashville, TN: Freedom Forum First Amendment Center.

5. *TV Guide,* January 1994.

6. Jennings, Peter. Presentation to the Religion Newswriters' Association, New York, April 30, 1994.

7. As the situation has gradually changed, this recognition has dawned. *The Producer Newsletter,* an online publication intended for local news personnel, reported on the religion trend in late 1997 and quoted one local news director as noting that religion is a good topic for the particular demographic targets of local news. See Wilson, Ted. 1997. This is not Sunday school. *The Producer Newsletter,* December 2.

8. Lloyd, Roy (Director of Electronic News, National Council of Churches). Personal interview, New York, April 12, 1993.

9. Govier, Gordon. 1994. Religion reporter at ABC. *The Communicator* [published by the Radio-Television News Directors Association], May, pp. 23-4.

10. Lloyd, interview, April 12, 1993.

11. Carpenter, Joel. 1985. Tuning the gospel: Fundamentalist radio broadcasting and the revival of mass evangelism, 1939-45. Paper delivered to the Mid-America American Studies Association, University of Illinois, Urbana, April 13, p. 15.

12. Schultze, Quentin. 1987. The mythos of the electronic church. *Critical Studies in Mass Communication* 4:245-61.

13. Hadden, Jeffrey and Charles Swann. 1981. *Prime-time preachers.* Boston: Addison-Wesley, p. 76.

14. Schultze, Quentin, ed. 1988. *Evangelicals and the mass media.* Grand Rapids, MI: Academie Press, p. 20.

15. Barnouw, Eric. 1966. *A tower in Babel.* New York: Oxford University Press, p. 100.

16. Hadden and Swann, *Prime-time preachers,* p. 267.

17. Jennings, Ralph. 1969. Policies and practices of selected national religious bodies as related to broadcasting in the public interest. Ph.D. diss., New York University, p. 16.

18. Ellens, J. Harold. 1974. *Models of religious broadcasting.* Grand Rapids, MI: Eerdmans, p. 27.

19. Jennings, Ralph, Ph.D. diss., p. 3; U.S. Federal Communications Commission. 1946. Public service responsibility of broadcast licensees [known as the "Blue Book"]. Washington, DC: Author, pp. 10-13.

20. Jennings, Ralph, Ph.D. diss., p. 29.

21. Barnouw, *Tower in Babel,* p. 46.

22. *New York Times,* November 21, 1938, p. 7.

23. *New York Times,* November 27, 1938, p. 46.

24. Quoted in Ralph Jennings, Ph.D. diss., p. 109.

25. Ibid., p. 60.

26. Pomeroy, W. David (Director of Broadcasting, National Council of Churches). Telephone interview, March 3, 1992; McClurken, William (former Director of Broadcasting, National Council of Churches). Telephone interview, August 3, 1992.

27. Hadden and Swann, *Prime-time preachers,* p. 78.

28. Marsden, George. 1982. Preachers of paradox: The religious new right in historical perspective. In *Religion and America: Spirituality in a secular age,* edited by Mary Douglas and Stephen Tipton. Boston: Beacon.

29. Voskuil, Dennis. 1990. The power of the air: Evangelicals and the rise of religious broadcasting. In *American evangelicals and the mass media,* edited by Quentin Schultze. Grand Rapids, MI: Academie Press, p. 85.

30. Fore, William F. (former Assistant General Secretary for Communications, National Council of Churches). Telephone interview, April 11, 1992.

31. Moyers, Bill. Personal conversation, September 17, 1992.

32. Santos, John (Producer, WNET). Personal interview, April 13, 1993.

33. Jennings, Ralph (public radio general manager, Fordham University). Telephone interview, February 22, 1993.

34. Jennings, Peter, RNA presentation, April 30, 1994.

35. Ibid.

36. Ibid.

37. Ibid.

38. Ibid.

39. *USA Today,* January 26, 1994, p. 3D.

40. *Dallas Morning News,* February 12, 1994, p. 33A.

41. Wehmeyer, Peggy. Telephone interview, April 25, 1994.

42. Ibid.

43. Ibid.

44. Ibid.

45. Ibid.

46. Ibid.

47. Ibid.

48. Ibid.

49. *Business Wire,* January 13, 1994.

50. Collins, Sean (producer, National Public Radio). Personal interview, April 22, 1994.

51. *Denver Post,* April 24, 1994, p. 4G.

52. Greenhalgh, Jane (producer, National Public Radio). Personal interview, April 21, 1994.

53. Ibid.

54. Sarasohn, Sara (producer, National Public Radio). Personal interview, April 21, 1994.

55. Greenhalgh, interview, April 21, 1994.

56. Sarasohn, interview, April 21, 1994.

57. Ibid.

58. Neary, Lynn (journalist, National Public Radio). Personal interview, April 21, 1994.

59. Ibid.

60. Ibid.

61. Ibid.

62. Ibid.

63. Ibid.

64. Ibid.

65. Dinges, John (editorial director, National Public Radio). Personal interview, April 21, 1994.

66. Ibid.

67. Ibid.

68. Collins, interview, April 22, 1994.

69. Dinges, interview, April 21, 1994.

70. Ibid.

71. Ibid.

72. Ibid.

73. Collins, interview, April 22, 1994.

74. Dinges, interview, April 21, 1994.

75. Ibid.

76. Ibid.

77. Collins, interview, April 22, 1994.

78. Dinges, interview, April 21, 1994.

79. Franklin, James (news director, WMAQ Radio, Chicago). Remarks to a meeting of the communication unit, National Council of Churches, Chicago, February 10, 1994.

80. Dinges, interview, April 21, 1994.

81. Producer of *Fresh Air* during staff interview, March 24, 1993.

82. Ibid.

83. Gross, Terry (host, *Fresh Air,* WHYY-FM). Personal interview, March 24, 1993.

84. Ibid.

85. Ibid.

86. Ibid.

87. Ibid.

88. Producer of *Fresh Air,* interview, March 24, 1993.

# 10

# THE CHALLENGE OF STANDARDS

From a practical and professional standpoint, what was seen in the previous chapters provides some insight into normative standards for religion news in contemporary times. Before turning to the larger cultural, theoretical, and political context in Chapter 11, let's pause here to look at the question of whether some common ground might be found between news professionals and news audiences.

We might begin by elaborating some of the principles that define the ideal role and position of religion in newspapers and broadcast news that emerges from what we have found. These should not be seen as prescriptive necessarily but might lay the groundwork for a dialogue directed at developing *model* policy and practice in contemporary religion coverage.

*Religion news is no longer only news about "religions."* We are well past the time when religion can be defined by the denominations and institutions that dominated in the 1950s. Today, religion is a more varied field, defined by contemporary spiritual, moral, and ethical quests and often expressed in individual actions quite outside the domain of traditional religions.

At the same time, religion journalism must avoid developing an "anti-institutional" bias. There is a natural tendency to accord more value and attention to the vibrancy of personal experience, to work at the "cutting edge" of nontraditional religious experience. It seems somehow more "authentic." And yet there is still news in the world of "religions." The membership patterns of Americans, particularly recent immigrants, are changing the religious topography substantially. As the conventional religions respond to these changes, they continue to be important stories as well. Religion coverage thus needs to strike a balance between these three "fields": the conventional religions, the new ones, and the wider field of religious consciousness and experience expressed outside the boundaries of the historic faith groups.

*Religion is not "fading away."* The secularization hypothesis should never have been taken to imply that religion was *unimportant,* even if it was in decline, but we should recognize that religion is far from declining. This is particularly so if we take into account a new definition of religion.

*Religion needs to be understood substantively as well as functionally.* Much religion coverage has tended to focus on the outward manifestations of religion *in* politics or contemporary social and cultural change or on the politics or economics *of* religion itself. Such coverage is important, of course, and a good deal of the resurgence of interest in religion on the part of the news business can be traced to the political activism of religious organizations and to their own internal politicization, as in the case of the Southern Baptist Convention of recent years.

However, there is more to religion than just its politics and economics. As the critical incidents discussed in Chapter 1 demonstrate, there is an essential, fundamental nature to religion that is unique and that must be more generally understood and made transparent if journalism can be said to be doing its job.

*The religious dimension of stories that have not traditionally been defined as "religious" needs to be recognized.* Religion plays a unique and often confusing role in contemporary politics worldwide. Religious sensibilities are involved in contemporary political and cultural debates on everything from the environment to economics. Religious activism on these matters has sometimes found its way into coverage, but the cultural contribution of religion to discourse about them has rarely been recognized in media practice.

*Journalism needs to maintain an "institutional memory" regarding religion.* One of the hallmarks of the best religion coverage has been the consistency of perspective brought to bear by the best religion writers. The quality of their own research and writing is important, of course, but they also tend to provide implicit policy regarding religion at the papers where they work. Few media (outside of commercial broadcasting) have had formal policies regarding religion. Instead, the general approach to coverage has been the province of the journalists covering it.

As the religion beat becomes more complex and more prominent, this will not be adequate. Newspapers and broadcast news staffs need to begin serious internal dialogues about their approach to the religion story. This will have the dual benefit of improving the quality and scope of coverage and of expanding the staff ownership and consciousness of the religion beat. As we noted in our 1989 report, even the best religion "shops" tended to be rather insular. It will be an important measure of the improving status of the beat that more and broader story conferences are devoted to it.

*Religion specialists need to be treated as internal expert consultants.* In *Bridging the Gap,* Dart and Allen suggest that religion reporters should be looked on as "fact checkers" on other stories, so as to ensure an improvement in the consistency and quality of coverage. A broader kind of "fact checking" can and should be expected. If religion is an important story, it is important to get it right on a number of levels, and the religion reporter should be looked on as critical to this task. Religion is a broad and complex beat. No single religion reporter can be enough of a generalist to provide detailed feedback on every story. However, at the level of generalism on which most religion writing needs to be done, the religion writer can and should be helpfully involved.

*Religion needs to be understood as transcending the local and personal level.* There is a great deal of very tempting material to be mined in the private realm of religion. We do, in fact, need to know much more than we do about the nature of contemporary religious experience, and some very good journalism can be done there. However, journalism is also about the general culture and the broader realm of public discourse, and religion stories that articulate the local with the translocal also need to be addressed. It is in a way a "re-ghettoization" of religion to see it relating only to the private sphere. To do so condemns it to a fundamentally different status than "elite" beats such as politics, business, education, science, and economics.

There is evidence that the new trends in broadcasting, particularly local broadcasting, are moving very much in the direction of this local and personal approach. A report on trends in local television news coverage in late 1997 suggested four reasons for increased attention to religion. First, religion can provide an angle that gives an edge in competition with other stations for coverage of important local stories. Second, it adds to the diversity of newscasts. Third, it can humanize complicated and esoteric issues. Fourth, it can satisfy public demand for more uplifting and inspirational news.[1]

Anne Ryder, who has won Emmy Awards for her religion stories at WTHR-TV in Indianapolis, confirmed these sentiments at a conference the same year.[2] "People simply like these stories because they are new and different and are closer to home," she said.

*Journalism and journalists need to become "self-assured" regarding religion.* As has been noted, one of the root problems of religion coverage is entirely an *internal* one. It is that the traditionally marginal status of religion has left the "institutional culture" of the news business without working operational definitions of religion news, and—more importantly—without operational justifications (rooted in professional judgment) for it. It is not that these things do not exist at all. They of course are well worked out at many newspapers that have had long-standing commitments to religion coverage. However, the sense of self-assurance that comes with experience and practice on any beat is less evident in the field of religion than in other, more "senior" beats.

Due in part to the cultural conditions we have discussed, these insights result from a view that is, in many ways, unprecedented. Religion has never been the focus of much sustained research. These considerations then should provide an important baseline against which future research and experience can be judged. It has taken place in a field where very little previous work exists.

When it has looked at religion, industry research has tended to do so within imposed categories of coverage. Studies have given some insight into the readership of, and interest in, the "religion page," or "religion section," for instance. Other research has assessed levels of readership interest in opinion and commentary columns. Research on readership behavior has sometimes addressed religion stories but has often not allowed stories to be multiply classified, so a story on religion and politics might be classified as "politics," not as "religion." When this is done, religion interest of the type seen here is eliminated at the outset. Most previous industry research on the topic has been of little value in assessing the issue of religion news according to the broad definitions and interest found in this study.

## Defining Religion

It should be clear that we cannot afford to limit the definition of religion coverage we apply. To do so constricts the broad and rich insight and input obtained from audiences. It also eliminates the broader and more diverse field that the religion beat can be. Therefore, we made the strategic decision in this exploration to allow a definition and categorization of religion to emerge out of the data rather than be imposed on it. And there is more to be learned from looking rather directly at the way these various voices chose to frame the question.

## The Readers

First, as said earlier, the readers heard from here seem to be much more knowledgeable and sophisticated consumers of religion journalism than was expected. They know the difference between the front page and the feature page of the paper. They understand the significance of the "church page" or of a "religion section." More important, they seem to understand what is appropriate for each. They understand not only the difference between "hard news" and softer fare but what kinds of things fit in each category.

None of them were asking for inappropriate coverage, such as material of a "church announcement" type appearing in the news section of the paper. Instead, they seemed to be saying that, in an era where religion looms large in public and private life, many newspapers did not reflect that fact.

Some did make charges of specific "bias" on the part of journalists against religion, or against a specific religion or faith group. This did not obviate the overall sense that they knew much more about journalism and about what could reasonably be expected from it than they are often given credit for.

Some were more interested than others in the idea that journalists are *biased* in their coverage. However, this was tempered by an understanding of such things as the reality that the scandals that rocked certain churches (e.g., the Assemblies of God) are justifiable as "hard news." Members of groups less affected by "negative coverage" are less likely to think that deliberate bias is at the base of the problems in religion coverage. All those heard from agree, however, that religion is not as commonplace nor as competently handled as it should be when it does appear. Only the Catholics took significant exception to this, in that they were less interested in secular religion coverage than were the other groups.

How did these readers define "religion news"? They defined it much more broadly and globally than was expected. Some defined religion news as coverage of formal and institutional "religions." However, all of them wanted to define religion coverage much less restrictively, as it needs to deal with matters of belief whether they fit into formally constituted religious settings or not.

Their ideas progressed from there. Religion news needs also to reflect the fact that religion is part of day-to-day life in the United States. Many noted that they could read the daily newspaper for days at a time without seeing anything that indicated religion is at all important to people. Further, readers clearly did not wish to see religion confined to their *local* or *parochial* interests. A number of them pointed out that the press is the only place they can turn for news about religion in general—about religions besides their own.

Nor did the religious press form a significant *substitute* for many of them. The Assemblies of God members were more heavily involved in subscribing to and reading religious periodicals but saw these to be rather limited in their purpose. The secular press cannot, to their way of thinking, be expected to cover issues of spirituality, transcendence, and faith except in limited and very concrete terms. Readers felt they needed to depend on the specifically religious press for that. Catholics felt the same way about their own publications. In contrast, Methodists were able to find inspiration even in the most seemingly "secular" material in the daily press.

The national surveys amplified these ideas, confirming that religious people are also newspaper readers. This should not have surprised anyone, but somehow it did. The idea that religion was not of interest to journalism seemed inferentially to indicate that it was not of interest to its *readers*. This turned out not to be true.

We know from other surveys that the typical American reports a high degree of religious belief and behavior. It was thought possible that regular newspaper readers might be atypical in this regard and, consistent with the idea of "secularization," less interested in religion than cohorts who read newspaper less frequently. However, regular newspaper readers did not significantly differ from the general population in this regard. Demographic controls also did not appear to affect this pattern.

There were some variations in newspaper readership among subgroups, however. Members of traditionally evangelical denominations (Southern Baptists, Missouri Synod Lutherans, etc.) were less likely than others to read a newspaper every day. By a smaller margin, those respondents who consider themselves born again also were less likely than others to be daily readers.

Born-again readers showed the strongest interest in *religious* periodicals. They were more likely than others to read both religious newspapers and religious magazines. However, only a minority of all respondents reported reading religious magazines or newspapers. Even among those who consider religion "very important," less than a third read religious magazines.

Taken together these findings suggest that the majority of readers who consider themselves religious do not read religious publications. It would not be surprising to find them sharing the view of some of our congregational interviewees that the secular media are where they turn to find significant information about the world of religion.

When asked to compare religion with other topics that newspapers cover, readers confirmed that it is neither the *most* nor the *least* important to them. There were clear *regional* differences in how important religion coverage is to readers. Respondents in the Southeast expressed a higher degree of interest than those in the West and Northwest. Other demographic characteristics, such as education and income, made less difference.

There was general dissatisfaction with the coverage of religion. When asked how satisfied they are with the coverage of a variety of beats by the paper they read most often, respondents ranked religion at the bottom of the list. This tended to hold for papers of all sizes, except that the smallest papers (those with circulations under 50,000) were perceived as doing a slightly better job. When asked directly how frequently they read articles about religion when they appear in the newspaper, some interesting gender and belief differences emerged. Men were more likely than women to report frequent reading. Born-again respondents reported much lower levels of reading than did others.

Our final analysis in the surveys was of the *type* of religion coverage that interests readers. Overall, they clearly want to see coverage that is far less local and parochial. Consistent with the findings from the congregational research, respondents employ a broad definition of religion coverage, one that entails religion on a local, national, and international level and that sees religion as an important dimension of much of the rest of the news. Although the local items ranked fairly high in their interest, respondents placed national and institutional items high as well. There seemed to be less interest, for instance, in newspapers covering spiritual or inspirational matters.

These findings suggest that some assumptions about readership interest in religion are misperceptions. Readers understand the news process fairly well and understand what kinds of things qualify as news. They see much that *could* fit in the newspaper that does not. They are not expecting newspapers to cover their own local group so much as they expect religion in general to find its way into the news in general. They would like to see more evidence in the papers they read that religion is an important part of daily life for many Americans. They want to see religion *mainstreamed* in the newspaper.

## The View From Inside the Media

Journalism is a *cultural* practice. It is about manipulating symbols and presenting narrative in such a way that they are relevant to the cultural context within which that journalism functions. Therefore, the journalist works within a set of cultural, value, and institutional constraints. These constraints function on both the formal and the informal level.

*Formal* constraints include such institutional and structural factors as how much budget, how much time, and how much space are devoted to religion. The major factors influencing the religion beat divide into questions of staffing and questions of placement. It is seen as an advance by most interviewees that more and more papers are now staffing the religion beat with expert reporters. Further, it is seen as an advancement that such papers have a generalized commitment to the religion beat that goes beyond the commitment and interest of a particular reporter. In the past, it was sometimes the reporter's *own* interest and motivation that explained a paper's religion coverage. Now, more and more papers are *deciding* to have improved religion coverage and *then* addressing the question of how to staff it.

Placement is another arena of change. The "church page" approach to religion (short rewrites of promotional copy from churches themselves packaged as news on a page that also carries church ads) has given way to the idea of a much more serious and journalistic "religion section" at many papers. There still may be church ads and announcements in some of these, but it is the philosophy that is different. Religion is now on the press agenda, and some papers have continued to maintain a special section or department to address it. However, more papers are *also* beginning to see religion as copy that can appear *outside* an identified religion section, that can, in fact, compete with other news and feature coverage for placement anywhere in the paper, including page 1A. Two of the larger papers where we conducted interviews do not have identified religion pages or sections. Religion is simply "run of paper." Most of the others have a section but see religion *also* competing for space on an equal footing for placement elsewhere.

*Informal* constraints include such things as the status of the beat within the "institutional culture" of the paper and the status and cohort relationships of the religion writer. There are many stories of journalists who do not consider religion a serious beat. The received practice in journalism of the past was for it to be something taken up either by people who had a particular "axe to grind" or people who weren't able to do anything else. Indeed, there are still places and occasions that illustrate the fact that the earlier perception of religion has not yet gone away. Even those interviewees who worked in conditions where religion news is valorized had such stories to tell.

However, religion is now becoming a higher-status topic. There are many reasons for this. The most prominent one seems to be that religion has recently become more "newsworthy," and colleagues and supervisors have now seen that it can be an interesting and challenging area. This "newsworthiness" of religion also needs to be elaborated a bit, however. Religion has become better copy in recent years because it increasingly *resembles* other beats and journalists feel less constrained from investigating it. These two trends are, of course, interrelated. As one interviewee pointed out, journalists and editors are instinctively more comfortable when religion can be covered in the same way (using the same analytic categories) that politics, economics, and scandals are. As the seeming influence of the religious "establishment" has faded, press attitudes of deference toward it have faded as well. The emergence of scandals, controversies, and politicization within religious groups, be they organized or independent, has helped push these trends along.

In all the cases here, there is a consensus that religion coverage is improving, is being elevated, and is becoming a more important beat all the time. As we see these "good examples" struggling with the task, we see developing a set of standards and practices in religion coverage that defines its rising importance *and* its trajectory toward a place of more prominence in the news business. There is no single, unitary vision of how it is best done and no single, unitary standard by which it is judged, even at the papers we studied.

Religion is a diverse, rich beat. It has become complex, as religious faith and practice have become diverse, idiosyncratic (in some cases), and privatistic. As one interviewee said, "It has it all—scandal, sex, power, money, hopes, dreams, corruption, altruism." As religion has become easier for newspapers to cover, many of them have taken the opportunity. Perhaps to oversimplify, religion's "special" status has begun to fade, along with the "establishment," and this has emboldened journalism to look into its closets.

## ■ Change Is the Story

Both religion and the religion beat have changed in the past 10 years. As religious institutions have seemed to fade and religious practice to become more diverse and privatized, the religion story has become the story of change and diversity. We are in a period of transition both in the world of religion and in the world of the religion writer.

At this point, it appears to most interviewees that this change is an improvement. As coverage moves, as a matter of course, from coverage of religion in the "old" ways to religion as part of the "mainstream" of newspaper coverage, readers and writers must come to understand each other better. We must end this report with some optimism that this can happen.

The following thoughts about these issues come from radically different perspectives. The first is from the pastor of a large and growing Assemblies of God parish. In another context, he would be expected to be the spokesperson for a conservative perspective critical of, even dismissive of, the role and position of secular journalism vis-à-vis religion. Instead, he says,

> I don't expect them [the press] to understand "spiritual" things, but remember that we're talking about *religion* now, and I expect them to use the same type of professionalism in the area of religious news and stuff that they use in the area of political or medical or scientific or any other of those areas. . . . I'm not willing to let them off the hook for religious stuff because they don't understand. They were able to do an adequate job, a good job, of reporting the scandals, they can do a good job in general if they want to.[3]

The other voice is someone on the "other side" of the religion-journalism process. He is the managing editor of one of the newspapers in our study. We might reasonably expect such a person, in such a role, to be dismissive of religion as a beat that has the same weight and import as others, but he says,

> You can't have a newspaper without a sports section. You can't have a newspaper without a business section. And I think we've proved that you can't have a *good* newspaper without a *religion* section. Everyone does a certain amount of religion. But traditionally it's driven by a desire to produce revenue from church ads. I think it is absolutely necessary to have religion as a viable part of the paper's public service.[4]

With such concordant opinions on what should be the opposite "sides" of this question, it seems reasonable to suggest that the religion beat has great potential to find a place as an important part of the public service provided by the news media. It further seems that, with a better understanding of each other's needs and perceptions, religion news can become more universally accepted by both groups as an important contribution to social and cultural life.

This does not show that newspapers will be able to increase circulation or broadcasters to increase ratings or make more money by doing a better job of covering religion. The issue is not "what people will buy"; it is what they *want* and what they *think*. In fact, the issue cannot really be one of circulation, anyway. The data clearly indicate that religious and religion-interested people are already present in media audiences.

The discussion here is, instead, about what these media *should* be doing. The newspaper's—or a network's—self-description and self-understanding is an important dimension of both the formal and informal standards and practices in the news business. The comments by the managing editor quoted here (and by Peter Jennings in an earlier chapter) clear justify improving religion coverage as part of the overall mission of the news business. It is a question of how such coverage serves the needs and interests of the readers and the community more than it is one of clear evidence that improved coverage would somehow bring in more readers.

The question of "needs" versus "wants" will always be there. However, many news decisions are made based on a sense of the "needs" of the audience and the communities they serve. This information informs such planning and understanding.

We know that people tend to read and watch sex, violence, and sports. At the same time, a large part of their overall satisfaction with the newspapers they read and the television programs they watch is based in the service of interests beyond those. People may not attend to education or health news as frequently as they scan the scandals, but they nonetheless base their feeling about a given medium on whether it attempts to cover those more marginal areas. Thus, what the journalists and audiences here are calling for is a type of religion coverage that fits the conditions of today. They want to see religion news in the mainstream of media practice. By developing categories and definitions of religion that are sufficiently broad and diverse, religion news can find such a place.

Taken somewhat in isolation, then, a plausible argument can be made that some commonality exists between evolving audience and evolving industry perceptions and practices around religion. The voices heard from here can be rather easily put into dialogue and an agreement crafted between them. But policy and practice in the public media is not only a matter of the private choices of individual audience members and industry actors. It exists within a larger set of criteria and constraints, as we have seen, and these constraints markedly affect the range of options available for coverage and for the symbolic construction of the religion story.

The next and final chapter discusses these larger questions. Although common ground exists between audiences and producers of news in theory, we need to understand the potential pitfalls in practice. That is the question to which we now turn.

## Notes

1. Wilson, Ted. 1997. This is not Sunday school. *The Producer Newsletter* [an online newsletter], December 2.

2. Ryder, Anne. Speech to the North American Conference of the World Association for Christian Communication, Ft. Lauderdale, December 5, 1997.

3. Interview included in Hoover, Stewart, Barbara Hanley, and Martin Radelfinger. 1989. *The RNS-Lilly study of religion reporting and readership in the daily press.* Philadelphia: Temple University, and New York: Religious News Service.

4. Ibid.

# 11

# TO *BE* THE DISCOURSE OR
# MERELY TO *COVER* IT

As we reflect on our explorations, we might begin by asking ourselves what we learned about where we might look first for an explanation of the status of religion in the news. There are many directions we could go, and many of the received or proposed explanations have some merit. A few of them are reviewed here.

Chapter 3 considered the extent to which the institutions of American religion may themselves be part of the answer. History told us much here. Many of the most important established faiths have strong, traditional justifications for the practices regarding the media and the public sphere. For Protestantism, its roots are in movements that eschewed the sort of publicity and cultural projection now demanded in the media age. For Catholicism, there are deep traditions of suspicion of publicity. For all of religion, there is skepticism regarding the prerogatives of the media to interpret and symbolically construct religious institutions, themes, and practices. Those should be the prerogative of religion itself, or so the thinking goes. There is, further, the fact that much of religion is today undergoing transformation that makes it increasingly difficult for journalists to cover it in traditional ways.

There is also the possibility that part of the answer lies in a broad, informal acquiescence to a particular notion of secularization. Much of the rational discourse that dominates the academy and the schools has for decades assumed that religion would recede over time. That religion is reconstructing rather than receding is now beginning to dawn but has yet to be fully realized and understood.

There is also evidence that part of the explanation lies in the nature of American cultural discourse in general. The history of broadcast policy on religion reviewed in Chapter 9 was enlightening on this point. Stephen Carter's argument, that religion has traditionally found only the most re-stricted place in public, makes some sense, although it is far from a settled point. It is true that American public culture has at least a problematic relationship with religion, and in recent years, as religious antagonism and activism have increased, public discussion has increasingly contemplated religion with some suspicion.

The most vibrant arguments are, as we have seen, those proposing that the problem is entirely the result of journalistic bias, ignorance, or both. This range of critiques, which we looked at in some detail, does not provide the whole explanation. Although it is true that the culture of journalism has had a certain negative view of religion (as described in countless accounts, including many in this book), it does not necessarily follow that this prevents journalists from giving religion the same treatment they give other fields, such as politics and business, about which they are also skeptical. Indeed, many of the voices of criticism demand only that religion be treated similarly to other beats, not that it be singled out for either more or less extensive coverage.

This book has been, after all, about the prospects and prerogatives of improved journalistic treatment. The cultural composition of the journalistic profession cannot and will not change overnight, and for many complex reasons, it is unlikely to change in large measure anyway. Instead, we have tended to follow the lead of advocates such as Jimmy Allen, who have argued that what the readers and viewers have a right to expect is only that religion receive equivalent coverage to that received by other beats and that arguments about professionalism and quality can help perfect coverage in due course.

## ◼ What Professionalism Might Achieve

We began by suggesting that the most appropriate way to understand the relationship between religion and the media is to do so within three distinct domains: American religious culture, the realm of journalistic practice, and the sphere of public discourse. This approach derives from the premise that the media play an important role in articulating "the religious" for modern eyes and ears. Further, the reality of contemporary religion must be seen on its own terms, as must the realities of a set of discursive practices we have called *the public sphere* and its definitions of the appropriate role or place for religion in public and private life.

In the final analysis, the distance between the worlds of religion and of journalism is remarkably small. There is much agreement among the various voices here on the necessity of putting religion higher on the news agenda and on the potentially more nettlesome question of what the nature of the treatment of religion should be. In sum, readers and media decision makers share very similar visions of religion in the news: It should be coverage that represents the underlying religiosity of the communities that local newspapers serve, and it should demonstrate as well the extent to which religion is an important dimension of "other" stories.

An ever larger number of voices are calling for religion to be more central in news content, and important and significant moves in that direction are under way. We have taken this as an opportunity to look a bit more critically at the nature of this "improved" coverage as well as at the historical conditions that have led to religion being so problematic for journalism in the first place. We have also begun to consider the extent and limits of a *normative* approach to religion treatment and to make some initial recommendations in that light.

## ◼ Contemporary Religious Evolution

We are now at the end of the "establishment era" of American religious institutions. In an earlier time, the position and prominence of the major faith groups gave them a particular profile and position within the political, social, and cultural spheres. This prominence, combined with the problematic nature of religion in public discourse per se, dictated a particular relationship between religion and the media.

First, religion was seen as primarily a *private* matter, open to very little coverage in the first instance because it was not involved in, or relevant to, public discourse. Second, when religion was covered, it was treated with a certain *tacit deference.* It was seen as an *institutional* story when it existed outside the private sphere, but its institutions were rarely subjected to the kind of scrutiny typical of "hard news" journalism. A measure of this is the fact that the *New York Times* and other papers in that era actually covered and reprinted sermons from prominent pulpits in their Monday editions.

Religion has now changed, and the conventions of covering it are also changing. Religion has begun to resemble other beats in important ways. The scandals of the televangelists, accounts of financial and other malfeasance, followed by the clergy misconduct stories have stripped away some of the legitimacy that had led to this tone of journalistic deference toward religious institutions. More important perhaps, these incidents have also made it possible to cover religion as if it *were* politics or crime or vice. The politicization of religion in recent years has also taken away some of its mystery. Religious groups and individuals are today more and more active in attempting to prosecute their agendas in the mediated public sphere, and religion is sometimes seen more as a "pressure group" than as a legitimate, authentic object of inquiry.

There has also been important change in the nature of religious expression and action. The authority of all religious institutions is increasingly being questioned. The legitimacy of these bodies in everything from theology to personal morality is also under scrutiny. Individual and personal judgment has begun to replace the institutions and the historic doctrines. American religion is now seen more as a "cafeteria" where ideas, norms, beliefs, commitments, symbols, and icons are gathered from a variety of sources and assembled by individuals (and affinity groups) into a personal, highly individualized (or small-group based) religious pastiche.

These shifting religious sands mean that some of the most important challenges that religion poses to the media are becoming exacerbated. Religion is now *more* complex and potentially more *controversial* than ever. In the case of broadcast policy regarding religion, the whole relationship to the religious community was conditioned by attempts to avoid controversy and to minimize exposure to problems of complexity whereby media decision makers might be interpreted as "favoring one religion over another." The resulting policies meant that in its regulations and practices broadcasting reified the essential problematic construction of religion in American public discourse. Religion might well exist as an authentic, vibrant force on the personal and individual level, but on a broader, public level, it could only be expressed in the most general terms, terms we labeled the "broad truths." These broad truths enjoyed a status not unlike the "civil religion" or "civic piety" described by sociologists.[1]

The place of religion in the "personal" sphere is established through two of the trends already discussed. First, religion historically has been accorded the greatest latitude on this personal, individual, "private" level. Second, contemporary religious evolution has elevated the realm of private choice and personal action to a high status. Religious authority over many issues and in many contexts now resides with the laity. Thus, religious expression lodged in the personal sphere seems more attractive, more authentic, and more authoritative.

## ■ The Sphere of Public Discourse

We began by suggesting that the sphere of public discourse plays an important role in the way religion is covered. Ruel Tyson described the practice of journalism as "consensus making" and "consensus made," meaning that journalistic writing both refers to and contributes to ongoing public understandings of the stories covered. We have said this slightly differently in these pages, holding that there is a *sphere of discourse* to which this writing is directed and to which it must "make sense."

This general or consensual view of the status of religion and the place of religion coverage was extensively elaborated by Stephen Carter in *The Culture of Disbelief*.[2] Religion is allowed to achieve a substantial resonance within the private sphere but is severely limited in public. People may talk openly about religion, but as Carter claims, they are not to act as though it is anything more than a "hobby" to them. He notes that an extensive legal and policy superstructure has arisen to enforce this view of religion in public life.

This situation in turn affects the way religion is understood and treated by the "secular" media. As institutions whose whole raison d'être is articulation in the public sphere, their treatment of religion is framed by a general perception that downplays its importance. Further, the day-to-day business of crafting media messages takes place in settings that are themselves "public," so the general reluctance of public discussions to accord much credibility to "the religious" further attenuates its presence there.

For both the public sphere itself and media contemplations of the question of religion, the idea of "secularization" has had rather profound implications.

The assumption has been that religion is of passing concern anyway, and as the dominant religious institutions seemed to be fading in influence from the 1950s through the 1970s, the progress of secularization seemed to be moving ahead apace. Thus, there was no real necessity to question the profile of religion in the public environment. Its relative quietude there was seen as a result of natural social evolution.

The notion of secularization has further been convenient because of its concordance with evolving American constitutional doctrine regarding religion. Religion has been assumed to be both important and potentially challenging to democratic pluralism. The First Amendment's treatment of religion has been read to enforce a federal disestablishment and over the years has also come to imply a fully secular state. A number of observers have suggested that a misreading of the juxtaposition of the *press and religion* in that Amendment has been naively interpreted within journalistic circles to imply a separation of religion *from* the media as well.

A further implication of the situation is the sense that since religion is essentially a private matter, *expertise* is not an issue. If faith is relevant only at the individual and private level, questions of authority are resolved there rather than in public. As a consequence, expertise about the articulation of religion at the public level is made problematic. If questions of religion exist primarily in the private sphere, there is little necessity of having a public purchase on them. This has meant that some in the news media have not felt that any particular expertise about religion is necessary to its coverage. In particular, it has meant that little priority has been given to questions of continuity, consistency, and institutional memory in the area of religion.

The overarching theme here is that what is lacking is a *consensual public language of religion*. As Joan Connell observed earlier, we lack such a "second language" of religion, and that has made the practice of journalism particularly difficult. It can be simply (perhaps too simply) stated as a question of *discomfort*. Public discourse and journalistic discourse about its own practices are uncomfortable with the notion of religion. For the public setting this has meant that there is relatively little experience with religious articulation and with religious discourse. For journalists, this has meant that religion coverage can suffer from two "sides."

The first "side" is that which sees religion from a perspective of secular rationalism. The journalists and editors who have been said to be "tone deaf" to religion because of their own lack of religiosity do not understand it, or worse yet, denigrate it. This is the side represented by the objects of the Rothman-Lichter critiques, for example. The other "side" is, in some ways, more troubling. Many of our informants have identified cases where people in the newsroom who are themselves religious are nonetheless unwilling or unable to engage in professional-level dialogue about it. This is a problem obviously grounded in conventional canons of journalism where religion is seen as the most private and intense of personal values, and thus it has great potential for undermining the cool "objectivity" still commonly thought to define good journalism.

But why *should* journalism take religion more seriously? As was discussed in Chapter 3, a strong normative argument can be made for the necessity of bringing religion fully into public discourse. Observers from Tocqueville to Carter have posited that the success of our democracy depends in some measure on our ability to take account publicly of the vibrant claims of the religious sphere. What Wuthnow terms "vocabularies of public life" must come to terms with the foundational ideas and values rooted in religion.

This is not a simple task. A result that would replicate the more or less meaningless "broad truths" historically sought by *broadcast* religion policy would not be satisfying. But neither is the current situation, where there are few occasions or settings where the disparate appeals and claims of the various interest communities within the religious landscape come together. A middle ground between a bland and enforced commonality, on the one hand, and a cacophony of voices, on the other hand, must be found. As many of our informants have said, journalism *and* the media are implicated in the search for this middle ground.

This is not made any easier by the fact that the institutions and practices of the media hold a particularly prominent place in the realm of public discourse. They are the "gatekeepers" through which others gain access to that sphere. Thus, voices from the world of religion are both the *objects* of journalistic activity *and* potential sources of *pressure.* Unlike more private members of the public, individuals and groups from the world of religion can seem to carry a necessary gloss of "publicity" and "public relations" when they are encountered by journalists.

Overall, the definition of religion in public discourse is a complex yet truncated one. Religion is generally assumed to be an authentic and vibrant dimension of life. Its vibrancy, in fact, makes it culturally ominous. It has been the source of much disharmony and suffering, so we contemplate it with some apprehension. The discursive solution to this fear has been to limit its influence in public life to the extent possible. This apprehension has also led some journalists and editors to compartmentalize their own faith so as to insulate their work life from it. It has led others to treat religion with open

disinterest or disdain. Religious activism tends to contribute to these perceptions. But, at the same time, religion is attractive for its authenticity and its
vibrancy. It is also making more and more "news," and journalism is going
to be paying more attention to it.

## ■ The Practice of Journalism

Journalism now finds itself at a crossroads with regard to religion coverage.
There is a widespread consensus that the prospects of the beat are improving,
and much attention is being given to it in a number of new places, including
broadcasting. These trends will undoubtedly continue. The deeper question,
the one raised here, is what that coverage will be. Is an increase in the
quantity of coverage enough, or should some attention be given as well to
the nature of that coverage? We have been attempting to develop an argument
that the quality of religion coverage needs to be assessed against some sort
of normative standard, a standard that recognizes the fundamental contribution religion can and should make to public discourse.

But what is the role that journalism should play in this process? That role
certainly cannot be one of unquestioningly introducing religious claims into
the public sphere, abandoning its standards in deference to the authenticity
of "the religious," whether privately or publicly articulated. We have seen
that the approach of journalism to religion is conditioned by a powerful set
of cultural definitions that affects both the sphere of discourse into which
journalism interjects itself and the discourses within journalism that define
its practices. For our purposes here, it is important to focus on the mechanism
by which these forces come into play.

Sociologists would call this mechanism "the cohort." The social context
within which professionals form and shape their stories has important determinative effects. In our earlier report, we referred to two types of "standards"
within which journalists function: the *formal* and the *informal*. The former
are policies, procedures, and accepted practices that, although not necessarily written down, are formalized through conventional use. The latter are
influences that flow through colleagues, associates, competitors, and social
networks in general. The "newsroom culture" or "corporate culture" to which
many refer is, in fact, the context where these informal cohort influences
come into play.

Thus the atmosphere of a given newsroom regarding religion may not be
a matter of formal policy so much as it is a set of informal understandings

within the culture of that newsroom. The ambivalence of the news business to religion is expressed more in this informal, cohort-conveyed way than it is in any formal policies (outside, as we have seen, the specific case of broadcasting). The Rothman and Lichter-based critiques are rooted in an assumption about the influence of cohorts on news practice. But this determinism can flow in a number of different directions. It is logical to assume that, in some cases, Rothman and the Lichters are right. A general disinterest in or disdain fpr religion can lead to a cohort culture that devalues it. We have much anecdotal evidence of this happening.

However, there is evidence that the opposite can also occur. We have conducted interviews in a number of the sites Rothman and the Lichters would call representative of the "media elite" and find that the cohort influences there have been coming in recent years to accord religion more value as a matter of "good journalism." But what of situations where the newsroom culture includes people who are not as ignorant of religion as Rothman and the Lichters found, or who are actually deeply religious? It is fairly easy to assume that, in many of these cases, religion would receive fairer treatment just as a matter of course. This is the implication of such things as inquiries into the religious "bona fides" of prominent journalists such as ABC's Peggy Wehmeyer.

However, we also have evidence here of an opposite outcome. The construction of religion as something that is more authentically and vibrantly "private" introduces a challenge for some journalists, particularly those who hew to a particularly reified conception of the notion of journalistic objectivity. Among our informants, we encountered the following anecdotes:

- People in the newsroom, often in editorial or supervisory positions, who are widely known to be deeply religious yet do not engage in newsroom discourse about religion stories or the religion beat
- A crusty editor who denigrated religion and yet was the first out the door to see the Pope when he came to town
- An editor who privately recommended his own pastor as "a good interview" to a religion writer new on the beat at a major paper but who consistently declined to publicly engage in discussion of the beat in editorial meetings.

These were regarded by other interviewees as fairly typical.

Of course, familiarity can breed contempt. There are many, many people in newsrooms who come from religious backgrounds. For some, their experiences have left an indelible and negative impression of religion in general (those who had unhappy experiences in parochial schools is a commonly noted example). Yet, against these obstacles, religion has begun making more and more "news," and a newer, more complete interpretation of it has begun to emerge.

We find now that another dimension has also begun to emerge, that of an appreciation for the authentic expression of religion and the role it can play in addressing what is widely seen as a cultural crisis over "values." Many have observed, for instance, that as the age cohort that dominates in many newsrooms has begun to get older and to have older children the importance of values and of solutions to this crisis have seemed more pressing. There is also the issue of the crisis of meaning itself. To the extent that it can be said to be "new," more and more newsrooms are addressing it, and religion is thought to be at least implied in these considerations.

What is the nature of religion coverage that is emerging, then? This "new wave" is one that addresses the private, individual, and (presumably) authentic sphere where Stephen Carter says religion has always been allowed great scope and leeway. A number of our interviews could be said to reveal a sense of "discovery" of the religious sphere and of the intensity and vibrancy of it. There is a danger there, however, that the result will be merely a "reprivatization" of religion rather than a genuine, public encounter with it.

One of the dynamics that feeds this sense of discovery is the trend toward personal autonomy and personal authority. We have already observed that this is a central trend in contemporary religious evolution, and a great deal of very interesting journalism can no doubt be based on it. Authority now lies more and more with "laity," so to speak, and as one informant said, those voices are now more "authentic" than others. But somewhere along the line, this all must have public purchase. The private and diverse claims of religion will have limited significance unless a way can be found to integrate them into a consensual discourse. Although the notion of journalistic responsibility in such matters is controversial, at least one of our more prominent informants said that there is clearly a role implied here for the media. They must find a way to be involved in that encounter between the "private" and the "public" emanations of religion.

This will not be an easy task. The truncation of religion in public and the lack of a "language" of religion there have left us with few tools and little experience at crafting a public discourse of religion. We may not even really know yet what it would look like. Yet there are some things we can say about the contemporary situation that illustrate the extent to which journalistic practice is already, as a matter of course, contributing to such discourse.

## ▓ Normative Roles and Normative Structures

We return then to the essential questions of media responsibility and media practice. Notwithstanding some important issues surrounding the contemporary self-identity and practices of religious groups and individuals themselves, the role of journalism in shaping the religion story in the public realm is central. What are the extents and limits of this role, and what can be argued in the way of a development of a more normative understanding?

We have already seen how an expanded role for the media in public religious discourse makes sense in light of the critiques of religion coverage with which we are all so familiar, and in light of the broader social good that could result from a greater understanding of America's religious culture. However, as has also been seen, there is some controversy over this role and over whether there can be in any way an expectation of "responsibility" on the part of journalism. The question centers around the classic conventions of journalism, where the graying of the boundary between objective truth-seeking by the journalist and any other role has been seen as problematic.

In the simplest terms, the question is whether journalism is to *be* this improved discourse, or whether it is merely to *cover* the discourse. If it is to be the former, the self-perception of professional journalists cannot accommodate it. If it is to be the latter, is it really serving any purpose? Coverage of the "culture wars" is generally thought to be inadequate if it merely recounts the various sides of the various battles without doing something more to interrogate them and make them accessible to readers and viewers. Thus, merely covering the discourse is not quite enough.

Perhaps a fuller answer is available in the interaction between journalistic practice and the "consensus" to which it addresses itself. The best religion journalism is actually about making various private claims *understandable* in public. This process is, in fact, implicit in the understandings our informants have of their work.

Here again is Terry Gross of *Fresh Air* talking about their approach:

Our philosophy of covering issues is if we're confused we'll cover it. . . . We're not political experts so our attitude is if we're having trouble

keeping up, our listeners must be, too, and we better find somebody who
can explain what is happening.[3]

The clear implication here is that the program is aimed at an idealized set of
"listeners" out there, a category that is completely consistent with the realm
of public discourse to which we have been referring. The idea is that there is
a consensual set of perceptions of a given issue and that topical content needs
to recognize the necessity of presenting information and ideas in a way that
articulates into those perceptions.

And again, Peggy Wehmeyer talking about her self-positioning vis-à-vis
the abortion issue:

> I think they [pro-life interest groups in the audience] think that my own
> position on abortion might have something to do with the way I cover
> things. I don't have the luxury of even thinking about what I think about
> abortion. I am too busy trying to conduct an interview. What my source
> thinks is the issue, not what I think.[4]

The point here is that she sees the journalist positioning her- or himself so
as to make the *source*'s view clear, not somehow shaping the story to bring
her own view into play. There can be quite a bit of discussion about the extent
to which it is possible to fully distance oneself in such cases, but that is not
the issue here. What we are exploring is the extent to which the practice of
daily journalism, oriented as it is toward presenting and clarifying issues and
ideas for an idealized "general audience," does, in fact, see itself as acting
to serve the extension of public discourse, whether it succeeds in describing
things in those terms or not.

This "inquiring mind" approach to journalism has a function. It places the
journalist in the position of proceeding intelligently but yet acting as a
"proxy" for a readership or audience that cannot know all the ins and outs of
a given topic. In spite of the arguments made elsewhere for specialization,
there is still a sense in which all journalists are generalists first. This is a
situation that applies as readily to religion as it does to politics. Reflecting
on the issue of generality in an on-air commentary, NPR anchor Scott Simon
put it this way:

> Reporting makes news personal, not ideological. Back in 1980 I covered
> the campaign of independent John Anderson and informal polls on the
> campaign planes then revealed that most of the reporters traveling with

President Carter, Ronald Reagan, or Mr. Anderson said they would vote
for the candidate they covered. Perhaps we all saw ourselves becoming
White House correspondents. But the candidates were all nice men
personally, and I think that over the many months crossing the country
together reporters simply got to like the men they got to know and
wished them well.

Reporters believe most passionately in the best story. They don't root
for plane crashes or bombings to occur but tend to get enlivened when
they do. Reporters believe in news. Some of the men and women
Speaker Gingrich might suspect of being Democrats have still been his
most valuable press agents.[5]

The generalism implied by such a culture must have, as its "target," the
interpretation of stories with the goal of supporting general understanding.

Thus, it is argued, there *is* a middle ground between the idea of journalistic
practice *becoming* public discourse, and its merely *covering* public discourse. The very nature of conventional journalism at its best *serves* public
discourse because it neither advocates nor inflames, it *clarifies*. Good religion journalism is informed but general. It does not advocate for any single
position, and it does not attenuate positions to the "poles" of a given issue
(thus adding to misunderstanding and conflict). Instead, it attempts to make
clear to an idealized general audience the essence of religious issues, trends,
and conflicts in a general language that is accessible to them. In a well-
functioning sphere of public discourse, that general language would be the
"public language" of religion advocated earlier.

The coverage of an issue directly germain to this argument—Lynn Neary's
work on the "culture wars—illustrates the necessity of finding a forum and
a voice besides the advocates themselves. She put it this way in Chapter 3:

What was missing was a sense that we have to sort these things out in
a public way. This all does have to be played out publicly, we can't just
leave it to individual sentiment and choice.[6]

Things also must be done in a certain way. John Dinges noted that the
media could take a superficial approach to coverage which relates to public
discourse, but that would be inadequate:

In public radio we think we have a very strong mission, a societal
democratic mission. I think people are expanding that notion to say,

"That doesn't mean just having 'good government' forums. That might mean having discussions with people, forums with people in which they talk about spiritual values."[7]

Throughout these discussions with journalists, they consciously refer to a general level of discourse. For some, this realm is described as "our readers" or "our listeners." For others, it is articulated in even more general phrases such as "people think so-and-so." For example,

I think for most people outside of places like Colorado Springs, this is all new and interesting stuff. . . . I was at a party and this woman came up who knew I was at NPR to say that she'd heard that report and knowing my work, she had to ask if that was really the way I thought it was with those women. It is like a window to their world.[8]

Such conversations provide a valuable reference for the journalist. While we might say that such contacts risk idiosyncrasy or fallacious inference, it is important to see that in this particular anecdote there is more care and calculation involved. The speaker, a working radio journalist, recognizes that this woman she met depends on journalism for her "window" into this realm of religiosity she might otherwise know little about. Thus, such a listener represents the kind of generalized, consensual discourse to which stories are ideally directed.

### ◼ Controversy and Complexity

And what of the twin problems of controversy and complexity? It is clearly the case that these issues continue to play a role. They are deeply embedded in the history of religion treatment. As we have seen, they were directly involved in the early development of broadcast policy regarding religion. They have continued to emerge in newsroom-level discussions about the future of the beat. Particularly interesting is the insight uncovered here that, for supervisory-level people who do not directly cover the beat, the issue of controversy may lead to a kind of reticence. To paraphrase one informant's comments, the issue is really one of not knowing what to do if someone complains.

We have also found several answers to the problems of complexity and controversy in our interviews here. Most fundamentally, the question of complexity seems to be tailor-made for good journalism rather than an excuse for avoiding it. As several informants said, in several different ways, if the world of religion seems complex and unexplainable, it is the role of the professional journalist to attempt to demystify and explain it.

The issue of controversy is even more squarely met by several of the voices here. There is a general consensus that controversy also should be a reason *for* covering religion, not for avoiding it. The fact that there are competing claims and that there is activism and struggle in the world of religion makes it "good copy."

What these reactions to the problems of complexity and controversy have in common is—for want of a better word—*maturity*. Each of them reflects a level of self-assurance that might not have typified religion journalism in an earlier era. Many of the anecdotes detailing the problems of religion coverage reveal a sense of timidity and reticence rather than self-assurance.

Fortunately, this insecurity seems to be on the decline. The answer to the question of controversy and complexity in religion is, in the end, the same answer that is appropriate in any other area of journalistic practice. Journalists, as professionals, do the best job they can with coverage and understand that any criticisms they receive must be seen in light of their own professional judgment. Valid criticisms must be taken on board, but in the end, they are responsible for the scope and nature of their own work. Religion is no longer thought to be trivial or "fluff." It is a serious, important beat that merits the same professionalism *in* coverage and in discourse *about* coverage that other beats receive.

## Notes

1. Cf. Bellah, Robert. 1975. *The broken covenant: American civil religion in time of trial.* New York: Seabury.

2. Carter, Samuel. 1993. *The culture of disbelief.* New York: Basic Books.

3. Gross, Terry. Personal interview, March 24, 1993.

4. Wehmeyer, Peggy. Telephone interview, April 25, 1994.

5. Simon, Scott. 1996. Commentary. *Weekend Edition Saturday,* National Public Radio, April 20.

6. Neary, Lynn. Personal interview, April 21, 1994.

7. Dinges, John. Personal interview, April 21, 1994.

8. Neary, interview, April 21, 1994.

# INDEX

# ABOUT THE AUTHOR

**Stewart M. Hoover** is an internationally known researcher in media audience and reception research, specializing in studies of religion and the media. He has conducted research on the institutional, cultural and meaning implications of religion in an era dominated by the media industries. Among these studies have been a number focused on the use of the media by religion, particularly around the phenomenon of televangelism. His most recent book looks at media use and construction of religion, in the form of the cultural conditions and implications of religion journalism. He has authored *Mass Media Religion: The Social Sources of the Electronic Church* (1988) and *Religion in the News: Faith and Journalism in American Public Discourse* (1998) and has co-edited *Religious Television: Controversies and Conclusions* (1990) and *Rethinking Media, Religion, and Culture* (1997). He has authored numerous journal articles, reviews and commentaries. He directed the first major public conference on Media, Religion and Culture, in 1996, and serves on numerous scholarly study committees and other initiatives. In addition to his work on religion and media, he has conducted research on media and culture in the developing world, having published work on foreign and local culture in the Eastern Caribbean. He is Professor of Media Studies at the University of Colorado, where he holds appointments in Religious Studies and American Studies.